Four Gems of Tasawwuf
by Shaykh Ahmad ibn 'Ajiba

Four Gems of Tasawwuf

by

Shaykh Ahmad ibn 'Ajiba

Translated by Aisha Abdurrahman Bewley

Four Gems of Tasawwuf

Published by: Diwan Press Ltd.
                         311 Allerton Road
                         Bradford
                         BD15 7HA
                         UK
Website: www.diwanpress.com
E-mail: info@diwanpress.com

Author: Shaykh Ahmad ibn 'Ajibah
Translated by: Aisha Abdurrahman Bewley
Edited by: Abdalhaqq Bewley

A catalogue record of this book is available from the British Library.

ISBN-13:   978-1-914397-11-0 (paperback)
                   978-1-914397-10-3 (casebound)
                   978-1-914397-12-7 (ePub and Kindle)

CONTENTS

INTRODUCTION
TO IQADH AL-HIMAM,
THE COMMENTARY ON THE HIKAM

PREAMBLE

by the slave in need of his Lord Who has no need of
anything, Ahmad ibn Muhammad ibn 'Ajiba al-Hasani

The best thing, which hearts have intended, tongues
have expressed and pens have written, is praise of
the Victorious, the All-knowing, the Generous, the
Benefactor. Praise belongs to Allah who fills the hearts of His
friends with love of Him, singles out their spirits to witness
His immensity and paves the way for their secrets to bear
the burden of direct knowledge of Him. Their hearts rejoice
in the meadows of the gardens of His gnosis, their spirits
walk in the meadows of His *malakut* and their secrets swim
in the seas of His *jabarut*. So their thoughtful reflection
produces precious jewels of knowledge, and the gems of
their wisdom and the fruits of their understanding roll
fluently off their tongues. Glory be to the One who chooses
them for His presence and singles them out for His love.
Some are wayfarers and some *majdhub*, some are lovers
and some are loved. He annihilates them through love of

1

His Essence and then causes them to go on by witnessing the traces of His Attributes. Peace and blessings be upon our master Muhammad, the fount of knowledge and light, the mother lode of gnosis and secrets. May Allah be pleased with his righteous Companions and the pure people of his House.

In the ranks of the sciences, *tasawwuf* is one of the proudest, greatest, and most important. It is their most radiant sun and brightest moon. And how could that not be the case when it is the core of the *shari'a*, the very pathway of the *tariqa* and through it shine out the lights of the *haqiqa*? This is the central topic of the wisdom sayings of Ibn 'Ata'allah's *Hikam*, which are no less than gifts direct from the Divine and secrets direct from the Lord. The book articulates thoughts from the Pure Presence and presents secrets from the *jabarut*.

I once heard the shaykh of my shaykh, Moulay al-'Arabi ad-Darqawi, may Allah be pleased with him, say that he heard the *faqih* al-Banani say, "The *Hikam* of Ibn 'Ata'allah is almost a direct revelation. If it were permissible to do the prayer by reciting something other than the Qur'an, it would have been with the words of the *Hikam*," or words to that effect.

My shaykh, the gnostic and perfected and realised being, Sayyidi Muhammad al-Buzidi al-Hasani, has asked me to write a medium-sized commentary on the *Hikam*, defining its terminology and clarifying its meaning, relying in that upon the strength and power of Allah, the treasures of His knowledge and wisdom, and the words of past Sufis which are appropriate to the task. I have therefore responded to his request, hoping that it will provide people with enjoyment and benefit; success is only by Allah, on Him I rely and to Him I turn. I have entitled the book: "The Awakening of High Aspiration: a Commentary on the *Hikam*." May Allah make this an undertaking which is sincerely for Him alone, by the rank of our noble Chosen Prophet, may the best of blessings and purest peace be upon him always.

We have written two separate introductions to this book: the first outlining the definition of *tasawwuf*, its subject matter, its founder, its name, its sources, its legal ruling, understanding its parameters, its degree of excellence, its relationship to other sciences, and its benefits; and the second detailing the biography of its author, Shaykh Ibn 'Ata'allah al-Iskandari, mentioning some of his virtues and noble characteristics.

FIRST INTRODUCTION: THE SCIENCE OF TASAWWUF

1. Definition

Imam Al-Junayd said, "[*Tasawwuf*] is that the Real makes you die to yourself and live by Him." He also said, "It is that you are with Allah without attachment." It is said that it is adopting every exalted characteristic and relinquishing every base characteristic; that it is noble character appearing at a noble time among noble people; that it is that you own nothing and nothing owns you; and that it is abandoning the self to Allah so that it wants whatever He wills. It is also said that *tasawwuf* is based on three qualities: holding to poverty and loss, spending on and showing preference to others, and abandoning management and choice; that it is having all hope in Reality and no hope from creation; that it is *dhikr* through gathering, ecstasy through listening, and acting through following; that it is refusing to budge from the door of the Beloved even if He shuts you out. It is further said that it is the purity of proximity after the turbidity of remoteness; that it is sitting with Allah without worry; and that it is being protected from the sight of created existence.

Abu Hamza al-Baghdadi said, "The sign of the true Sufi is that he is poor after being wealthy, lowly after being mighty, and obscure after being well-known. The sign of the false Sufi is that he is wealthy after being poor, mighty after being lowly and well-known after being obscure."

Al-Hasan ibn Mansur said, "The Sufi is alone in the Essence: no one accepts him and he accepts no one." It is said that the Sufi is like the earth – all kinds of ugly things are thrown onto it but only beautiful things emerge from it, and both good and evil people tread upon it; and that there is nothing uglier under the sun than an avaricious Sufi.

Ash-Shibli said, "The Sufi is cut off from creation, connected to the Real, as is indicated by the words of the Almighty, *'I have chosen you for Myself.'* (20:41)" He also said, "The Sufis are children in the lap of the Real." It is said that a Sufi is someone whom the earth does not carry nor the sky cover over, meaning that he is not encompassed by created existence.

Shaykh Ahmad Zarruq said, "*Tasawwuf* has been defined, delineated and explained in about two thousand different ways. The basis of all of them, however, is true sincerity in turning to Allah Almighty. They are simply facets of this, and Allah knows best." Then he said, "The fact that there is such great disagreement about the One Reality simply indicates how difficult it is to grasp its entirety. As all the different definitions derive from a single source, which contains within its compass everything that has been said about it, then the expression used is according to what has been grasped of it. Thus all the statements about it are actually a matter of detail rather than substance, each person expressing that which corresponds to his degree of knowledge, action, state, tasting and so forth. That is the source of the differences found within *tasawwuf* and that is why, when Abu Nu'aym wrote about most of the people he deals with in his *Hilya*, he added a saying of theirs appropriate to their particular state. It is said that that is the nature of *tasawwuf* – it means that everyone with a portion of true sincerity in turning to Allah has a portion of *tasawwuf* and that everyone's *tasawwuf* only consists in their true sincerity in turning to Allah, so understand that."

Shaykh Zarruq also said, "A rule when it comes to sincere-turning-to-Allah is that its precondition is that it must be done in a way which is pleasing to Allah Almighty and with means that are pleasing to Him. Anything which has a precondition is not valid without that precondition being fulfilled. Since '*He is not pleased with thanklessness (kufr) in His slaves*' (38:7), it is necessary to make one's faith true, '*and if you are thankful, He will be pleased with you*'. So acting according to Islam is essential. And because of this there can be no *tasawwuf* except with correct *fiqh* since the outward judgements of Allah Almighty can only be known through it. In the same way there can be no *fiqh* without *tasawwuf* since there can be no action without sincere-turning-to-Allah. And neither of these are possible without faith since the validity of both of them is dependent on it. So they must be combined together due to their essential mutual dependence in law, just as spirits are inseparable from bodies – the spirit only knows existence through the body and the body only knows existence through the spirit, the one completes the other."

Malik said regarding this matter: "If someone practises *tasawwuf* without *fiqh*, he is a heretic (*zindiq*); if someone practises *fiqh* without *tasawwuf*, he is a deviant (*fasiq*); and if someone combines the two then he achieves realisation." The heresy of the first lies in his denial of personal responsibility by absolute attribution of all his actions to Allah (*jabr*), thereby denying Divine wisdom (*hikma*) and rulings. The deviancy of the second lies in the fact that his knowledge is devoid of the quality of sincere-turning-to-Allah, which is the very thing that stops people disobeying Him, and is devoid of that sincerity which is a precondition for all action. And the realisation of the third lies in his embodiment of the reality (*haqiqa*) due to the absoluteness of his adherence to the Real. Therefore, recognise and understand that there can be no true reality (*haqiqa*) except through absolute adherence to the Real, and that no human being may achieve perfection except through the embodiment of that.

2. Subject matter

The subject matter of *tasawwuf* is the Sublime Essence itself since it seeks to know it either through evidential proof or through direct witnessing and vision, the former applying to those who are on the path and the latter to those who have arrived. It is also said that its subject matter is the self (*nafs*), heart (*qalb*) and spirit (*ruh*) since it seeks their purification and refinement. There is no great difference between this definition and the first since "he who knows himself knows his Lord."

3. Founder

The founder of this science was the Prophet ﷺ taught to him by Allah through Divine revelation and direct inspiration. The first thing brought down by Jibril was the *shari'a*. When that was established, he then brought down the Reality (*haqiqa*), giving it to some people but not all.

The first to speak about it openly was Sayyiduna 'Ali, may Allah ennoble his face. Then Hasan al-Basri, whose mother Khayra was the client of Umm Salama, the wife of the Prophet ﷺ and whose father was the client of Zayd ibn Thabit, took it from him. When Hasan al-Basri died in 110 AH, Habib al-'Ajami took it on, and then Abu Sulayman Dawud at-Ta'i took it from him. When he died in 160 AH, Abu Mahfuz Ma'ruf ibn Fayruz al-Karkhi took it on, and then Abu-l-Hasan Sari ibn Maghlis as-Saqati took it from him. Then when he died in 251 AH, the baton was passed on to the Imam of this *tariqa* and the one who made the signs of the Reality manifest, Abu-l-Qasim Muhammad ibn al-Junayd al-Khazzaz.

Imam al-Junayd's family came from Nihawand although he himself grew up in Iraq. He studied *fiqh* with Abu Thawr and gave fatwa according to his school, even though he spent a lot of time in the company of Imam ash-Shafi'i. He then kept the company of his uncle, as-Saqati, and that of Abu-l-Harith al-Muhasibi and others. Imam al-Junayd's words and deep insights are preserved in many books. He died, may Allah be pleased with him, in 297 AH and the location of his tomb in Baghdad is well-known and much-visited. The knowledge of *tasawwuf* then spread through his companions and continued on from them and will remain ever-present until as long as the *deen* lasts.

In an alternative chain, the knowledge was passed on from Sayyiduna 'Ali to the first of the *qutbs*, his son al-Hasan; and then from him to Abu Muhammad Jabir; then to the *qutb*, al-Ghazwani; then to the *qutb*, Fath as-Sa'ud; then to the *qutb*, Sa'd; then to the *qutb*, Sa'id; then to the *qutb*, Sidi Ahmad al-Marwani; then to Ibrahim al-Basri; then to Zaynu'd-din al-Qazwini; then to the *qutb*, Shamsu'd-din; then to the *qutb*, Taju'd-din; then to the *qutb*, Nuru'd-din Abu-l-Hasan; then to the *qutb*, Fakhru'd-din; then to the *qutb*, Taqiyyu'd-din al-Fuqayr; then to the *qutb*, Sidi 'Abdu-r-Rahman al-Madani; then to the great *qutb*, Moulay 'Abdu-s-Salam ibn Mashish; then to the famous *qutb*, Abu-l-Hasan ash-Shadhili; then to his successor, Abu-l-'Abbas al-Mursi; then to the great gnostic, Sidi Ahmad ibn 'Ata'allah; then to the great gnostic, Sidi Dawud al-Bakhili; then to the gnostic, Sidi Muhammad, the Sea of Purity; then to his son, the gnostic, Sidi 'Ali ibn Wafa; then to the famous *wali*, Sidi Yahya al-Qadiri; then to the famous *wali*, Ahmad ibn 'Uqba al-Hadrami; then to the great *wali*, Sidi Ahmad Zarruq; then to Sidi Ibrahim Afham; then to Sidi 'Ali as-Sanhaji, known as ad-Dawwar; then to the great gnostic, Sidi 'Abdu-r-Rahman al-Majdhub; then to the famous *wali*, Sidi Yusuf al-Fasi; then to the gnostic, Ahmad ibn 'Abdullah; then to the gnostic, al-'Arabi ibn 'Abdullah; then to the great gnostic, Sidi 'Ali ibn 'Abdu-r-Rahman al-'Amrani al-Hasani, [known as Sidi 'Ali al-Jamal]; then to the famous gnostic, the shaykh of shaykhs, Sidi Moulay al-'Arabi ad-Darqawi al-Hasani; then to the perfect realised gnostic, our Shaykh, Sidi Muhammad ibn Ahmad al-Buzidi al-Hasani; and finally to the slave of his Lord and the least of His slaves, Ahmad ibn Muhammad ibn 'Ajiba al-Hasani, and from him many others have taken. All favour belongs to Allah, the High, the Great.

4. Name

The name of this science is *tasawwuf* although there is some disagreement about the etymology of this name. There are five main positions.

The first is that it is derived from *sufa* (a tuft of wool) because with Allah the Sufi is like a tuft of wool at the mercy of the wind, having no say in the direction of his own management.

The second is that it is derived from *sufa* (the hair of the back of the neck) because of its softness. So the Sufi is hidden and soft like that hair.

The third is that it is derived from *sifa* (attribute), since the Sufi embodies praiseworthy attributes and casts off blameworthy ones.

The fourth is that it is derived from *safa'* (purity). This derivation is considered the soundest, and for this reason Abu-l-Fath al-Busti said in a verse of poetry:

People disagree about the word "Sufi",
  Ignorantly supposing it to come from wool (*suf*).
I give this name to no one but a pure (*safi*) young man,
  who is purified (*sufi*) until Sufi becomes his name.

The fifth is that it is derived from the *Suffa* (verandah) of the Mosque of the Prophet, which was where the people of the *Suffa* lived. This is because the Sufi adopts the same characteristics as those attributed to them by Allah in the Qur'an, when He says about them: *"Restrain yourself patiently with those who call on their Lord morning and evening, desiring His face."* (18:28) And, as Shaykh Zarruq maintained, this quality of theirs is the source of every derivation.

5. Sources

Its sources are the Book, the *Sunna*, the Divine inspirations of the righteous and the Divine openings of the gnostics. Certain elements from the science of *fiqh* have also been included because of the pressing need of the science of *tasawwuf* for them. Al-Ghazali codified these sources in the *Ihya'* in four places: *the Book of Worship, the Book of Everyday Practice, the Book of Things Leading to Destruction*, and *the Book of Things Leading to Salvation*. However, apart from those things connected to obligatory acts of worship, these elements are a not a precondition [of *tasawwuf*], rather they help make it complete. Allah Almighty knows best.

6. Legal Ruling

Al-Ghazali said about its legal ruling, "It is an individual obligation for every Muslim (*fard 'ayn*) since, apart from the Prophets, peace be upon them, no one's heart is free of sickness or defect."

Ash-Shadhili said, "Anyone who does not immerse himself in this science of ours dies persisting in grave wrong action without being aware of it."

And since it is an individual obligation, it becomes obligatory to travel to someone from whom this matter may be taken, someone who knows how to convey it and is recognised as a dispenser of the medicine of the heart, even if doing that involves disobeying one's parents, as is attested to by several scholars including, al-Bilali, as-Sanusi and others. Shaykh as-Sanusi said in the commentary of al-Juzayri, "The self when it overpowers you is like an enemy when he attacks you: just as you must fight and seek help against your enemy, even if that entails disobedience to your parents, so too must you fight and seek help against your own self." How apt are the words of the poet:

I stake my soul on Your love,
  sail the currents of Your ocean,
climb steep crags for Your passion
  drink even poison from Your cup.
I spurn all who would stop me,
  my ear is deaf to detractors.

I will risk all for Your love,
   quit my folks for Your pleasure.

7. Understanding its parameters

Understanding its parameters involves knowledge of its technical terms and the words which are used by the People of Sufism, such as *ikhlas* (sincerity), *sidq* (truthfulness), *tawakkul* (reliance), *zuhd* (doing-without), *wara'* (scrupulousness), *rida* (contentment), *taslim* (submission), *mahabba* (love), *fana'* (annihilation), *baqa'* (going on); and such as *dhat* (Divine Essence), *sifat* (Divine Attributes), *qudra* (Divine Power), *hikma* (Divine Wisdom), *ruhaniyya* (spirituality), and *bashariyya* (mortality); and such as the real nature of *hal* (spiritual state), *warid* (spiritual inspiration), *maqam* (spiritual station) and other such terms. At the beginning of his *Risala*, al-Qushayri gives a clear explanation of these terms, and I have also written a book containing the true definition of one hundred sufic terms, entitled *Mi'raj at-Tashawwuf ila Haqai'q at-Tasawwuf.* Anyone who wants to understand the language of the People [of *tasawwuf*] should read this.

The truth about the technical terms of this science is that they refer to those matters which a wayfarer must study during the course of his journey [to Allah] so that he may understand them and act by them. For instance, it is necessary to know that *ikhlas* (sincerity) is a precondition for any action, that *zuhd* (doing without, abstemiousness) is a pillar of the Path, that *khalwa* (retreat) and *samt* (silence) are required elements of the path, and other similar matters. These are the technical terms of this science and they must be fully grasped before it is possible to begin to know or act by them. Allah Almighty knows best.

8. Degree of Excellence

As was mentioned earlier, the subject matter of *tasawwuf* is the Divine Essence, which is by definition that which is most excellent. It follows, therefore, that the science of it is also by definition the most excellent, since its beginning revolves around fear of Allah, its middle around behaviour towards Allah, and its end around direct knowledge of Allah and attachment to Him alone. That is why al-Junayd said, "If I knew of anything under the sky nobler than this science about which we speak, I would have done everything to pursue it."

Shaykh as-Saqalli says in his book, *Anwar al-Qulub fi'l-'Ilm al-Mawhub*, "Anyone who believes in this science is among the elite; anyone who understands it is among the elite of the elite; and anyone who gives expression to it and discourses on it is an inexhaustible ocean and an unreachable star." Someone else said, "If you see someone who has had belief in this Path opened to him, congratulate him; if you see someone who has had understanding of it opened to him, envy him; and if you see someone who has had articulation of it opened to him, honour him greatly; but if you see someone who criticises it, shun him and flee from him as you would from a lion. There is no science that cannot be dispensed with it at some time or another, except *tasawwuf.* There is never a single moment when it can be done without."

9. Relationship to Other Sciences

In terms of its relationship to other sciences, *tasawwuf* encompasses them all, and indeed is a precondition for them, since there can be no knowledge or action without sincere-turning-to-Allah. In this way, *ikhlas* (sincerity) is a precondition for all sciences. This is with respect to their legal soundness, repayment and reward. As for their outward form, however, although they appear to exist independently of *tasawwuf,* they are in fact deficient or inadequate without it. That is why as-Suyuti said, "The relationship between *tasawwuf* and other sciences is like the relationship between rhetoric and grammar, in other words it perfects it and adorns it."

Shaykh Zarruq said, "The relationship of *tasawwuf* to the *deen* is that of the spirit to the body since *tasawwuf* is the [indispensable] station of *ihsan* which the Messenger of Allah, may Allah bless him and grant him peace, explained to Jibril, as being 'to worship Allah as if you saw Him for if you do not see Him He sees you' since *tasawwuf* is nothing if not what is expressed in these words. For the nub of *tasawwuf* is *muraqaba* (watchfulness) after *mushahada* (witnessing), or *mushahada* (witnessing) after *muraqaba* (watchfulness), otherwise it can have no existence and no trace of its existence can become manifest, so understand." Perhaps when he says "*muraqaba* (watchfulness) after *mushahada* (witnessing)", he is referring to *baqa'* (going on) by means of seeing all created existence by Allah.

10. Benefits

The main benefits of *tasawwuf* are refining the heart and gaining direct knowledge of the Knower of the Unseen. Or you could say that its benefits are bringing about generosity in the self, peace in the heart and good conduct towards every creature.

Know that the knowledge which we have been talking about is not a matter of rattling off words; rather it is a matter of *dhawq* (tasting) and *wijdan* (ecstatic experience). It cannot be acquired from books, only from the people of tasting. It cannot be obtained by talk or tale, but only by serving men of Allah and keeping company with the people of perfection. Allah only grants success to those He grants success through their keeping the company of someone to whom He has granted success. Success is only by Allah.

Iqadh al-Himam

The science of *tasawwuf* is nothing other than the result of right action and the fruit of purified states and if anyone acts by what he knows, Allah will give him knowledge of what he does not know, and this is the reason Shaykh Ibn Ata'illah begins his *Hikam* by mentioning action:

مِنْ عَلامَةِ الاعْتِمَادِ عَلَى العَمَلِ، نُقْصَانُ الرَّجَاءِ عِنْدَ وُجُودِ الزَّلَلِ.

1. A sign of your reliance on action is losing hope when you slip up.

Reliance on a thing means to depend on it and to put your trust in it. Actions can be either movements of the heart or the body. If the movement is in harmony with the *shari'a*, it is called obedience. If it is contrary to the *shari'a*, it is called disobedience. The people of this science divide actions into three categories: actions of the *shari'a*, actions of the *tariqa*, and actions of the *haqiqa*. This can be re-phrased as actions of Islam, actions of *iman* and actions of *ihsan*; or actions of worship, actions of slavehood and actions of pure slavehood, which is freedom; or you might say actions of the people of the beginning, actions of the people in the middle and actions of the people of the end. *Shari'a* is that you worship Allah; *tariqa* is that you aim for Allah; and *haqiqa* is that you witness Allah. You could also say that *shari'a* is putting the outward right, *tariqa* is putting the inward right, and *haqiqa* is putting the secret right.

Putting the limbs right is achieved by three things: *tawba* (sincere repentance), *taqwa* (active fear of Allah) and *istiqama* (going straight). Putting the heart right is achieved by three things: *ikhlas* (sincerity), *sidq* (truthfulness) and *tuma'nina* (tranquillity). Putting the secret right is also achieved by three things: *muraqaba* (watchfulness), *mushahada* (witnessing) and *ma'rifa* (gnosis). You could also say that putting the outward right is by avoidance of what is prohibited and obedience to what is commanded; putting the inward right is by ridding oneself of vices and adorning oneself with virtues; and putting the secret, which is the *ruh* (spirit), right is by abasing it, breaking it until it is disciplined and content with *adab*, humility and good character. Know that we are speaking about the actions necessary for purifying the limbs, heart and *ruh*. and they have already been specified for each category. As for knowledge and gnosis, they are the fruits of purification and refinement. When the secret is pure, it becomes filled with knowledge, gnosis and lights.

Moving to a station is not valid until one has mastered what comes before it. 'Whoever has a radiant beginning has a radiant ending.' So a person does not move to the actions of the *tariqa* until he has performed the actions of the *shari'a* and his limbs are content with that, so that he fulfils all the conditions of repentance and the pillars of *taqwa* and all the various types of right action. That consists in following the Messenger 🙷 in his words, deeds, and states. Once someone's outward is pure and illuminated by the *shari'a*, he then moves from the outward actions of *shari'a* to the inward actions of *tariqa*, which consist in purifying oneself of the attributes of human nature as will be discussed. When he is free of the attributes of human nature, he is adorned with the attributes of spirituality, which take the form of proper *adab* with Allah in His *tajalliyat*, which are His outward manifestations. Then the limbs have rest from their toil and all that remains is good *adab*. One of people of realisation said, 'Anyone who reaches the reality of Islam is unable to be lax in his actions. Anyone who reaches the reality of *iman* is unable to conceive of acting by other than Allah. Anyone who reaches the reality of *ihsan* is unable to turn to anyone except Allah.'

In travelling through these stations, the *murid* should not rely on himself or his own actions, power, or strength. He should only rely on the bounty of his Lord, His granting him success and His direction and guidance. Allah says: '*Your Lord creates and chooses whatever He wishes. The choice is not theirs.*' (28:68) And He says: '*If your Lord had wanted to, He would have made mankind into one community but they persist in their differences, except for those your Lord has mercy on.*' (11:118) The Prophet 🙷 said, 'None of you will enter the Garden by virtue of his actions.' They asked, 'Not even you, Messenger of Allah?' He said, 'Not even me, unless Allah envelops me in His mercy.'

Reliance on the lower self, on the *nafs*, is a sign of misery and wretchedness. Reliance on action comes from lack of certainty that all things will come to an end. Reliance on generosity and states comes from lack of the company of true men. Reliance on Allah comes from realisation of direct knowledge of Allah. The sign of reliance on Allah is that your hopes are not lessened when you fall into disobedience, nor are they increased when good comes from you. You can say that the fear of such a person does not increase when he is in a state of heedlessness, just as his hope does not increase when he is in a state of awareness. His fear and hope are always in equal balance because his fear is the result of witnessing Allah's majesty and his hope is the result of witnessing Allah's beauty.

The Majesty and Beauty of the Real are not affected by increase or decrease. So increase and decrease cannot arise as a result of them, which is not the case with someone who puts his trust in his own actions, since, when the actions of such a person are few, his hope is little, and when his actions are many, his hope is great because of his *shirk* in respect of his Lord and his demonstration of his own ignorance. If he were to be annihilated to himself and go on by his Lord, then he would have rest from his toil and achieve gnosis of his Lord.

For this it is essential for him to have a perfected shaykh who will bring him out of the toil and trouble of his lower self to the rest and ease of witnessing his Lord. A perfected shaykh is the one who gives you rest from toil and trouble, not the one who directs you to it. 'Whoever directs you to action, tires you out. Whoever directs you to this world, cheats you. Whoever directs you to Allah has been true to you,' as Shaykh Ibn Mashish said. Being directed to Allah means being directed to forgetting the self. When you forget yourself, you remember your Lord. Allah Almighty says: '*Remember your Lord when you forget*' (18:24), meaning that when you forget everything except Allah you will have remembered your Lord. The cause of all toil and trouble is remembering the self and being concerned with its affairs and portions. Whoever forgets the self finds nothing but stillness and rest.

As for the words of Allah: '*We created man in trouble*' (90:4), they are specific to the people of the veil; or you could say specific to those whose lower selves are still alive. As for those who have died to themselves, the Almighty says: '*If he is one of Those Brought Near, there is solace and sweetness and a Garden of Delight*' (56:88), meaning he will have the solace of reunion and the sweetness of beauty and the garden of perfection. The Almighty says: '*They will not be affected by any tiredness there*' (15:48). Rest, however, is only obtained after toil and trouble; and victory is only obtained after seeking. 'The Garden is surrounded by adversity.'

O you passionately in love with the meaning of Our beauty,
  Our dowry is expensive for the one who proposes to Us:
An emaciated body and spirit full of care
  and eyes which do not taste sleep,
And a heart which does not contain other than Us.
  If you want to pay the price,
Then be annihilated if you wish for eternal annihilation.
  Annihilation brings one near to that annihilation.

Remove the sandals when you come

to that quarter, for in it His radiance appears.

Cast off both beings and remove

what is between us from between us.

When you are asked, 'Who do you love?'

Say, 'I am the One I love and the One I love is me.'

We read in *Hall al-Rumuz*: 'Know that you will not attain to the stages of nearness until you ascend six steep slopes. The first is weaning the limbs from opposing the *shari'a*; the second is weaning the self from its normal familiarities; the third is weaning the heart from human frivolities; the fourth is weaning the self from all traces of natural turbidity; the fifth is weaning the spirit from all echoes of sensory experience; the sixth is weaning the intellect from illusory imaginings. After the first slope you look down at the founts of wisdom of the heart. After the second you look at the secrets of divinely granted knowledge. After the third there appears to you the signs of the intimate conversations of the *malakut*. After the fourth, the lights of the stages of nearness shine out to you. After the fifth, the lights of the witnessings of love appear to you. After the sixth slope, you descend to the meadows of the Holiest Presence and there you withdraw, by what you witness in them of the subtleties of intimacy, from the densities of the sensory.

'When Allah desires you to become one of His selected elite, He will give you a draught from the cup of His love. That drink will increase your thirst, as tasting will increase your yearning; nearness will intensify your quest; and intoxication will increase your restlessness.'

Excellent people have been puzzled by the words of the Almighty: *'Enter the Garden for what you did'* (16:32) since the Prophet ﷺ said, 'None of you will enter the Garden by his actions.' The answer to that is that the Book and Sunna alternate between the *shari'a* and the *haqiqa*; or you could say between prescription and realisation. They prescribe in some places and speak of the reality in others, regarding the same thing. The Qur'an may legislate about something in one place while the Sunna explains its reality, and the reverse also occurs. The Messenger ﷺ explained what Allah revealed. Allah says: *'We have sent down the Reminder to you so that you can make clear to mankind what has been sent down to them.'* (16:44)

Allah's words: *'Enter the Garden for what you did'* is legislation for the people of Wisdom, who are the people of the *shari'a*, and the words of the Prophet ﷺ explain the reality of the matter for the people of Power, who are the people of *haqiqa*. The words of the Almighty: *'But you will not will unless Allah wills'* (81:29) is the *haqiqa*, whereas the words of the Prophet ﷺ, 'When one of you intends a good action, a good action is written for him' is the *shari'a*. In short, the Sunna qualifies the Qur'an and the Qur'an qualifies the Sunna. So a person is obliged to have two eyes: one looks at the *haqiqa* while the other looks at the *shari'a*. If you find that the Qur'an legislates in one place, you will certainly find the *haqiqa* in another, and the reverse is true. There is no contradiction between the ayah and the *hadith*, nor any confusion.

There is another response, which is that when Allah Almighty called people to *tawhid* and obedience, He knew that they would not undertake it without a clear incentive and so He promised them a reward for their actions. Once their feet were firm in Islam, the Prophet ﷺ dispensed with that and encouraged them towards the attainment of sincere slavehood and the realisation of the station of pure sincerity. So he told them, 'None of you will enter the Garden by his actions.' Allah knows best. Here the answers of the people of the outward are of no use at all.

When someone moves from outward actions to inward actions, the effect of that must appear on the limbs. The Almighty says: '*When kings enter a city, they lay waste to it.*' (27:34) When that movement occurs it inevitably appears in the form of divestment (*tajrid*).

إِرَادَتُكَ التَّجْرِيدَ مَعَ إِقَامَةِ اللهِ إِيَّاكَ فِي الْأَسْبَابِ مِنَ الشَّهْوَةِ الْخَفِيَّةِ، وَإِرَادَتُكَ الْأَسْبَابَ مَعَ إِقَامَةِ اللهِ إِيَّاكَ فِي التَّجْرِيدِ انْحِطَاطٌ عَنِ الْهِمَّةِ الْعَلِيَّةِ

2. Your desire for divestment
when Allah has established you in the world of means
is a hidden appetite.
Your desire for the world of means
when Allah has established you in divestment
is a descent from high aspiration.

The word for divestment, *tajrid*, literally means 'taking off and removing'. The word is used for things like removing a garment or shedding a skin. As for the Sufis they divide *tajrid* into three types: divesting the outward alone, divesting the

23

inward alone, and divesting both of them together. Outward divestment is to abandon worldly means and break physical habits. Inward divestment is to abandon psychological attachments and illusory obstacles. To withdraw from both of them is to abandon both inward attachments and physical habits. You could say that outward divestment is abandoning all that distracts the limbs from obeying Allah and inward divestment is abandoning all that distracts the heart from being present with Allah. Joining the two brings about the isolation of both heart and body for Allah. Perfect divestment outwardly is to abandon means and divest the body of normal clothing, and inwardly it is to divest the heart of every blameworthy quality and adorn it with every noble quality. That is perfect divestment.

When someone divests his outward and not his inward, he is a liar. Like someone who plates base metal with silver, his inward is ugly and his outward beautiful. If someone divests his inward and not his outward, he is like someone who plates silver with base metal. He is good but this is rare since usually when someone is involved with his outward, he is also involved with his inward. If someone's outward is occupied with the physical, his inward is occupied with it, for energy cannot go in two directions. The one who divests both his inward and his outward is the perfect truthful one. He is that purified pure gold which is suitable for the treasuries of kings.

Shaykh Abu-l-Hasan ash-Shadhili said, 'The *adab* of the divested *faqir* consists in four things: respect for the old, mercy towards the young, demanding justice from his own self and refusing to go to its aid. The *adab* of the *faqir* in the world of means also consists in four things: befriending the pious, avoiding the impious, attending the group prayers, and giving comfort to the poor and wretched with what he has been given. Every *faqir* should, however, take on the *adab* of the divested since perfection lies in that. Part of the *adab* of those established in the world of means is that they should remain employing those means, in which Allah has established them, until Allah Almighty Himself takes them out of it either by the tongue of their shaykh, if they have one, or through some other clear indication, such as its becoming absolutely impossible for them to continue in it. Only then should they move to divestment.'

The desire of a *faqir* to enter a state of divestment when Allah has established him in the world of means is a hidden appetite because the self might only intend by that to escape from responsibility while it has not yet acquired sufficient certainty to endure the hardships of poverty. When poverty actually hits him, he is shaken and upset and rushes back to the world of means, which is worse than not leaving it in the first place. This is how it reveals itself to be an appetite and it is hidden because outwardly the *faqir* displays renunciation and asceticism, which is a noble and sublime state, while inwardly he conceals his true intention which was to escape from responsibility, or desire for honour or *wilaya* or whatever. He did not intend the attainment of true slavehood and the breeding of certainty. He also shows a lack of *adab* towards Allah by wanting to leave the situation in which He has placed him and by failing to remain patient until he is given permission to do so.

The sign of someone having been established by Allah in the world of means is that he continues to have success in it, that it does not place in his path any impediments which cut him off from the *deen*, that he obtains everything he needs, and that abandoning it would make him look expectantly towards creation and have anxiety about provision. When these conditions cease to exist, then he should move to a state of divestment. We read in *at-Tanwir*, 'What Allah demands of you is that you should remain in the situation in which He has established you until He Himself removes you from it, just as He placed you in it in the first place. The business is not that you abandon the means but that the means abandon you.

'One of the people of Allah said, "Once I abandoned a certain means and then I returned to it and then the means left me and I did not return to it." When I had resolved to take on divestment, I went to Shaykh Abu-l-'Abbas al-Mursi. I told myself, "It is unlikely that I will reach Allah Almighty in the state I am in which is occupation with outward knowledge and socialising with people." Before I even spoke to him, he said to me, "A man who was occupied with outward knowledges and advanced in them kept my company and tasted something of this Path. He came to me and told me, 'Sidi, I will leave what I am doing and devote myself to your company.' I told him, 'The business is not that. Rather remain where you are and what Allah has allotted you from us will reach you.'" Then the Shaykh looked at me and said,

"That is how the true men (*siddiqun*) are. They do not leave anything until Allah Himself removes them from it." So I left him and Allah washed away those thoughts from my heart and I found rest in submission to Allah Almighty.' Nonetheless they, as the Messenger of Allah ﷺ stated, "... are people whose companion is not wretched."

'He said, "The only reason he forbade him to take on divestment was because his self was greedy for it. When the self is greedy for something, it is easy for it, and what is easy for it has no good in it. Something is only easy for the self when it has a portion of it."' Then he said, 'If he desires to gain benefit, the *murid* should not divest himself from a position of power until this power leaves him. If divestment takes place in that state, then weakness will soon come, followed by people who produce arguments who will unsettle him and tempt him and it is very possible that, if his Lord does not reach him with His kindness, he will indulge in worldly company. Then he will revert to what he left and harbour a bad opinion of the people of divestment and say, "They are based on nothing! We entered that land and found nothing there."' The one who must divest himself is the one who finds divestment difficult at first since it is only difficult for his *nafs* because he is holding a sword to its neck and if he moves his hand at all, its throat will be cut.

If someone who is in a state of divestment wants to return to the world of means without express permission, it is a descent from high aspiration to low aspiration or a fall from a greater *wilaya* to a lesser *wilaya*. The shaykh of our shaykhs, Sidi ʿAli, said that his shaykh Sidi al-ʿArabi said to him, 'My son, if I had seen anything higher, nearer and more beneficial than divestment, I would have told you of it, but with the people of this Path it has the status of the elixir: a *qirat* of it is more valuable than all the gold in the world. That is how highly we rate divestment in this Path.' I heard the shaykh of our shaykh say, 'The gnosis of the one divested is better and his thought clearer because purity comes from purity and turbidity comes from turbidity. Purity of the inward comes from purity of the outward and turbidity of the inward comes from turbidity of the outward. Whenever you increase in the sensory, you decrease in the meaning.'

In one report we find: 'When a scholar takes something of this world, his rank is decreased with Allah, even if He is noble with Allah. As for the one who is permitted means, he is like the one who is divested, since when that is the case his use of means becomes a form of worship. So divestment without permission becomes means, and means with permission becomes divestment. Success is by Allah.'

NOTE: All this is about those who are travelling on the Path. As for those who have arrived and are firm, there is nothing to be said about them since they have been taken from themselves, seized by Allah and defended by Allah. Allah has taken charge of their affairs, preserved their secrets and guarded their hearts with armies of lights. The darkness of 'other-than-Allah' has no effect on them. That was the state of the Companions in respect of means, may Allah be pleased with them and give us the benefit of their blessings! Amen.

Know that in the case of the realised gnostics, the one involved with means and the one who is divested both work equally for Allah. Each of them has true turning to Allah. One of them said, 'The one who is divested and the one involved in means resemble two slaves of a king. He says to one of them, 'Work,' and to the other, 'Stay in my presence. I will support you by my allotment.' But the true turning in the divested person is stronger because of his lack of impediments and severing attachments, as is known.'

The aspiration of divested *fuqara* is usually such that they are as the Prophet ﷺ described: 'Allah has men such that if they were to make an oath by Allah, Allah would keep it for them.' Our shaykh said, 'Allah has men such that when they aspire to a thing, it comes about by the permission of Allah.' The Prophet also said, 'Beware of the insight of the believer. He sees by the light of Allah.' The shaykh feared that because of this someone might imagine that aspiration can pierce through the walls of the decree and accomplish something which is not destined. This is why he said:

$$ سَوَابِقُ الْهِمَمِ لَا تَخْرِقُ أَسْوَارَ الْأَقْدَارِ $$

3. Things aspired to in advance do not breach the walls of the decree.

Aspiration (*himma*) is the energy which comes out from the heart when it desires something and is concerned with it. If that matter is an exalted thing, such as gnosis of Allah and seeking His pleasure, it is called high aspiration. If it is a base thing, such as seeking this world and its wealth, it is called low aspiration. Aspirations which are realised do not breach the walls of the decree, because when a gnostic or *murid* aspires to something strongly, Allah Almighty immediately causes that to coincide with His Power so that his command is by Allah's command. The shaykh of our shaykh, Moulay al-'Arabi said, 'When a sincere *murid* is annihilated in the Divine Name, whenever he aspires to something, it is achieved. If he is annihilated in the Divine Essence, the thing he aspires to is formed even before he aspires to it.' That is true. In a report, Allah Almighty says: 'I am Allah. When I say to a thing, 'Be!' it is. So obey Me and I will make you say to things 'Be!' and they will be.' We also find in a sound *hadith*, 'When I love him, I am his hearing, sight, and hand,' and Allah affirms, 'If he asks Me, I give to him.'

Nonetheless, there is more to the matter than that alone. Nothing comes into being except what is already part of destiny and contained by the decree. So the aspiration of a gnostic is directed to a thing and when it finds the decree for it there, it brings it immediately into effect. That is by Allah's permission. If, however, his aspiration finds the walls of the decree erected against it, it does not try to breach it; rather it shows *adab* and reverts to its core attribute, which is slavehood. It is not grieved or sad. It rejoices because its reverts to its proper place and true attribute. Our shaykh's shaykh, Sidi 'Ali, said, 'When we will something to happen and it happens, we have one joy. When it does not happen, there are ten joys.' That was due to his full gnosis of Allah. One of them was asked, 'By what did you recognise your Lord?' He replied, 'By the breaking of resolve.'

So strong aspiration can be effective in making things happen. If the person who has it is defective, as is the case with someone with the evil eye or a sorcerer by virtue of their wickedness, and they look at a thing with the intention of producing an evil effect, none of that breaches the walls of the decree. It only happens because it is what the One, the Conqueror has willed. Allah Almighty says: '*They cannot harm anyone by it, except with Allah's permission,*' (2:102) and: '*We have created all things in due measure,*' (54:49) and: '*But you will not will unless Allah wills.*' (81:29) The Prophet ﷺ said, 'Everything is by the decree and according to destiny, even incapacity and dexterity.' Weak aspiration cannot accomplish anything. It is the same for good and evil.

The metaphor he uses of breaching walls implies strength on both sides, but the barrier is stronger and the strength of the incapable slave is of no use against it. Since aspiration cannot breach the walls of the decree, there is no point in your pondering and choosing, so he continues:

أَرِحْ نَفْسَكَ مِنَ التَّدْبِيرِ، فَمَا قَامَ بِهِ غَيْرُكَ عَنْكَ لَا تَقُمْ بِهِ لِنَفْسِكَ

4. Give up the management of affairs.
Since Someone Else has taken it on for you,
why take it on yourself!

Management (*tadbir*) means linguistically 'to look to matters and their ends'. As a technical term Shaykh Zarruq says that it means 'the determination of matters which will occur in the future which are feared or hoped for, by judgement not by entrustment. When there is entrustment and it is a matter of the Next World, it constitutes a good intention; if it is for something natural, it constitutes an appetite; if it is for this world, it is just wishful thinking.'

There are three types of management: blameworthy, desirable, and permissible. The blameworthy is that which is accompanied by unyieldingness and excessive planning, whether it is for the *deen* or this world, since it contains lack of *adab* and hastens fatigue if the Living, Self-Subsistent does not bring it about. You will never achieve it by yourself. Something you start doing for yourself is not normally helped by the winds of destiny and is frequently followed by cares and trouble. That is why Ahmad ibn Masruq said, 'Whoever abandons management has rest.' Sahl ibn 'Abdullah said, 'Leave management and choice. They cause problems for people in respect of their livelihood.' The Messenger of Allah ﷺ said, 'Allah put ease and rest in contentment and certainty.'

Shaykh ash-Shadhili said, 'Do not choose in any of your affairs. Choose not to choose and flee from that choice, from your flight and from everything to Allah Almighty. "*Your Lord creates and chooses whatever He wills.*" (28:68)' He also said, 'If you must manage, then manage to not manage. It is said that whoever does not manage is managed.' The shaykh of our shaykhs, Sidi 'Ali said, 'One of the attributes of the perfect *wali* is that he only needs what his Master has brought about for him in that moment,' i.e. he only wants what issues from the Decree.

As for the desirable form of management, it is to take care of the obligations for which you are responsible and the voluntary actions which are recommended while entrusting other things to destiny. This is called a righteous intention. The Prophet ﷺ said, 'The intention of the believer is better than his action.' He also said, reporting from Allah, 'When My slave desires to do good action and does not do it, I write a full good action for him.' This is what is understood from the words of the Shaykh, 'Since Someone Else has taken it on for you, why take it on yourself.' It is the act of obedience in which there is no harm in managing. That is why Ibrahim al-Khawwas said, 'All knowledge is contained in two statements: 'Do not burden yourself with what you have enough of and do not waste what you get.' 'Do not burden yourself with what you have enough of' refers to the blameworthy form of management and 'do not waste what you get' refers to the desirable one.

Shaykh ash-Shadhili said, 'You have no say in all the choices and measures of the *shari'a*. They are chosen by Allah and you simply hear and obey. This is the place of divine understanding and divine knowledge. It is the earth down to which descends the knowledge of the reality from Allah for the one who is mature,' meaning his intellect is mature, gnosis complete and his *haqiqa* is in balance with his *shari'a*. But he must not relax in that and become distracted from Allah.

The permissible form of management lies in undertaking worldly or natural matters while entrusting their outcome to whatever emerges of the decree without depending on any of it. That is what is understood of the words of the Prophet ﷺ: 'Management is half of livelihood provided that it is not repeated time after time.' The permitted amount is that it passes through the heart like the wind, entering one side and emerging from the other. This is management by Allah, and that is the business of the realised gnostics. The sign of it being by Allah is that when the opposite of what someone has intended by his management issues from destiny, he is neither constricted nor upset.

Submit to Salma and go wherever she goes.

Follow the winds of fate and turn wherever they turn.

We read in *at-Tanwir*: 'Know that things are either blameworthy or praiseworthy according to what they lead you to. Blameworthy management is the kind which distracts you from Allah, makes you fail to rise to serve Allah and impairs your conduct with Allah. Praiseworthy management is the kind which leads you to nearness to Allah and connects you to His pleasure.' The rest of his words deal with management and he also wrote a book on it called Illumination of the Dropping of Management. It is excellent. The perfect *wali*, Sidi Yaqut al-'Arishi said, 'Everything that can be said is contained in two verses:

There is only what He wills,
   So leave your cares and abandon them.
Leave your preoccupations
   which distract you and you will have rest.'

Preoccupation with management and choice indicates the dullness of the inner eye, and abandoning them or taking them on by Allah indicates the opening of the inner eye. So the author now mentions another clearer sign of the opening or dullness of the inner eye:

اِجْتِهَادُكَ فِيمَا ضُمِنَ لَكَ وَتَقْصِيرُكَ فِيمَا طُلِبَ مِنْكَ دَلِيلٌ عَلَى انطِمَاسِ البَصِيرَةِ مِنْكَ

5. Your exertion in respect of what is guaranteed to you and your deficiency in respect of what is demanded from you

are proof of the dimness of your inner eye.

Exertion in respect of something means to devote your efforts and energy to obtaining it and deficiency in respect of something means neglecting it and squandering it. The inner eye is the sight of the heart in the same way that ordinary eyesight is the sight of the senses. Whereas ordinary eyesight only sees sensory things, the inner eye sees meanings. You could say that the inner eye only sees the subtle and ordinary eyesight only sees the dense; or the inner eye only sees the timeless and ordinary eyesight only sees the in-time; or the inner eye only sees the Maker and ordinary eyesight only sees what is made.

When Allah desires to open someone's inner eye, He makes his outward occupation serving Him while his inward is occupied with loving Him. When inward love and outward service become great, the light of the inner eye grows strong until it overpowers ordinary sight, and the light of ordinary eyesight merges with the light of the inner eye so that it only sees the subtle meanings and timeless lights which the inner eye sees. This is the meaning of the words of Shaykh al-Majdhub:

My vision vanished into perfect vision,
  and I was annihilated to all that vanishes.
I reached the truth, lost sight of otherness,
  and continued in that state in pure delight.

When Allah wants to disappoint His slave, He makes his outward occupation serving phenomenal being while his inward is occupied with love of created things. Then he continues like that until the light of his inner eye is extinguished and the light of ordinary eyesight overcomes the light of the inner eye so that he only sees the sensory and only serves the sensory. Then he exerts himself to obtain his allotted provision, which is, in any case, guaranteed for him, and is deficient in respect of the obligations demanded from him. If he replaces exertion with total absorption and deficiency with abandonment, dimness turns into blindness, which is disbelief. We seek refuge with Allah! That is because this world is like the river encountered by the troops of Talut. The only drinkers who are saved are those who scoop up a little with their hands, not those who slake their thirst, so understand! Shaykh Zarruq said that.

Shaykh ash-Shadhili said, 'The inner eye is similar to the outer eye. The least thing that falls into it prevents it from seeing, even if that does not lead to blindness. There is danger in anything which impairs sight and renders thought turbid. The mere desire for such a thing removes good altogether. Acting by it, however, removes from a person a portion of his Islam and gives rise to its opposite. If he continues in evil, his Islam will slip away, and if he reaches a stage which involves attacking the Community, wrongdoing due to love of rank and position, and love of this world rather than the Next World, then know that his Islam has completely disappeared. Do not be deluded by anything you see in the outward; it has no inner reality because Islam is love for Allah and love for His righteous slaves.'

Exertion in respect of what is guaranteed for us is completely blameworthy, whether it is by action or word, whether we desire to hasten its arrival by supplication or any other method. He indicates that when he says:

لَا يَكُنْ تَأَخُّرُ أَمَدِ الْعَطَاءِ مَعَ الْإِلْحَاحِ فِي الدُّعَاءِ مُوجِبًا

لِيَأْسِكَ، فَهُوَ ضَمِنَ لَكَ الْإِجَابَةَ فِيمَا يَخْتَارُهُ لَكَ لَا فِيمَا تَخْتَارُ

لِنَفْسِكَ، وَفِي الْوَقْتِ الَّذِي يُرِيدُ، لَا فِي الْوَقْتِ الَّذِي تُرِيدُ

6. Do not let a delay in the timing of the gift,

even when you have made intense supplication for it,

be the cause of your despair.

His reply to you is guaranteed;

but in the way He chooses, not the way you choose;

and at the time He desires, not the time you desire.

Intense supplication is to repeat a supplication for something you want again and again. Supplication is asking, which is accompanied by *adab* on the carpet of slavehood in the presence of the Lord. The cause of a thing is that which is the source of its existence. Despair prevents desires from being realised. Know that One of Allah's names is *al-Qayyum* which is an intensive form of the word *qiyam* which means establishment. Allah established the creation of all things, from His Throne to His earth, and the essential nature of every created form is that it has a limited lifespan and known end. Everything has a specified form and an allotted provision. '*When their time comes, they cannot delay it a single hour nor bring it forward.*' (7:34) When your heart becomes attached to any of the requirements of either this world or the Next, then return to the promise of Allah and be content with the knowledge of Allah and do not be greedy. There is fatigue and abasement in greed. Our shaykh's shaykh, Moulay al-'Arabi, said, 'Ordinary people fulfil their needs exhibiting their greed for them and yielding to them. We fulfil our needs by abstinence in respect of them and being distracted by Allah from thinking of them, considering them to be of little importance.'

If you must make supplication, let your supplication be for slavehood, not to seek your portion. If you leave portions, they will come to you. If seeking overwhelms you and you do seek something, and then the time of giving is delayed for you, do not suspect Allah's promise when He says: '*Call on me and I will answer you.*' (40:60) Do not despair of obtaining it. Allah has guaranteed to you that He will grant you what He wishes of the good of this world and the good of the Next. His kindness to you may prevent that request being answered since it is not right for you. Shaykh ash-Shadhili says, 'O Allah, we are unable to avert harm from ourselves when we know what we know, so how can we not be incapable of that when we do not know what we do not know?'

One of the commentators said that Allah's words: *'Your Lord creates and chooses whatever He wills. The choice is not theirs'* (28:68) mean that He chooses the matter in which they have choice and He answers you at that time when it is best and most beneficial for you, and then He gives that at the time in which He wishes, not at the time when you want. He may delay that until the Abode of Generosity and Abiding, and it is *'better and longer lasting.'* (87:17)

In a *hadith*, the Messenger of Allah ﷺ said, 'Someone who makes supplication is inevitably one of three: either his request will be hastened to him, or its reward will be given to him later, or a like evil will be repelled from him.' Shaykh Abu Muhammad 'Abdu-l-'Aziz al-Mahdawi said, 'The one who does not leave his chosen supplication out of pleasure with what Allah chooses for him is drawn on bit by bit. He is one of those about whom it is said, "Fulfil his need, I dislike to hear his voice." It is by the choice of Allah, not by his choice for himself, that he is answered, even if he is not given to. Actions are according to their seals.'

So what is said about fulfilling the promise and carrying out what is promised is clear to you, but in the manner in which Allah wills and at the time He wills. In that He commands you to truthfulness and affirmation and forbids you doubt and hesitation in order to thereby complete the opening of your inner eye and the delight of the lights of your secret. Then he says:

لَا يُشَكِّكَنَّكَ فِي الوَعْدِ عَدَمُ وُقُوعِ المَوْعُودِ – وَإِنْ تَعَيَّنَ زَمَنُه

– لِئَلَّا يَكُونَ ذَلِكَ قَدْحًا فِي بَصِيرَتِكَ وَإِخْمَادًا لِنُورِ سَرِيرَتِكَ

**7. If something that is promised does not happen
even though the time for it is set,
do not doubt the promise!
Doing that will dim your inner eye
and snuff out the light of your secret.**

Doubting a thing means wondering whether it is going to happen or not. Dimming the inner eye means diminishing it and denying its capacity. The 'inner eye' is that human faculty which is capable of perceiving the inner meaning of things and the 'secret' is that human faculty prepared for the firm receipt of knowledge and gnosis. Know that *nafs*, intellect, *ruh* and secret are all names for the same thing but they are used according to the level of perception exhibited. When it perceives appetites it is called the *nafs*. When it perceives legal judgements it is called the intellect. When it perceives *tajalliyat* and *waridat* it is called the *ruh*. When it perceives realities and fixed states it is called the secret. But in each case the locus is the same. Putting out the light of a thing means expunging it after it has appeared.

When Allah promises something by means of the Revelation or through inspiration given to a Prophet or a *wali* or through strong *tajalli*, do not doubt that promise, *murid*, if you are true. If the time for its occurrence is not specified, the matter has wide scope and a long or short period may elapse before it takes place. So do not doubt that it will occur, even if it takes a long time. It took forty years for the realisation of the supplication of Musa against Pharaoh when he said: '*Our Lord, obliterate their wealth.*' (10:88) If it is tied to a particular time and it does not occur when that time comes about, you must still not doubt the truth of the promise. It may be due to reasons and unseen circumstances which Allah has concealed from the Prophet or *wali* concerned, connected with the way He wishes to manifest His force, might and judgement.

Reflect on the case of Yunus when he informed his people of the punishment as he had been told to and then fled from them. That was connected to their refusal to accept Islam. When they became Muslim the punishment was deferred. The same is true of the case of Nuh when he said: '*My son is one of my family and Your promise is surely the truth.*' (11:45) which coincided with the literal general meaning of Allah's promise to him. Then Allah said to him: '*He is definitely not one of your family. He is someone whose action was not righteous.*' (11:46), showing the specific nature of the original promise. He had only promised him that the righteous members of his family would be saved, even if Nuh had understood the promise to be all inclusive. It is Allah's knowledge which is all-encompassing.

This is a hidden secret. The Prophets and great and true men do not rest with the simple promise alone. Their agitation continues and they are not happy with anything other than Allah. They look at the vastness of His knowledge and the effects of His power. One example of this is the words of Ibrahim the Friend, when he said: '*I have no fear of any partner you ascribe to Him unless My Lord should will such a thing to happen. My Lord encompasses all things in knowledge,'* (6:80) and the words of Shu'ayb: *'We would never return it,'* i.e. to the religion of disbelief, *'unless Allah our Lord so willed. Our Lord encompasses everything in His knowledge.'* (7:89) There is also the case of our Prophet ﷺ on the Day of Badr when he called on His Lord so earnestly that his cloak fell from his shoulders, saying: 'O Allah, Your covenant and promise! O Allah, if this group is destroyed, there will be none left to worship you after today.' The Siddiq said to him, 'Enough, Messenger of Allah. Allah will fulfil His promise to you.' So the Chosen One looked to the reality of Allah's power over and above His outward promise while the Siddiq remained with the literal meaning. Each was correct but the Prophet had a wider view and more perfect knowledge. As for al-Hudaybiyya, the time of the promise was not clear in that case since Allah says: *'He knew what you did not know.'* (48:27) When 'Umar said, 'Did you not tell us that we would enter Makka?' the Prophet ﷺ answered, 'Did I tell you it would be this year?' 'No,' he replied. He said, 'You will enter it and do *tawaf* in it.'

My brother, grasp my hand in affirmation of what Allah has promised you and have a good opinion of Him and His friends, especially your shaykh. Beware of concealing denial or doubt or that that will dim your inner eye and be the reason for its becoming dull and also for snuffing out the light of your secret. You could go right back to square one, losing all the ground you have gained and destroying everything you have built up. Look for the best interpretation and cling to the best conclusion. We have already mentioned the words of the shaykh of our shaykh, Sidi 'Ali: 'When we will something to happen and it happens, we have one joy. When it does not happen, there are ten joys.' That was only due to the vastness of his learning and his firm gnosis of his Lord. Allah may acquaint His friends with the arrival of the decree but not acquaint them with the kindness accompanying it. When the decree arrives accompanied by kindness, it may be so light and easy that a person may think that it has not happened. We have witnessed this and what we mentioned previously both in ourselves and in our shaykhs and it neither decreased our sincerity nor extinguished the light of our secret. Praise be to our Lord.

NOTE. Sidi at-Tawudi ibn Sawda said, 'This wisdom-saying is obscure. Someone may well ask, "How can it be said that the time for something like this can be set? If it was by Revelation, Revelation has ceased; and if it is by inspiration, then doubt about it could not cause the dimming of the inner eye since belief in it is not mandatory."' Our reply to this is: 'Our words only apply to true *murid*s who are travelling the path or those who have arrived at the goal. They are asked to affirm the shaykhs in all that they say since they are the heirs of the Prophets and so they follow in their footsteps. The Prophets received Revelation and the *awliya'* receive true inspiration because when hearts are purified of impurities and from anything other-than-Allah and are filled with lights and secrets, only the Truth is manifest in them. When they make a promise or threat, a *murid* must believe it. If he has any doubt or hesitation about what Allah has promised on the tongue of His Prophet or a shaykh, that will dim the light of his inner eye and snuff out his secret. If the time is not specified, wait for the thing to occur, even if it takes a long time. If the time is set and the thing does not take place, interpret it like the Messengers as being dependent on hidden reasons and preconditions. That is the difference between the *siddiq* and *sadiq* because the *siddiq* has no hesitation or astonishment while the *sadiq* hesitates and then resolves. If he sees a breaking of norms, he is astonished and finds that strange. Allah knows best.'

The arrival of Divine Power is made known by outward majesty and inward beauty followed by the attributes of perfection. The *murid* may doubt Allah's promise of blessings and the openings which result from it. That is why the Shaykh says:

إِذَا فَتَحَ لَكَ وِجْهَةً مِنَ التَّعَرُّفِ، فَلَا تُبَالِ مَعَهَا إِنْ قَلَّ عَمَلُكَ ، فَإِنَّهُ مَا فَتَحَهَا لَكَ إِلَّا وَهُوَ يُرِيدُ أَنْ يَتَعَرَّفَ إِلَيْكَ، أَلَمْ تَعْلَمْ أَنَّ التَّعَرُّفَ هُوَ مُورِدُهُ عَلَيْكَ، وَالْأَعْمَالَ أَنْتَ مُهْدِيهَا إِلَيْهِ، وَأَيْنَ مَا تَهْدِيهِ إِلَيْهِ مِمَّا هُوَ مُورِدُهُ عَلَيْكَ ؟

8. If He opens up a way of making Himself known to you, do not let your lack of actions worry you.

**The only reason He opened up the way for you
was to make Himself known to you.
Do you not see that He has brought you
knowledge of Himself
whereas you only present Him with actions.
Where is what you present to Him
in comparison with what He has brought to you!**

'Opening up' here means preparation and ease. It is usually used for good things. Here it is followed by knowledge of beautiful things and the manner in which they arrive. What is meant by 'way' is an opening which enables you to perceive His Presence and the use of the expression 'making known' implies a desire for recognition to take place. You say, 'Someone made himself known to me,' when he sought to make himself known to you. Direct apprehension of this kind makes the reality of the knowledge of what is known firm in the heart so that it cannot leave it.

If Allah reveals Himself to you by His Name, the Majestic, or His Name, the Conqueror, and by that opens a door and a way to you for you to have direct knowledge of Him, then know that Allah has shown concern for you, has wanted to select you for His nearness, and has chosen you for His presence. So cling to *adab* with satisfaction and submission. Receive it with joy and happiness. Do not be concerned about any actions you may neglect because of it. It is a means to actions of the heart. He has only opened this door to you because He wants to lift a veil between you and Him. Do you not know that these manifestations of Divine Majesty are what He sends to you to bring you to Him whereas you aspire to reach Him by means of the bodily actions you present to Him. What a vast difference there is between the puny actions and diseased states you present to Him and the Divine gnoses and face-to-face knowledges He brings you.

So, *murid*, be happy about any manifestations of Divine Majesty and revelations of Divine Power which come to you, such as illnesses, times of hunger and hardship, terrors and all the other things that are heavy on the *nafs* and difficult for it like poverty, humiliation, annoyance from others and other things which the *nafs* hates. All the things of this nature which happen to you are, in fact, great blessings and generous gifts, which are signs of the strength of your sincerity, and the greater your sincerity the greater the amount of direct Divine knowledge you will have. Those with the greatest affliction are the Prophets and then the next best people and then the next best. When Allah wants to shorten the distance between Himself and His slave, He grants affliction power over him so that when he is purified and cleansed by that, he is ready for the Divine Presence, just as silver and gold are purified by fire so that they are fit for the king's treasury.

Shaykhs and gnostics continue to delight in these blows and to consider them to be gifts. The shaykh of our shaykhs Sidi 'Ali al-'Imrani called them 'the Night of Power' and said, 'Constriction is the Night of Power which is better than a thousand months.' That is because of the actions of the heart which the slave harvests from it. An atom's weight of them are like mountains of actions of the limbs. I wrote two lines of poetry about this:

When a time of need knocks at my door,
  I open the door to it with joy and happiness.
I tell it, 'Welcome and welcome again!
  Your time with me profits me more than the Night of
  Power!'

Know that these manifestations of majesty are a test from Allah and a gauge of people and the way that silver and gold are distinguished from copper. There are many pretenders who make a display of gnosis and certainty with their tongues. Then when the tempestuous winds of the decree strike them, they cast them into the deserts of despair and denial. If someone claims what he does not have, he will be exposed and disgraced by being tested. Shaykh Moulay al-'Arabi used to say, 'The greatest wonder of all is someone who seeks gnosis of Allah and is eager for it, but then, when Allah gives him knowledge, flees from it and denies it.' Shaykh al-Buzidi said, 'These revelations of majesty fall into three categories. One betokens punishment and expulsion, one discipline and admonition, and the third increase and ascension.' As for the category which betokens punishment and expulsion, it is for someone who has bad *adab* towards Allah and so Allah Almighty punishes him by it. He is ignorant of the reality of what is happening and becomes angry, despairs and denies and so that increases him in expulsion and distance from Allah. As for the category which betokens discipline, it is for someone whose *adab* is faulty and so Allah Almighty disciplines him and He teaches him through it and alerts him to his defective *adab* and he ceases his negligence. It is therefore a blessing for him in the form of retribution. As for the category which betokens increase and ascension, it is for someone on whom these manifestations of majesty descend without reason and so he has gnosis through them and disciplines himself in them and rises to the station of firmness and stability. That is why one of them said, 'Firmness is according to the amount of testing.'

LESSON. If you want majesty made easier for you, you must welcome it with its opposite, which is beauty. It will be transformed into beauty immediately, The method of doing that is that when Allah manifests Himself by His Name, the Constricter, outwardly, you should meet Him with expansion inwardly. Then it will become expansion. When He manifests Himself by His Name, the Strong, then meet Him with weakness. When He manifests Himself by His Name, the Mighty, meet Him with inward humility. That is how things are met with their opposite. Shaykh Moulay al-'Arabi says, 'These things all have one reality. If you drink it as honey, you find it to be honey. If you drink it as milk, you find it to be milk. If you drink it as colocynth, you will find it to be as bitter as colocynth. Therefore, my brother, drink what is pleasant and do not drink what is ugly.'

Then the Shaykh speaks about actions and their fruits, which are *adab*, being at peace under the descent of the decree without exercising management or choice, or trying to bring forward what has been delayed or delay what has been brought forward. That is the gauge of how to see if you receive what emerges as manifestations of Divine Power and Majesty with proper gnostic understanding.

$$ تَنَوَّعَتْ أَجْنَاسُ الْأَعْمَالِ لِتَنَوُّعِ وَارِدَاتِ الْأَحْوَالِ $$

9. Types of action are of various kinds due to the varied inspirations of different states.

The word 'action' here refers to physical movements while the word 'inspirations' refers to movements of the heart. Passing thoughts, inspirations and states all have the same locus: the heart. As long as the heart is subject to both dark and light thoughts, what occurs in it is called a passing thought (*khâtir*). When dark thoughts are cut off from it, a thought occuring in it is called an inspiration (*wârid*) or a state (*hal*), and the connection between them is figurative, not something cut and dried. They are both subject to change. When a state continues and subsists, it becomes called a station (*maqam*).

Outward actions vary according to inward states; or you might say that an action of the limbs follows an action of the heart. If contraction comes to the heart, it appears on the limbs as stillness. If expansion comes to it, it appears on the limbs as lightness and movement. If asceticism and scrupulousness come to the heart, they appear as abandonment and abstention. If desire and greed come, they appear as fatigue and exhaustion. Love and yearning appear as ecstasy and dancing. Divine gnosis and witnessing appear as rest and stillness. The same applies to other states and the appearance of resultant actions. These states may vary in one and the same heart, producing a variety of outward actions. Or a heart may be dominated by one state so that only one kind of action results from it. If contraction dominates a person, he will usually appear dispirited. Or he may be dominated by expansion or some other state. Allah knows best. The *hadith* states: 'There is lump of flesh in the body, the nature of which is that when it is sound, the entire body is sound, and when it is corrupt, the entire body is corrupt – it is the heart.' So this is the reason that the states of the Sufis vary. Some are worshippers, some are ascetics, some are scrupulous, and some are *murid*s and gnostics.

Shaykh Zarruq said in his *Qawa'id*, 'Rule: A life of piety (*nask*) entails adopting every path of virtue and turning one's back on everything else. If someone's desire lies in making that a reality, he is a worshipper. If his inclination is to concentrate on states, that implies scrupulousness. If he prefers to leave things out of the desire to be safe, he is an abstainer. If he abandons himself to what Allah desires, he is a gnostic.' He said in another rule: 'Different methods do not necessitate different goals. In spite of the different methods employed, such as worship, abstention and gnosis, every striver after unity pursues the way which leads to nearness to Allah on the Path of Nobility. All of them interconnect. So the gnostic must be involved in worship since there is no point to his gnosis if he does not worship the One he knows and he must be involved in abstinence since there is no reality to him if he does not turn from what is other than His Lord. The worshipper must also have aspects of both gnosis and abstention since there is no true worship without some gnosis and there is no devotion to worship except through abstention. The same is true for the abstainer, since there is no true abstention which is not accompanied by gnosis and worship. Anything else will make the blessings null and void. But the one who is dominated by action is a worshipper, the one dominated by doing without this world is an abstainer, and the one dominated by looking at how Allah disposes of things is a gnostic. All equally constitute Sufism, and Allah knows best.'

Since sincerity is a precondition for every action, he now mentions its effect:

$$ الْأَعْمَالُ صُوَرٌ قَائِمَةٌ وَأَرْوَاحُهَا وُجُودُ سِرِّ الْإِخْلَاصِ فِيهَا $$

10. Actions are simply set-up images.
Their life-breath is the existence
of the secret of pure sincerity in them.

The word 'actions' here refers to movements of both the body and the heart. The 'images' are the pictures of the particular activity formed by the mind. The 'life-breath' (*ruh*) is the secret of life which is lodged in living creatures. Here it refers to that quality by which perfection in actions is achieved. 'Pure sincerity' is when the heart is entirely devoted to the worship of the Lord together with its secret and its core. That is the true sincerity characterised by giving up all claims to personal strength and power, for an action is only made perfect by that, even if it is sound without it. Pure sincerity precludes showing-off and hidden *shirk* while its secret precludes conceit and self-regard. Showing off detracts from the soundness of actions, while conceit detracts only from their perfection. All actions are shapes and forms. Their life-breath is the existence of sincerity in them. Just as bodies can only subsist if they possess spirits since otherwise they are dead and prone, so actions of the body and heart only subsist by the existence of sincerity in them. Otherwise they are just set-up images and empty forms worthy of no consideration.

Allah Almighty says: '*They were only ordered to worship Allah, making their deen sincerely His, as people of pure natural faith,*' (98:5) and: '*Worship Allah, making your deen sincerely His.*' (39:2) The Messenger of Allah ﷺ reported that Allah says, 'I am the furthest removed from anything which is associated with Me.' The Messenger of Allah ﷺ also said, 'That which I most fear for my community is hidden *shirk*. It lies in showing off.' In one version, 'Fear this hidden *shirk*, It creeps like an ant.' They asked, 'What is hidden *shirk*?' 'Showing off,' he replied. In another *hadith*, the Prophet ﷺ was asked about sincerity and said, 'Not until I ask Jibril.' When he asked him, he said, 'Not until I ask the Lord of Might.' When he asked Him, He told him, 'It is one of My secrets which I have entrusted to the hearts of those of My slaves who love Me. No angel can see it to enable him to record it and no shaytan can see it to enable him to corrupt it.' One of the people of Allah said, 'This refers to station of *ihsan*: which is to worship Allah as if you were seeing Him.'

Pure sincerity has three degrees: the degree of the common people, the degree of the elite, and the degree of the elite of the elite. The sincerity of the common people involves the elimination of created beings from their dealings with Allah while at the same time seeking their share of both this world and the Next, such as the preservation of the body, money, expanded provision, palaces and houris. The sincerity of the elite involves seeking their share of the Next world rather than this world. The sincerity of the elite of the elite involves not seeking any share whatsoever. So their worship is in order to fully realise their slavehood and fulfil the demands of their Lord, or out of love and yearning for the vision of His face. As Ibn al-Farid said:

My request is not for the bliss of the Garden.
  My only desire is to see You.

Another said:

All of them worship out of fear of the Fire
  and see salvation as a generous prize,
Or seek to dwell in the Garden
  and relax in meadows and drink of Salsabil.
I have no opinion of Gardens or the Fire.
  I do not seek any recompense for my love.

Shaykh Abu Talib said, 'Sincerity with the sincere is to eliminate all creatures from one's dealings with the Real. The first of creatures is the self. Sincerity among the lovers is not to do an action for the sake of the self. Otherwise it is affected by looking for recompense or desiring a share for the self. For the people of realisation, sincerity is to eliminate all creatures from dealings with of the Real by not seeing them in respect of actions and by not relying on them or relaxing with them in states.'

One of the shaykhs said, 'Make your actions sound through sincerity and make your sincerity sound by freeing yourself from any claim to strength and power.' One of the gnostics said, 'Sincerity is not achieved until you are nothing in other people's eyes and and they are nothing in yours.' That is why another said, 'Whenever you fall in people's eyes, you become great in the sight of Allah. Whenever you become great in people's eyes, you fall in the sight of Allah.' This happens when you take note of them and are watchful of them.

I heard our shaykh say, 'As long as the slave continues to be watchful of people and to have awe of them, his sincerity will never be fully realised.' He also said, 'Watchfulness of Allah will never be combined with watchfulness of creation because it is impossible to see Him and see other-than-Him with Him.' The upshot of all this is that it is not possible to ever be free of the self and purified of subtle showing-off without a shaykh. Allah knows best.

This means that obscurity is part of sincerity. Indeed, it is usually only achieved through it since it is something the self has no share in. That is why he said:

$$\text{اِدْفَنْ وُجُودَكَ فِي أَرْضِ الْخُمُولِ، فَمَا نَبَتَ مِمَّا لَمْ يُدْفَنْ لَا}$$
$$\text{يَتِمُّ نِتَاجُهُ}$$

11. Bury your existence in the earth of obscurity.
For anything which grows without first being buried
will never produce proper fruit.

'Bury' means cover up and conceal. 'Obscurity' means loss of standing in other people's eyes. 'Fruit' is a metaphor for wisdom, gifts and knowledge which the slave harvests from his gnosis of Allah. That happens when his *nafs* dies and his *ruh* comes to life. *Murid*, conceal your *nafs* and bury it in obscurity until it is intimate with it, happy with it and finds it sweeter than honey, and until self-display becomes more bitter than colocynth. If you bury it in the soil of obscurity and its roots spread out in it, then you will pluck its fruits and obtain its yield: the secret of sincerity and realisation of the station of the elite of the elite. If you do not bury it in the earth of obscurity and allow it to give itself renown, its tree dies or its fruits drop off. When the gnostics harvest from the gardens of gnosis they have planted and the treasures of wisdom they have buried, and the storehouses of their understanding become full, you will be at their door poor, begging or trying to steal.

Sayyiduna 'Isa asked his companions, 'Where does grain grow?' They replied, 'In the earth.' He said, 'The same applies to wisdom. It only grows in a heart which is like the earth.' One of the gnostics said, 'If you bury your *nafs* in earth below earth, your heart will rise to heaven above heaven.' Once the Messenger of Allah ﷺ was sitting with al-Aqra' ibn Habis, a great man of the Banu Tamim, when one of the poor Muslims went past. He asked al-Aqra', 'What do you say about this one?' He replied, 'Messenger of Allah, this is just one of the poor Muslims. If he were to propose marriage, his proposal would not be worth accepting, and if he were to intercede, his intercession would not be granted, and if he were to speak, his words would not be listened to.' Then a wealthy man passed by them and the Messenger of Allah asked him, 'And what do you say about this one?' He replied, 'If he proposed marriage, his proposal would be accepted, if he interceded his intercession would be granted, and if he were to speak, his words would be listened to.' The Messenger of Allah ﷺ said, 'The former (the poor man) is better than everything the earth contains and better than this last one.'

There are many *hadith*s and sayings which praise obscurity. Even if it contained nothing but rest and freeing the heart from this world, that would be enough. Al-Hadrami wrote:

Live obscure among people and be pleased with that.
   That is sounder for this world and the *deen*.
If someone associates with people, his *deen* is not safe
   and he vacillates between action and inaction.

One of the wise said, 'Obscurity is a blessing but the *nafs* rejects it. Self-display is an affliction yet the *nafs* desires it.' He also said, 'The end of this Path of ours will only be reached by people who sweep rubbish heaps with their spirits.'

Someone who is tested by having rank and leadership must make use of path of ruin in such a way that it will lower his reputation, making sure that he does not overstep from doing things which are disliked into the realm of what is actually forbidden. He should do such things as begging in shops and houses, eating in markets and where people will see him, sleeping in them, drinking from a water-skin, carrying rubbish on his head, walking barefooted, making a display of greed, miserliness and avarice, wearing the *muraqqa'a* and large prayer beads, and anything else which burdens the *nafs* and is permitted or disliked, but not unlawful.

Shaykh Zarruq said, 'Just as it is no use planting crops in bad land, it is not permitted to seek obscurity in a way which is not pleasing to Allah. But making that analogous with suicide is not sound because loss of physical life prevents every good, whether mandatory or recommended, and losing it when it is possible to prolong it is forbidden by consensus according to the words of Allah: '*Do not cast yourselves into destruction.*' (2:195) Whereas in the case of obscurity the opposite is true. Nothing is lost and instead perfection is obtained by it, which is denial of rank and position, when its basis is permissibility.' Some men of knowledge even assert that loss of the ephemeral life of the body is, if anything, more likely to be permissible than loss of the everlasting life represented by gnosis, so reflect. I heard our Shaykh say, 'The true *faqir* kills his *nafs* using the minimum amount of what is permitted and the false *faqir* falls into forbidden things and never kills his *nafs*.' He said, 'We have enough scope in what is permissible to spare us from ever having to resort to unlawful and disliked things.'

Begging is disliked or forbidden if done with the aim of obtaining food for your body when you already have enough. If it is undertaken with the aim of nurturing the spirit, then it is not unlawful. In his commentary on al-Bukhari, al-Qastallani mentioned from Ibn al-'Arabi that it is mandatory for the *faqir* in the early stages. Look at what he says there. He mentions enough about it in his Basic Research. Look there at what he says about not taking from other creatures. This will be discussed later, Allah willing.

This path of ruin which I have mentioned can also entail notoriety since obscurity means being masked from people's eyes and this may in fact entail great exposure. The reality of obscurity is losing status in other people's eyes, concealing the secret of *wilaya*. Everything that serves to lower your status in their sight and negate any hint of *wilaya* is in fact obscurity, even if there is some display outwardly. That is why our shaykh used to say, 'This Path of ours is obscurity in the outward and outwardness in that obscurity!' An-Najibi said in al-Inala, 'As for those among the Sufis who say that the *muraqqa'a* is ostentation, the response is found in the fact that Salman al-Farisi from Iraq to Syria travelled to visit Abu-d-Darda' on foot wearing a coarse mantle. He was told, 'You have made yourself ostentatious.' He said, 'True good is the good of the Next World. Here I am a slave who dresses as a slave. When I am free, then I will wear a robe of honour and not worry about its borders.'

Another illustration of this is the report that al-Ghazali was carrying ox-hides on his back when he met his shaykh, al-Kharraz, sweeping the market and using a water-skin to give people water. I heard that many times from my Shaykh but have never found anyone else who knew about it. There is also the story of ash-Shushtari with his shaykh. Ash-Shushtari was a government minister and scholar and his father was a governor. When he wanted to set out on the Path of the People (of Sufism), his shaykh told him, 'You will not get anywhere until you sell your goods, wear tattered garments, take a banner and enter the market.' He did all that and asked his shaykh, 'What should I say in the market?' He said, 'Say, "I begin by mentioning the Beloved."' So he entered the market, waving his banner and said, 'I begin by mentioning the Beloved.' He kept that up for three days and then the veils covering his heart were rent asunder and he began, in the marketplace, to sing about direct knowledge of Allah.

There is a companion story about a man who was with Abu Yazid al-Bistami. For thirty years the man did not leave his gathering or part from him. He said one day, 'Master, for thirty years I have fasted in the day and prayed during the night and abandoned my appetites and yet I have not found in my heart anything at all of what you have mentioned. I still, however, believe and affirm all you say.' Abu Yazid said to him, 'Even if you continue to pray for another thirty years, if you remain as you are now, you will still never find a single atom of it.'

'Why, master?' he asked.

'Because,' he replied, 'you are veiled from it by your *nafs*.'

'Is there any remedy for this,' the man enquired, 'so that the veil can be removed?'

'Yes, there is,' Abu Yazid replied, 'but you will neither accept it nor carry it out.'

'Yes, I will,' he insisted, 'I will do what you say.'

'Go immediately to the barber,' Abu Yazid said to him,

'and have your hair and beard shaved off. Take off these fine clothes and replace them with a coarse woollen robe. Hang a nosebag round your neck and fill it with walnuts. Then gather some children around you and shout in your loudest voice, "Children! I will give a nut to whoever gives me a slap!" Then enter the market where you are respected looking like this until everyone who knows you has had a good look.'

'Abu Yazid!' he exclaimed, 'Glory be to Allah! Do you say this to someone like me and think that I will do it !'

'Your words, "Glory be to Allah" are *shirk*.'

'How can that be?' he asked.

'Because,' Abu Yazid explained, 'you esteem your *nafs* and so it is that that you are really glorifying.'

'I cannot do this, Abu Yazid, and I will not do it, but direct me to something less than this that I can do.'

'You must start by doing this,' Abu Yazid told him, 'so that your high standing falls from you and you humble your *nafs*, then after that I will tell you what is appropriate for you.'

'I cannot do this.'

'Yet you said that you would both accept and do it. I know for sure that no one can aspire to be privy to the secrets of the Unseen which are veiled from the common people until he makes his *nafs* die and breaks the norms within which the common people are enmeshed. Then normal patterns will be broken for him and secrets will appear to him.'

There is also the story of Abu 'Imran al-Barda'i with his shaykh Abu 'Abdullah at-Tawdi in Fes. He shaved his head, put on a rough robe and took a loaf of bread, calling out for someone to save him from it. He did all that. There is the story of Shaykh 'Abdu-r-Rahman al-Majdhub, who ate figs from people's trees and sang in the markets. We also have the story of the shaykh of our shaykhs, Sidi 'Ali al-'Imrani, and his ruining his reputation in Fes which is famous. There is also the case of Shaykh Moulay al-'Arabi who wore a sack and gave people water from a water-skin and did other things all of which are well known. These stories indicate that obscurity is not what the common people understand it to be. It is not staying inside houses or fleeing to mountains. For those with realisation, doing that is, in fact, tantamount to ostentation. Obscurity, as Shaykh Zarruq said, '...is for the *nafs* to fully realise its lowest characteristic and be constantly aware of it. Its lowest characteristic is abasement and all that burdensome for it. So the *faqir* does his best to adopt the attribute of humility and pluck its fruit in order to attain to effective action and the perfection of realisation.'

If it is said that doing things like this will mean exposing oneself to people's words and make them fall into slander, I reply that it depends on the aim and intention. If someone does any of these things with the aim of killing his *nafs*, achieving sincerity and healing his heart, he will forgive and excuse those who talk about him. In his book, Sidi 'Ali said, 'We excuse those who excuse us and also excuse those who do not excuse us.' In his *Qawa'id*, Shaykh Zarruq said, 'The legal ruling is general for the common people because its aim to establish the outward *shari'a*, raise its standard and make its words victorious, while the ruling of *tasawwuf* is for the elite because it concerns the relationship of the slave with his Lord and nothing else. So it is valid for a *faqih* to object to a Sufi, but not valid for a Sufi to object to a *faqih*. One must return from *tasawwuf* to *fiqh* in respect of legal judgements, but not in respect of inner realities.'

NOTE: These remedies which we have mentioned apply to those who are in a state of illness. As for anyone who has been cured and perfected his annihilation, he is the slave of Allah whether he shows it or hides it. Abu-l-'Abbas al-Mursi said, 'If someone desires to make a display, he is the slave of display, and if someone desires concealment, he is the slave of concealment. The slave of Allah is the same whether he is displayed or concealed.'

Since purification of the finer points of ostentation and self-deception is only achieved through reflection, and reflection is only fully realised through retreat, he said:

$$ مَا نَفَعَ الْقَلْبَ شَيْءٌ مِثْلُ عُزْلَةٍ يَدْخُلُ بِهَا مِيدَانَ فِكْرَةٍ $$

12. Nothing benefits the heart like a period of seclusion through which it enters the arena of reflection.

To benefit means to make the desired result arrive. The heart is the faculty which is ready-made to receive knowledge. The word 'seclusion' here means the isolation of the heart with Allah, and refers to a spiritual retreat (*khalwa*) in this instance, which involves the separation of its possessor from any intercourse with other people. The heart is rarely isolated unless its possessor is also isolated. The word 'arena' is used for reflection since thoughts recur in the same way that horses do when running round a circular track and 'reflection' here means the heart travelling to the Presence of the Lord. There are two sorts of reflection: reflection which entails confirmation and faith, and reflection which entails witnessing and vision, as will come.

The reason that there is nothing more beneficial to the heart than seclusion accompanied by reflection is because seclusion is like a fever and reflection is the remedy for it. The remedy is of no benefit without the fever and the fever is of no benefit without the remedy. So there is no good in seclusion without reflection nor in reflection without seclusion since what is desired from the seclusion is the freeing of the heart; what is desired from freeing the heart is to let it move around in reflection; and what is desired from the reflection is the acquisition of knowledge which will be firmly fixed in the heart. When knowledge of Allah is firmly fixed in the heart, that is its cure and its restoration to health. Then it is what Allah calls 'a sound heart' (*qalbin salim*). Allah Almighty says about the Rising: '*The Day when neither wealth nor sons will be of any use – except to those who come to Allah with a sound and flawless heart.*' (26:89)

It is said that the heart is like the stomach. When bad humours dominate it, it becomes ill and only fever helps it. The fever expels the impurities and prevents a lot of bad humours. We find in a *hadith*: 'The stomach is the seat of illness and fever is the chief factor in healing.' The same can be said of the heart. When random thoughts gain control over it and the senses overpower it, it becomes ill and may die unless a fever comes to help it and causes it to flee from its usual haunts, which is socialising with other people. If you withdraw from other people and reflect, the cure takes place and your heart is set straight. Otherwise, it will remain ill until you meet Allah with a sick heart, full of doubt and destructive thoughts. We ask Allah for true good health.

Al-Junayd said, 'The noblest of gatherings is sitting with reflection in the arenas of *tawhid*.' Shaykh ash-Shadhili said, 'The fruit of retreat is obtaining the gifts of grace. They are four in number: the removal of the veil, the descent of mercy, the realisation of love and a truthful tongue in speech. Allah Almighty says: *"When he had separated himself from them and what they worshipped besides Allah, We gave to him...."* (19:49)'

Know that there are ten benefits in *khalwa*.

- The first is safety from disasters of the tongue. When someone is alone, there is no one else to talk to. The Prophet ﷺ said, 'May Allah show mercy to a person who is silent and so safe, or who speaks and gains good.' In general no one is safe from its harm except for someone who prefers seclusion to mixing with other people. Shaykh Sidi 'Ali said, 'When I see a *faqir* preferring seclusion to society, silence to speech, and fasting to satiety, I know that his melon is succulent. When I see him preferring socialising, speech and satiety over their opposites, I know that his melon is hollow.' We read in *al-Qut*, 'A lot of speech entails lack of scrupulousness, lack of *taqwa*, a lengthy calling to account, the unrolling of the scroll, a great number of claimants connecting the wronged to the wronger, a great deal of testimony from the noble scribes, and constant turning away from the Noble King, because words are the gateway to the major sins of the tongue: lying, slander, backbiting, and false testimony. It says in tradition, 'Most of the sins of the sons of Adam will be committed by the tongue,' and, 'The people with the greatest number of wrong actions on the Day of Rising will be those who most delve into what does not concern them.'

- The second benefit is protecting the eyes and being safe from the tribulations of sight. Anyone who withdraws from people is safe from looking at them and at what they possess of this world and its adornments. Allah says: '*Do not direct your eyes longingly to what We have given certain of them to enjoy, the flower of the life of this world, so that We can test them by it.*' (20:130) So Allah forbids the *nafs* to covet things of this world and to compete with its people. Muhammad ibn Sirin said, 'Beware of too much looking. It leads to an excess of appetite.' One author said, 'Those who look a lot are full of constant regrets.' It is said, 'The eye is a source of destruction.' If someone gives his eye free rein, he seeks his own destruction. Looking with the eye at things makes the heart dispersed.

- The third benefit is the preservation of the heart from showing off, flattery and other illnesses. One man of wisdom said, 'Anyone who socialises with people flatters them. Anyone who flatters them shows off to them. Anyone who shows off to them, falls into what they fall into and so is destroyed as they are destroyed.' One of the Sufis said, 'I asked one of the Abdal devoted to Allah, "What is the route to realisation?" He replied, "Do not look at creatures. Looking at them is darkness." I replied, "I cannot avoid it." He said, "Then do not listen to their words. Their words are hardness." I replied, "I cannot avoid it." He said, "Do not deal with them. Dealing with them is loss, regret and alienation." I replied, "I am among them and so I must deal with them." He said, "Then do not rely on them. Relying on them is destruction." I said, "This might be possible." He said, "You look at those who play, listen to the words of the ignorant, deal with cheats, rely on those who are destroyed, and you want to experience the sweetness of obedience when your heart is with other than Allah! Most unlikely! This will never be!" Then he left me.' Al-Qushayri said, 'When the masters of striving want to protect their hearts from ruinous thoughts, they do not look at the pleasant things of this world.' He said, 'This is one of their major principles in striving in the states of discipline.'

- The fourth is abstention with regard to this world and being content with what you have of it. That comprises the honour and perfection of a slave and is a reason for his being loved by his Lord since the Prophet ﷺ said, 'Abstain from this world and Allah will love you, and abstain from what belongs to other people and other people will love you.' There is no doubt that someone who isolates himself from people and does not look at their desire for this world and their pursuit of it will be safe from following them in that and safe from the pursuit of ruinous characteristics and demeaning behaviour. Few of those who mix with the people of this world are safe from what they do. It is reported that the Prophet 'Isa said, 'Do not sit with the dead or your hearts will die.' They asked, 'Who are the dead, Spirit of Allah?' He replied, 'Those who love this world and desire it.'

• The fifth benefit is protection from bad company which is immensely corrupting and contains terrible dangers. One tradition reads: 'The metaphor of a bad companion is that of a forge. Even if it does not burn you with its sparks, its foul smell still clings to you.' Sidi 'Abdu-r-Rahman al-Majdhub said, 'Sitting with other than good people is ruinous, even if you are pure.' Allah Almighty revealed to Dawud, 'Dawud, why do I see you withdrawn and alone?' He said, 'My God, I turned from creation for Your sake.' He said, 'Da'ud, be vigilant and go back to your brothers but do not keep the company of any brother who is not conducive to your gaining My pleasure. He is your enemy and will make your heart hard and distance you from Me.' If you want company, then you should choose the company of the Sufis. Their company is a treasure which will never be exhausted. Al-Junayd said, 'When Allah desires good for a person, He puts him with the Sufis and denies him the company of the reciters.' He said, 'By Allah, someone who has success only achieves it through keeping company with someone who has himself achieved success.'

- The sixth benefit is devotion to worship and *dhikr* and resolve to have *taqwa* and good action. There is no doubt that when a person is alone, he devotes himself to the worship of his Lord and concentrates his limbs and heart on it since there is nothing to distract him from that. We read in *al-Qut*, 'As for *khalwa*, it frees the heart from people and concentrates the *himma* on the Creator and strengthens the resolve to be firm.'

- The seventh is experiencing the sweetness of acts of obedience and great delight in the intimate conversations which fill his secret. This is well tested and sound. Abu Talib said, 'The *murid* is not truthful until he experiences sweetness, energy and strength in *khalwa* which he does not find when in society, and until his most intimate moments are when he is alone, his solace is in retreat and the best of his actions are done in secret.'

- The eighth benefit is rest for the heart and body. Mixing with people results in fatigue for the heart due to concern with their business and fatigue for the body due to striving to fulfil their desires and doing what they want. Even if there is a reward in that, the person doing it misses what is greater and more important, which is the concentration of the heart in the presence of the Lord.

- The ninth benefit is protection for oneself and one's *deen* from being exposed to the evils and quarrels which ordinary socialising makes inevitable. The *nafs* is eager to rush to involve itself in such things when it is joined to the people of this world and to contend with them for it. Ash-Shafi'i said:

For anyone who tastes this world, I too have eaten it,
  and its sweetness and punishment were forced upon me,
And I only found that it was nothing but delusion and falsehood
  like a mirage appearing in the desert.
It is nothing but a rotting corpse,
  which the dogs of concern are attracted to.
If you avoid it, you will live in safety from its people.
  If you are attracted to it, its dogs will snap at you.

- The tenth benefit is consolidation in the practice of reflection and contemplation, and it is the greatest goal of *khalwa*. A tradition says, 'Reflection for an hour is better than seventy years of worship.' 'Isa used to say, 'What bliss there is for someone whose words are *dhikr*, whose silence is reflection, and whose glance is a lesson! The cleverest of people is the one who humbles his *nafs* and works for what comes after death.' Ka'b said, 'Anyone who desires the honour of the Next World should reflect a lot.' The best worship of Abu-d-Darda' was reflection. That is because by it one reaches the realities of things, makes the truth clear from falsehood, is aware of the hidden snares and ruses of the *nafs* and the delusion of this world, and by it one comes to know the devices to use to protect oneself from them and be purified of them.

Al-Hasan said, 'Reflection is a mirror which shows you your good and bad. It also, when you reflect on His signs and works, acquaints you with the immensity and majesty of Allah. It also acquaints you with His blessings and gifts, His majesty and hidden secrets. Because of that it gives you radiant states which remove the sickness of your heart and make you go straight in obedience to your Lord.' Shaykh Ibn 'Abbad said, 'These are the fruits of the retreat of the people of the beginning. As for the people of the end, they are always in retreat, even if they are in the midst of people, because they are strong and veiled by gatheredness from separation and by meaning from the sensory.' Retreat and mixing are the same for them because they take their share from each but none takes a share from them.

If the *murid* is attached to seclusion, silence, hunger and wakefulness, his *wilaya* is complete, Divine concern appears to him, lights shine on him and the forms of otherness are effaced from the mirror of his heart. The shaykh indicated that when he expresses amazement at its opposite:

كَيْفَ يَشْرِقُ قَلْبٌ وَصُوَرُ الْأَكْوَانِ مُنْطَبِعَةٌ فِي مِرْآتِهِ ؟

**13. How can a heart be illuminated
if the images of created things
are imprinted on its mirror?**

The images referred to are the things themselves and their representations in the senses and imagination. Created things are all types of creatures, small or large. The word 'imprinted' means firmly fixed, since if something in imprinted and stamped on something, its image is transferred to it. The word 'mirror' used in respect of the heart is a metaphor for the faculty of insight which is the eye of the heart by which the meaning of things, both beautiful and ugly, is perceived. Allah made the heart of the human being like a polished mirror in which is reflected whatever stands in front of it. It can only face in one direction at a time. When Allah shows concern for one of His slaves, He fills its reflection with the lights of His *malakut* and the secrets of His *jabarut* and the heart is not attached to the love of any of dark beings or false illusions. So the lights of faith and *ihsan* are imprinted on the mirror of his heart and the moons of *tawhid* and suns of gnosis shine in it.

That was what ash-Shushtari was alluding to when he said, 'Lower the eye and you will see ... Be annihilated to creation and your secrets will appear to you. By polishing the mirror, your denial will be swept away.' Then he said, 'The starry heavens orbit within in you and shine and sparkle, and the suns and the moons rise and set within you. Polishing the mirror of your heart sweeps away your denial of the Truth to the point that you recognise Allah in everything and your heart becomes the hub of the whole universe of lights and the moons of *tawhid* and suns of gnosis appear in it.'

When, by His justice and wisdom, Allah desires to disappoint a slave, he occupies himself with dark phenomena and physical appetites so that it is those things which become imprinted on the mirror of his heart and, because of that, he is veiled from the rising of the suns of gnosis and the lights of faith by their phenomenal darkness and imaginary forms. As the images of created things pile up in him, the light of faith is extinguished and the veil thickened. Then he can only see material existence and can only reflect on material existence. That can lead to the veil becoming impenetrable and the total extinction of the light of faith so that the heart does not even acknowledge the existence of light in its source. That is the station of disbelief – we seek refuge with Allah!

When the heart is less encrusted with rust, however, and the veil is thinner, people affirm the light even though they cannot really see it. This is the station of the common Muslims. They vary in nearness and distance, and strength and weakness of affirmation, each according to his certainty and lack of ties to this world and attachments to appetites and illusion. In a *hadith* it says that the hearts rust as iron rusts and that faith wears out as a new garment wears out. In another *hadith* it says that everything has a polish, and that what polishes the hearts is *dhikru'llah*. The Prophet ﷺ also said, 'When someone commits a wrong action, a black spot forms in his heart. If he refrains and asks forgiveness, it is polished away. If he repeats it, it grows in the heart until it overwhelms it. That is the rust which Allah mentions: *"No indeed! Rather what they earned has rusted up their hearts."* (83:14)'

Since you know that the heart can only face one direction at a time, you must realise that when it faces light, it shines and when it faces darkness, it goes dark. Darkness and light are never combined. So now you will understand the reason for the astonishment of the Shaykh when he asked how a heart could shine with the light of faith and *ihsan* when the dark forms of created things are imprinted on its mirror. Two opposites cannot co-exist. Allah Almighty says: *'Allah has not allotted a man two hearts in his breast.'* (33:4) So, *faqir*, you only have one heart. When you turn to creatures, you turn away from the Real. When you turn to the Real, you turn away from creatures and travel from the world of the *mulk* to the *malakut* and from the *malakut* to the *jabarut*. As long as you remain shackled to this world by your appetites you will never travel to your Lord.

The Prayer of the Qutb Ibn Mashish

In the Name of Allah, the All-Merciful, Most Merciful
May Allah bless our master Muhammad and his family
and Companions and grant them peace abundantly

The shaykh, imam and scholar, righteous *wali* and gnostic
of his Lord, Sayyidi Ahmad ibn Muhammad ibn 'Ajiba, may
Allah be pleased with him and benefit us by him, says:

We praise You, the One who manifests Himself to
the hearts of His *awliya'* with complete beauty
and radiance, so that their contemplation
wanders through the meadows of His *malakut*. We thank
You, the One who takes charge of the secrets of Your
Prophets and elite, so that they plunge into the seas of His
jabarut. We pray and bless the seed of existence and the
sunrise of happiness, our master Muhammad. It is from the
secret of his humanness that all other secrets burst forth
and from the divine nature of his attributes that all lights
burst forth. Bless him with a prayer and blessing which give
him what he truly possesses in terms of immense rank and
worth. May Allah be pleased with his good Companions
and the pure people of his House.

This is a subtle commentary on the prayer of the *Qutb*,
Sayyidi 'Abdu-s-Salam ibn Mashish, may Allah benefit us

by his mention and pour out on us some of what overflows from him. Amen. Our shaykh, the gnostic of his Lord, model of the wayfarers and teacher of those who have arrived, Sayyidi Muhammad ibn Ahmad al-Buzidi al-Hasani, recommended that I write this commentary and I have responded to his request, hoping to gain his love, and drink from the overflowing of his help. We will preface it with a biography of the Shaykh and something of what he said.

HIS BIOGRAPHY

He is the shaykh and imam, the gnostic who arrived at the goal, the great *wali* and famous *qutb*, the sun of his time and unique man of his age, our master 'Abdu-s-Salam ibn Mashish (which is sometimes read as Bashish, in the dialect of Mazin, meaning light, clever, intelligent servant) ibn Abi Bakr ibn 'Ali ibn Jurma ibn 'Isa ibn Salam ibn Mizwar (Berber for scion of his father, and it is used to designate the leader of a people) ibn 'Ali ibn Haydra, (which means "lion") ibn Muhammad ibn Idris al-Azhar ibn Idris the Great, ibn 'Abdullah the Perfect ibn al-Hasan al-Muthanna ibn al-Hasan as-Sibt ibn 'Ali, may Allah honour him, and may He pleased with all of them.

He died a martyr in the year 622 AH or a little after that. Ibn Khaldun said:

"Some people murdered him at Jabal al-'Alam. Ibn Abi-t-Tawajin al-Kutami, the magician who had claimed to be a prophet, sent people to kill him. Because of his false claim, the armies of Ceuta made war on this Abi-t-Tawajin when he was with the Banu Sa'id and he was killed. I was informed by someone I trust among the Banu Sa'id that one of their young men killed him. He was an immoral wrongdoer who used to force himself on people's daughters. A young man dressed up in women's clothing and when he was alone with him, he killed him, because that wrongdoer wanted to molest his sister. That is why he dressed himself in women's garments and was presented to him as if he was a girl. He killed him with a dagger."

According to the statement of Ibn Khaldun, the *qutb*, ibn Mashish, died in 624 AH. He was buried at the top of the mountain called al-'Alam. He said in *al-Mirath*:

"His historical traces there are numerous, from the cave he used for retreat and worship, his mosque with low walls, and the place from which dawn can be seen. Below his tomb there is a spring in which he did *wudu'*. He was murdered near it. It is said that he was doing *wudu'* at dawn and went to climb up to this place of worship when dawn became visible and they murdered him there. It is well-known that a lot of lizards attacked his murderers and they were driven off the high mountain and fell into deep chasms and were torn to pieces and nothing more was heard of them. Below this spring are located the remains of the house where he lived."

I myself visited that place and prayed in the remains of his mosque near the spring called Qushur, which is located to the right of it. There was no house there at that time. The habitation was at the foot of the mountain where there were both abandoned and inhabited houses in which the people of noble lineage and others lived.

He had four sons: Muhammad, Ahmad, 'Abdu-s-Samad and 'Allal. From the sons of Muhammad came the Banu 'Abdul-Wahhab and a group called the Rahmaniyyun who live near Chafchaoun. From the sons of 'Allal came the sons of al-Fijfaj, including a group in Marrakech.

He had two brothers: Musa and Yamlah. The sons of Musa included the Chafchaounis who settled in Fes, and the sons of Yamlah included Sidi 'Abdullah ibn Ibrahim who lived in Ouazzan.

He had six uncles: Yunus, 'Ali, Malha, Maymun, al-Fatuh, and al-Hajj. From Yunus's children descended the clans of Ibn Ra'isun, of Ibn Rahmun, and of Marsu.

It is transmitted from Sidi 'Abdullah al-Ghazwani that the tomb of Mawlana 'Abdu-s-Salam contains three graves. The one in the middle is the grave of the shaykh, the one behind his back is that of his son, Sidi Muhammad, and the one in front of him is the grave of his servant, Ibn Khudama.

It is related that one day, while his student Shaykh Abu-l-Hasan ash-Shadhili was with him, someone was reciting Qur'an opposite his retreat (*khalwa*). When the reciter reached the verse in *Surat al-An'am*: *"Were he to offer every kind of compensation, it would not be accepted from him"* (6:70), a divine *warid* came on him and cut him off from his sensory perception and he was drowned in it for a time. When he came back to himself, he raised his hands to the heaven in supplication. Part of his supplication was, "O

Allah, do not let anyone who already has wretchedness decreed for him by You reach me. If someone reaches me, I will be an intercessor for him on the Day of Rising. O Allah, do not send to us anyone whom You have judged to be wretched."

His high worth and majestic position is well known. He was immersed in the sciences of the People, the core of which is the knowledge of realisation of the qualities of the Prophet ﷺ. He obtained an ample portion of that and his path is the path of the greatest spiritual wealth.

Shaykh Abu-l-Hasan ash-Shadhili said, "I went to Iraq and met the righteous shaykh, Ibn Abi-l-Fath. I had not seen anyone like him. I was seeking the *qutb*. One of the *awliya'* said to me, 'You are looking for the *qutb* here when he is in your own land. Return to your land and you will find him.' I returned to the Maghrib and I met with my master, may Allah be pleased with him."

He also said, "One day while I was in front of the shaykh I said to myself, 'I wonder if the shaykh knows the Greatest Name.' The son of the shaykh said, 'Abu-l-Hasan, what is important is not the one who knows the Name. What is important is the one who is the same as the Name.' The shaykh said, 'My son was correct and has insight into you, Abu-l-Hasan.'" It is said that the child mentioned was three years old.

He also said, "While I was travelling at the beginning of my affair, I was unsure about whether I should cling to the deserts and wilderness, in order to devote myself to obedience and *dhikr*, or should return to the cities to keep the company of scholars and good men. A *wali* was described to me there who lived at the top of a mountain. I climbed up to him at night and said to myself, 'I will not go to him at this time.' I heard him saying, 'Who has entered the cave? O Allah, some people ask You to subject Your creation to them and so You have subjected Your creation to them, and they were pleased with Your doing that. O Allah, I ask you to make creation tortuous for me so that there is no escape except to You!' I turned to myself and said, 'My self! See from the same sea which this shaykh has scooped up!' In the morning, I went to him and trembled out of awe of him. I said, 'Sidi, how are you?' He said, 'I complain to Allah of the coolness of contentment and submission, just as you complain of the heat of management and choice.' I said, 'As for my complaint of the heat of management and choice, I have tasted it and am in it now. As for your complaint of the coolness of submission, I have not yet tasted it.' He said, 'I fear that the sweetness of the two will distract me from Allah.' I said, 'Sidi, I heard you say yesterday, "O Allah, some people..."' He smiled and said, 'My son, instead of you saying, '"Subject Your creation to me," say, "Lord, be for me." Do you think that you will miss anything? What is this cowardice?'"

As for what he said about the realities, and the words of advice he gave, a taste of what he said is: "Cling to freedom from doubt. Whenever doubt occurs, do *wudu'*. Cling to freedom from the filth of this world. Whenever you incline to an appetite, put it right by turning to Allah. Nothing – or almost nothing – corrupts like illusion. It is essential to have love of Allah with respect and integrity and to devote yourself to drinking from its cup to the point of intoxication. Whenever you recover or awaken, drink again until your intoxication and your sobriety are by Him alone and until you withdraw from love by His beauty, and from drinking, and from the drink and the cup, by what appears to you of the light of His beauty and the absolute purity of the perfection of His majesty. Perhaps you will become someone who does not recognise love, nor drinking, nor the cup, nor intoxication, nor sobriety."

Someone said to him, "Yes, and how many a person immersed in something does not recognise that he is immersed! Inform me and tell me about that which I am ignorant of, or that which has passed by me while I was heedless of it." He said, "You will have it. Love is an understanding from Allah." I say that it is when someone loves what is disclosed to him of the light of His beauty and the purity of the perfection of His majesty. The drinker of love drinks a mixture of attributes with attributes, qualities with qualities, lights with lights, names with names, descriptions with descriptions, and actions with actions. Seeing is expanded in it for whomever Allah wishes. The Drink is that which quenches the thirst of hearts, joints and veins.

Drinking comes through training after training and discipline after discipline. Each drinks according to his worth. Some drink without intermediary and Allah takes charge of that. Some drink by means of intermediaries such as angels, scholars and great men who have drawn near to Allah. Some are intoxicated by merely witnessing the cup, without having yet tasted anything from it. So how do you think it will be after they have tasted it, after they have drunk it, after their thirst has been quenched, after they have become drunk, after they have been drunk, after they have then become sober, and after that in the various degrees they attain? Intoxication is also like that.

The Cup is the recognition of the Truth. With it, whomever Allah wishes among the sincere of His creation, scoops up some of that pure, unadulterated, undiluted drink. Sometimes the drink is witnessed as a form for that cup, sometimes it is witnessed as a meaning and sometimes it is witnessed as knowledge. The form is the portion of bodies and selves. The meaning is the portion of hearts and intellects. The knowledge is the portion of spirits and secrets. What a sweet drink it is! Bliss to the one who drinks from it and continues in it, not being cut off from it! We ask Allah for His bounty. *"That is the bounty of Allah, which He gives to whomever He wishes."* (5:54) A group of lovers may gather and drink from one cup. They may drink from many cups. Drinks may differ according to the cups. The drink from the same cup may be different when many lovers drink from it. These words have been explained in the commentary I made on the *Khamriyya* of Ibn al-Gharif.

Part of his advice to his student Abu-l-Hasan was that he said to him, "Allah, Allah! Beware of people! Free your tongue from remembering them and your heart from resembling them. Say, 'O Allah, show mercy to me by my not remembering them, save me from their evil, enrich me with Your good so that I do not need their good, and remove me from among them by granting me eliteness. You have power over all things.'"

Shaykh Abu-l-Hasan said, "My beloved, and by him I mean my master 'Abdu-s-Salam ibn Mashish, advised me, 'Abu-l-Hasan! Only move your feet to a place where you hope to gain the reward of Allah. Only sit in a place where you are usually safe from disobeying Allah. Only accompany those who will help you to obey Allah. Only choose for yourself those who will increase you in certainty. And they are very few indeed!'"

He also said, "My master advised: 'Do not keep the company of someone who incites your *nafs* against you. You will grow weary. Nor that of someone who incites you against yourself. He will rarely last. Accompany someone who reminds you of Allah when he talks, who suffices when he is present and is remembered when he is absent. His remembrance is the light of the heart and his presence is the key to the Unseen worlds.'"

He also said, "Abu-l-Hasan, flee from the best of people. Most people flee from the worst. The best of them will injure you in your heart while the worst will merely injure you in your body. It is better for you to be injured in your body than in your heart."

He also said, "I asked my master about the words of the Messenger ﷺ 'Make things easy and do not make them difficult. Give good news and do not make people averse.' He said, 'Direct them to Allah. Do not direct them to other than Him. Whoever directs you to this world has defrauded you. Whoever directs you to action has tired you out. Whoever directs you to Allah has given you good advice.'"

He also said, "My master asked me, 'Abu-l-Hasan, what will bring you to a face to face meeting with Allah?' I answered, 'My poverty.' He said, 'If you meet Allah with your poverty, you will meet Him with the greatest idol. Allah will cast it aside. Glory be to Him! There is nothing but Him.'"

A man said to him, "Sidi, impose on me some *wazifas* and *wirds* which I can do." He said to him, "Am I a Messenger? The obligations are well-known and the forbidden things are well-known. Preserve the obligations and avoid disobedience. Guard yourself from love of this world, love of women, love of rank and giving way to your appetites. Be content with what Allah has allotted you. When He produces pleasure for you, then be thankful to Him. When He produces difficulty for you, be steadfast in that. The love of Allah is the axis about which good things revolve and the basis of every kind of noble quality. That is all contained in four things: scrupulousness, good intention, sincere action and the company of knowledge. This is only achieved by the company of a righteous brother or shaykh of good counsel."

Shaykh 'Abdu-s-Salam ibn Mashish studied with his shaykh Abu Muhammad, Sidi 'Abdu-r-Rahman al-Madani, who was called az-Zayyat because he lived in the Harra az-Zayyatin. In his youth, he devoted himself to worship in a cave in Jabal al-'Alam after he was touched by *jadhb* at the age of seven. After some time a man of the people of good and righteousness visited him and said, "I am your shaykh who has supported you from the time you were attracted until now." He then described to him all that had happened to him in terms of stages and gnoses and detailed that for him station after station, state after state. He specified the time of each state. Then he was asked after that, "Did he use to come to you or you to him?" He answered, "All of that happened." He was asked, "Did he simply fold up the distance of the place or did he journey?" "He folded it up," he said.

This shaykh of his took from the gnostic of his time, the *faqir*, the *qutb*, Taqiyyi-d-din, who was from Iraq. He took from the *qutb* Fakhru-d-din, from the *qutb* Nuru-d-din Abu-l-Hasan, from the *qutb* Taju-d-din, from the *qutb* Shamsu-d-din in Turkey, from the *qutb* Zaynu-d-din al-Qazwini, from the *qutb* Abu Ishaq Ibrahim al-Basri, from the *qutb* Muhammad Abu-l-Qasim Ahmad al-Mirwani, from the *qutb* Abu Muhammad Sa'id, from the *qutb* Sa'd, from the *qutb* Muhammad Fath as-Su'ud, from the *qutb* Abu Muhammad Jabir, from the first of the *qutbs*, Sayyiduna al-Hasan, from his father, Sayyiduna 'Ali ibn Abi Talib, from the master of the first and the last, our master Muhammad ﷺ.

Our lineage is connected to this shaykh by way of our shaykh, the gnostic al-Buzidi al-Hasan, from his shaykh the gnostic Moulay al-'Arabi ad-Darqawi al-Hasani, from his shaykh, the gnostic Sidi Ali al-'Imrani al-Hasani, from his shaykh, the gnostic Sidi al-'Arabi ibn Ahmad ibn 'Abdullah, from his father, Sidi Ahmad ibn 'Abdullah, from Sidi Qasim al-Khassasi, from the gnostic of Allah, Sidi 'Abdu-r-Rahman al-Fasi, from Sidi Muhammad ibn 'Abdullah al-Kabir, the father of Sidi Ahmad, and they both took from the Qutb Sidi Yusuf al-Fasi, from the gnostic Sidi 'Abdu-r-Rahman al-Majdhub, from his shaykh Sidi 'Ali as-Sanhaji known as ad-Dawwar, from his shaykh, Sidi Ibrahim Afham, from Sidi Ahmad Zarruq, from his shaykh Sidi Ahmad ibn 'Uqba al-Hadrami, from Sidi Yahya al-Qadiri, from the *qutb* Sidi 'Ali ibn Wafa, from his father Sidi Muhammad Bahr as-Safa, from Sidi Dawud al-Bakhili from Sidi Ahmad ibn 'Ata'llah, from the *qutb* Sidi Abu-l-'Abbas al-Mursi friom the *qutb* Sidi Abu-l-Hasan ash-Shadhili from the great *qutb*, the famous gnostic and author of the prayer which follows:

THE SALAT OF IBN MASHISH

الصلاة المشيشية

اللّهُمَّ صَلِّ عَلَى مَنْ مِنْهُ انْشَقَّتِ الاَسْرَارُ. وَانْفَلَقَتِ
الاَنْوَارُ. وَفِيهِ ارْتَقَتِ الْحَقَائِقُ. وَتَنَزَّلَتْ عُلُومُ سَيِّدِنَا ءَادَمَ
عَلَيْهِ السَّلامُ فَأَعْجَزَ الْخَلائِقَ. وَلَهُ تَضَاءَلَتِ الْفُهُومُ
فَلَمْ يُدْرِكْهُ مِنَّا سَابِقٌ وَلَا لَاحِقٌ.

O Lord, bless him, out of whom secrets and lights have burst,
in whom rose the truth, upon whom devolved the knowledge
of our master Adam, peace be upon him. Beside him all
creatures are incapable. To him understanding is a trifle. Not
one of us has attained his standard, before or after.

فَرِيَاضُ الْمَلَكُوتِ بِزَهْرِ جَمَالِهِ مُونِقَةٌ.
وَحِيَاضُ الْجَبَرُوتِ بِفَيْضِ أَنْوَارِهِ مُتَدَفِّقَةٌ.

The meadows of the *malakut* are embellished with the beauty
of his flowers. The cisterns of the *jabarut* spill over with the
flood of his lights.

وَلَا شَيْءَ إِلَّا وَهُوَ بِهِ مَنُوطٌ. إِذْ لَوْ لَا الْوَاسِطَةُ لَذَهَبَ
كَمَا قِيلَ الْمَوْسُوطُ. صَلَاةً تَلِيقُ بِكَ مِنْكَ إِلَيْهِ كَمَا هُوَ أَهْلُهُ.

There is nothing not dependent on him: for as it was said,
'without the means the end would have escaped us'.
Bless him in Your way, from You to him,
according to his merits.

87

اَللّٰهُمَّ إِنَّهُ سِرُّكَ الْجَامِعُ الدَّالُّ عَلَيْكَ.

وَحِجَابُكَ الْاَعْظَمُ الْقَآئِمُ لَكَ بَيْنَ يَدَيْكَ.

O Allah, he is Your gathered secret that tells of You,
Your great veil that stands before You.

اَللّٰهُمَّ اَلْحِقْنِي بِنَسْبِهِ. وَحَقِّقْنِي بِحَسَبِهِ. وَعَرِّفْنِي إِيَّاهُ مَعْرِفَةً
أَسْلَمُ بِهَا مِنْ مَوَارِدِ الْجَهْلِ. وَأَكْرَعُ بِهَا
مِنْ مَوَارِدِ الْفَضْلِ.

O Allah, attach me to his descendants, and make me realise
his honour. Let me know him with a knowledge by means
of which I will be safe from the springs of ignorance and by
which I will sip from the springs of goodness.

وَاحْمِلْنِي عَلَى سَبِيلِهِ إِلَى حَضْرَتِكَ. حَمْلاً مَحْفُوفًا بِنَصْرَتِكَ.
وَاقْذِفْ بِي عَلَى الْبَاطِلِ فَأَدْمَغَهُ. وَزُجَّ بِي فِي بِحَارِ
الْاَحَدِيَّةِ. وَانْشُلْنِي مِنْ أَوْحَالِ التَّوْحِيدِ. وَأَغْرِقْنِي فِي عَيْنِ
بَحْرِ الْوَحْدَةِ. حَتَّى لَا أَرَى وَلَا أَسْمَعَ وَلَا أَجِدَ
وَلَا أُحِسَّ إِلَّا بِهَا.

Convey me on his way to Your Presence, protected by Your
help. Let me face falsehood so that I may conquer it, drive me
into the sea of Oneness, snatch me from the mires of belief
in Unification (*Tawhid*) and let me drown in the sea of Unity
(*Wahda*) so much that I may not see, hear,
feel or sense except by It.

وَاجْعَلِ الْحِجَابَ الْأَعْظَمَ حَيَاةَ رُوحِي. وَرُوحَهُ سِرَّ
حَقِيقَتِي. وَحَقِيقَتَهُ جَامِعَ عَوَالِمِي بِتَحْقِيقِ الْحَقِّ الْأَوَّلِ.

Make the great veil the life of my spirit and its spirit the secret
of my truth and its truth the integrator of my universe through
the realisation of the first truth.

يَآ أَوَّلُ يَآ ءَاخِرُ يَا ظَاهِرُ يَا بَاطِنُ.

O First! O Last! O Manifest! O Hidden!

اِسْمَعْ نِدَآئِي بِمَا سَمِعْتَ بِهِ نِدَآءَ عَبْدِكَ سَيِّدِنَا زَكَرِيَّآءَ عَلَيْهِ
السَّلَامُ. وَانْصُرْنِي بِكَ لَكَ. وَأَيِّدْنِي بِكَ لَكَ. وَاجْمَعْ بَيْنِي
وَبَيْنَكَ. وَحُلْ بَيْنِي وَبَيْنَ غَيْرِكَ.

Hear my cry as you heard the cry of Your slave, our master
Zakariah, peace be upon him. Give me victory through You
– for You. Support me through You – for You. Join me to You
– separate me from other-than-You.

اللهُ اللهُ اللهُ

ALLAH (3)

إِنَّ الَّذِي فَرَضَ عَلَيْكَ الْقُرْءَانَ لَرَآدُّكَ إِلَىٰ مَعَادٍ.

He Who has imposed the Qur'an upon you
will surely bring you home again.

رَبَّنَا ءَاتِنَا مِنْ لَدُنْكَ رَحْمَةً وَهِيِّئْ لَنَا مِنْ أَمْرِنَا رَشَدًا.
(ثَلَاثًا)

Our Lord, give us mercy directly from You and open the way for us to right guidance in our situation. (3)

إِنَّ اللَّهَ وَمَلَئِكَتَهُ يُصَلُّونَ عَلَى النَّبِيِّ يَـٰٓأَيُّهَا الَّذِينَ ءَامَنُوا۟ صَلُّوا۟ عَلَيْهِ وَسَلِّمُوا۟ تَسْلِيمًا

Allah and His angels call down blessings on the Prophet. You who believe, call down blessings on him and ask for complete peace and safety for him.

سُبْحَنَ رَبِّكَ رَبِّ الْعِزَّةِ عَمَّا يَصِفُونَ وَسَلَمٌ عَلَى الْمُرْسَلِينَ وَالْحَمْدُ لِلَّهِ رَبِّ الْعَلَمِينَ

Glory be to your Lord, the Lord of Might, beyond anything they describe. And peace be upon the Messengers. And praise be to Allah, the Lord of all the worlds!

Allahumma (O Allah) - by eliding the vocative particle *ya'* he removes the distance which it indicates and replaces it with a *mim* to indicate gathering, which is why al-Hasan said, "If anyone says, '*Allahumma*,' it is as if he had called on Allah by all His Names because the *mim* within it indicates all, like *hum* (them)."

Bless - in other words show mercy and be kind to Sayyiduna Muhammad - **him out of whom** - meaning from him, from his light which is the seedbed of all existence and the reason for every existence. It is possible that the pronoun *man* (him) is causal, in which case the meaning is for whose sake ﷺ – **secrets have broken out** – the secrets of the Sublime Essence – **and lights have burst forth** – have shone out and appeared or exploded out and overflowed. The Essence was hidden and veiled before the manifestation of his light. The Real manifested Himself in it through His name the Inwardly Hidden. When He wanted to manifest Himself by His name the Outwardly Manifest, He brought forth a handful of His light and said, "Be Muhammad!" From that Muhammadan handful all existence, from the Throne to the surface of the earth, took on form. The secrets of the Essence only appeared from out of that luminous handful. So its outward is Essence and its inward is Attributes. Density, form, expression, shape and complexity appeared through those attributes. From his light ﷺ other lights have "burst forth", have manifested themselves, and these are the lights of the Attributes whose traces appear outwardly in manifestation, dense and subtle, limited and particular, connected and separate, exalting and abasing, lowering and raising, contracting and expanding, and other kinds of different effects and changes of state.

All of these are among the effects of the pre-eternal attributes, which are Power, Will, Knowledge, and Life. The Attributes are not separate from what is being manifested through them, but while the attributes are subtle and not perceived, they appear outwardly in sensory things. The

Essence is the source of the Attributes and the Attributes are the source of the Essence; they have one and the same position. Inasmuch as the Essence is manifest, the Attributes are manifest. Inasmuch as the Attributes are manifest, the Essence is manifest. So this has been designated by the terms "unity" and "source". The people of separation, who are the people of the veil, only witness the Attributes, meaning that they only see their effect. They are veiled from witnessing the Essence.

Everyone who enters into the world of being comes from that handful of light. They are an outward manifestation of it. The people of gatheredness, who are the people of attraction and annihilation, only witness the Essence and lose sight of the effects of the Attributes. The people of going on, who are the people of perfection, witness the Essence in the Attributes and gatheredness in separation. Their gatheredness does not veil them from their separation nor their separation from their gatheredness. They give everyone with a right the right due to him and everyone owed a share their fair share.

So the words of the Shaykh are an aspect of ascent: the "breaking out of secrets" being for the people of annihilation in the Essence, who are the people of attraction and intoxication; and the "bursting forth of lights" being for the people of subsistence in Allah, which is returning by Allah to the witnessing of effects. They are the people who have returned to the way of sobriety after attraction and annihilation.

It is possible that the "secrets" referred to are the secrets of the *jabarut* and "the lights" are the lights of the *malakut*.

Or you might say, "from whom the secrets of the *haqiqa* have broken out, and the lights of the *shari'a* have burst forth." Or, "from whom the secrets of *ihsan* have broken out, and the lights of *iman* and Islam have burst forth." Or, "from whom the secrets of the Unseen world have broken out, and the lights of the visible world have burst forth." Or, "from whom the secrets of power have broken out, and the lights of wisdom have burst forth."

It is also possible that the words describe a descent, in which case the Shaykh is giving precedence to the station of the people of *ihsan*, the people of eye-witnessing, by mentioning secrets first. Then he descends to the station of the people of evidence and proof. They are the people who witness the effect of the Attributes before witnessing the Essence. So the word, "secrets" applies to the people of annihilation in the Essence, and the word "lights" applies to the people of annihilation in the Attributes before their annihilation in the Essence. Most people who advance on the path begin by witnessing effects and then rise to witnessing the Effector: first the *shari'a* then the *haqiqa*, from Islam to *iman* and then *ihsan*, first the visible world and then the world of the Unseen, first Wisdom and then Power. So the traveller first reaches the *tawhid* of actions: the realisation that there is no actor but Allah. This is the final stage of the righteous. Then he reaches the *tawhid* of the Attributes: the realisation that there is no one living or powerful or willing or hearing or seeing or speaking but Allah. Then he reaches the *tawhid* of the Essence: the realisation that there is nothing in existence but Allah.

Then some go further to the station of going-on. One of the people of Allah indicated that by his words:

> He is annihilated, then he is annihilated, then he is annihilated,
> and so his annihilation is the source of his going-on.

I heard our Shaykh al-Buzidi say, "Our Path only has two annihilations in it: the annihilation of actions and the annihilation of the Essence. As for the annihilation of the Attributes, it is contained in the annihilation of the Essence." It is as he said because the Shadhiliyya Path is short. The first step that a person takes on it is that which he places in the station of *ihsan* and so he is annihilated first in the Name and then in the Essence. The end of the righteous is the beginning of the gnostics. All our words are about those who find a shaykh of instruction. As for those who do not find one, there is nothing to say about them since they have no secret.

Note: The manifestation of the Essence is specific to secrets and the manifestation of the Attributes is specific to lights, because the manifestation of the Essence is only perceived by the elite or the elite of the elite. One aspect of the business of the secret is that only a few grasp it, which is not the case with the manifestation of the Attributes, which is concerned with effects. Both the common and the elite perceive that. That is the nature of light – it is not concealed from anyone. The secret is also singled out for breaking out and light for bursting forth because breaking out comes first and then bursting forth follows it. One says, "The vessel broke when it was not separated and so it became veiled without a veil." How excellent is the one who said:

She was only veiled by the lifting of her veil.

The wonder is that manifestation veils!

Witnessers of the Essence fall into three categories: One category witness it after witnessing beings. They are the people of attraction and annihilation. When he is separated, you say, "he is broken". That is how the secrets have broken out. So the first is for the people of annihilation and the bursting forth of lights follows for the people of going-on after annihilation.

Know that the sensory lights are three: the light of the stars, the light of the moon and the light of the sun. The lights of meaning follow that description: the light of Islam being like the light of the stars, the light of *iman* being like the light of the moon, and the light of *ihsan* being like the light of the sun. Or you might say that the light of annihilation in the actions is like the light of the stars, the light of annihilation in the attributes is like the light of the moon, and the light of annihilation in the Essence is like the light of the sun. The first light disclosed to the *murid* is faint like the light of the stars and so he sees it diminishing and fading out, being overcome by the brightness of the Path. Then the moon of *tawhid* appears to him and it is said that its light is bright. Then the sun of gnosis rises and nothing concealed is hidden from him. Al-Majdhub said about that:

The day rises over the moons and only my Lord remains.
People visit Muhammad while, in my case, he lives in
my heart.

He also said:

The sun rises in my heart so that I see it with my eye.

Another said:

The sun of the day sets at night, but the sun of the heart
never sets.

I said in my *qasida* in *ra'* on the secret of the *Ruh*:

The subtle lights shine out of dense darkness,
while the moon lights up the blackness of the night.
But when the daytime sun pours forth its light, the night-
time darkness
is expunged completely from your deep heart's core.
The sun of the sensory sets when night descends,
but the sun of the Real never sinks beneath the horizon.

Know that these lights which burst forth from his light
🌺 are veiled by the secret of Wisdom in the state of their
manifestation, just as a beautiful woman must have a veil
and the sun has clouds, and so are veiled without a veil.
Again, how excellent is what is said!

She was only veiled by the lifting of her veil.
The wonder is that manifestation veils!

The shaykh, Mawlana 'Abdu-s-Salam, said to his
student Abu-l-Hasan, "Sharpen the eye of *iman*. Then
you will find Allah Almighty in everything, at everything,

with everything, under everything, near everything, surrounding everything by nearness, which is His attribute, and by encompassment which is His description. Abandon circumstances and limits, places and directions, company and spatial proximity, and moving through creatures. Obliterate everything by His attributes of being the First and the Last, the Outward and the Inward. He is He is He. 'Allah was and nothing was with Him, and He is now as He was.'"

The word, "sharpen" here means purify. The word, "obliterate" refers to obliteration and disappearance. The rest of his words are clear to the people of tasting. May Allah give us the benefit of mentioning them and place us on their path. Amen!

in whom rose the realities

In his pure heart the suns of the realities of the gnostics rose and shone forth, as did the secrets of Lordship and direct knowledge of the Divine. The heart of the Prophet ﷺ is likened to a clear sky in which many suns are shining and so it is filled with light upon light. Similarly the plural of reality (*haqa'iq*) is used, even if it is in actuality one, because the Prophet ﷺ had many realities joined in him, which were then divided among others. His inward was filled with the lights of realities and his outward was filled with the lights of legalities. Allah gave him ﷺ strength in both directions. His outward was filled with the *shari'a* and his inward was filled with the *haqiqa*. This was unique to him ﷺ or to the one who follows in his footsteps, whom

Allah makes worthy of it by the fact that he follows him. This is after being made firm.

I heard our Shaykh Moulay al-'Arabi say, "Striving and witnessing are not joined except in the man who is following in the footsteps of the Prophet 🌸." He inserted the words of Shaykh al-Yunusi in one of his supplications, "Adorn the outward with striving and adorn the inward with witnessing," since there is no striving in the outward before witnessing inwardly, as was stated.

The shaykh of our shaykh, Sidi 'Ali al-Jamal, said, "The perfect *wali* is the one whose outward is filled with legality and whose inward is filled with reality." This is rare. Assuming that it occurs, then worship of Allah is done in it by Power and there is no striving in it at all. It is usual for the people of the inward to conceal their actions because they are actions of the heart: reflection and investigation, witnessing and consideration. They only observe what is easy in respect of the obligations. Then they immerse themselves in reflection and investigation which is the best of the acts of worship. "An hour of reflection is better than a year of worship," as it says in *hadith*. One variant has "seventy years". They are both there because the former refers to the reflection of the people of the veil and the second to the reflection of people of gnosis. The poet said about this:

Every moment with my beloved is worth a thousand hajjs.

By hajj here the poet means a year. Abu-l-'Abbas al-Mursi said, "Allah has established some people for His service and some people are singled out for His love. *'We sustain each one, the former and the latter, through the generous giving of your Lord; and the giving of your Lord is not restricted.'* (17:20)"

The people of love are the people of reflection and the people of service are the people of outward worship. Or you could say that the people of love are the people of the worship of the heart and the people of service are the people of worship of the limbs. Or you might say that the people of love are the people of spiritual worship and the people of service are the people of sensory worship. In short, the *shari'a* must be informed by the *haqiqa* and the *haqiqa* must be informed by the *shari'a*. That must be the case. The one who says anything different is ignorant of the science of the inward.

I saw in the *Qut al-Qulub* by Abu Talib al-Makki that the angel who records actions said to one of the gnostics, "Sir, we rejoice at some of your actions," meaning, "Show them to us so that we can bring them near to our Lord." He said to him, "The five prayers are enough for me." Look at the words of the poet, al-Hallaj:

> The hearts of the gnostics have eyes which see
>   what those who look do not see,
> And tongues which speak secrets intimately,
>   unseen by the noble scribes,
> And wings which fly without feathers
>   to the Unseen Domains of the Lord of the worlds.

We added two more verses to it:

> And hearts wild with the passion of
>   ecstatic love for the *jabarut* with certain truth.

If you want to reach the one with meanings,
  then exchange your spirit a little in us.

This is the worship of the realised gnostics, inward and concealed. That is why they are concealed from many people. They are only recognised by those to whom Allah wants to give gnosis through them.

and upon whom devolved the knowledge of our master Adam, peace be upon him

Then he indicates the outward knowledge which the Prophet ﷺ taught by saying that there "devolved" upon his heart by inspiration and revelation the knowledge of Adam, peace be upon him. The Almighty says: *"He taught Adam all the names"* (2:31), meaning that Allah inspired him and cast into his natural form the recognition of all the names and all the languages of Arabic, Syriac and every other tongue that his descendants would speak. It was like that with our Prophet ﷺ. Allah taught him the names and what they named as well as recognition of their special qualities and benefits. The Prophet ﷺ knew the dialects of the Arabs and non-Arabs. He used to speak to each people in their own language and write to them according to their own linguistic usages. Allah acquainted him with the sciences of earlier people, their vanished laws and their historical records. He knew what events would happen in his community and the afflictions and surprises they would encounter. Allah singled him out for secrets with which He did not acquaint anything else in His creation.

He ﷺ singled out some people for secrets which he did not disclose to others, so that 'Umar said, "I visited the Prophet ﷺ when Abu Bakr as-Siddiq was with him and they were speaking about the science of the secret and the knowledge of *tawhid*. I felt like a barbarian in their presence not knowing what they were saying." Sidi 'Abdu-l-Warith said in his commentary on *al-Mabahith*, "The first time they were speaking about the science of the secret. When 'Umar entered, they were silent. Then they let him participate in the discussion. When 'Uthman entered, they stopped and then let him participate in the discussion. When 'Ali entered, they stopped and then they let him participate in the discussion." Another said that 'Ali understood these secrets before he participated in the discussion. Allah knows best.

These secrets are not part of the knowledge of the outward. They are part of the knowledge of the inward. Its place is mentioned in His words: **"in whom rose the realities,"** but discussion was drawn to it in this topic, and they are connected, since the science of the unseen is only realised after outward knowledge. It is what is connected to putting the outward limbs in order.

There are three knowledges. There is a knowledge connected to putting the outward right. It is called the science of *shari'a*, the knowledge of wisdom. There is a knowledge connected to putting the inward right. It is called the science of *tariqa*, the knowledge of *tasawwuf*. Both of these can be acquired. Then there is a bestowed knowledge which is called the science of *haqiqa*. It is the fruit and the goal. Every knowledge, whose knower does not reach the knowledge of *haqiqa*, is imperfect since the fruit of knowledge is action. The fruit of action is state. The fruit of state is tasting and ecstasy. It is the goal of gnostics.

A teaching shaykh is essential in order to move the *murid* from the knowledge of *shari'a* to the knowledge of *tariqa* to the realisation of *haqiqa*. Otherwise he always remains stuck in one of them. *Shari'a* puts the outward right; *tariqa* puts the inward right; and *haqiqa* puts the secret right. Or you could say: *shari'a* is to worship Him; *tariqa* is to aim for Him; and *haqiqa* is to witness Him. You could also say: *shari'a* is for the seekers; *tariqa* is for the wayfarers; and *haqiqa* is for those who have arrived. You could say: *shari'a* is for the one who seeks a wage; *tariqa* is for the one who seeks presence; and *haqiqa* is for the removal of veils. You could say: *shari'a* is for the common people; *tariqa* is for the elite; and *haqiqa* is for the elite of the elite.

The basis of *shari'a* is obeying commands and avoiding prohibitions. The basis of *tariqa* is divestment and adornment – divestment is purification from base qualities and adornment is being described by good qualities. If you wish, you could say that divestment is being free of animal and shaytanic qualities and adornment entails taking on *ruhani* qualities. Animal qualities are concern with food, drink and sex, and shaytanic qualities are things like envy, plotting, deceit, fraud, pride, anger, impetuosity, anxiety, avarice, coarseness, harshness, love of rank, wealth and leadership and countless other characteristics to the extent that one of them said, "The *nafs* has as many imperfections as Allah has perfections." Allah knows best. *Ruhani* qualities are a sound heart, generous self, good character, humility, forbearance, deliberateness, tranquillity, peace of mind, compassion, mercy, easiness, gentleness and other perfect qualities of character.

Whoever has all these knowledges is the *"Piercing Star"*. Anyone who is content with just one of them is imperfect and falls short. Someone who has *shari'a* without *haqiqa* is a deviant since that inevitably involves a conflict of values and opposition to the All-Powerful. Someone who has *haqiqa* without *shari'a* is a heretic because he declares Allah's laws invalid and nullifies wisdom. Whoever combines them both has realisation since he establishes power with *adab* and wisdom.

In truth, there is only *haqiqa* since there is no Doer except Allah and nothing in existence except Him. Nonetheless, when what issues from the element of power is in harmony with wisdom, it is called *shari'a* and obedience, and it is also called a luminous reality. If it is in opposition to it, it is called disobedience and is called a dark reality. So all is from Him and to Him.

Allah, who is the most truthful speaker, says: *"If Allah had willed, they would not have done it,"* (6:112; 137) and *"If your Lord had willed, all the people on the earth would have believed,"* (10:99) and *"Your Lord creates and chooses whatever He wills."* (28:68) The Almighty also says, *"But you will not will unless Allah wills."* (76:30) So *haqiqa* is the same as *shari'a* and *shari'a* is the same as *haqiqa* since both of them are commanded. How excellent is the one who praised the Prophet ﷺ by saying:

O adornment of creatures, O source of *haqiqa*!

You realised realities and they were dependable.

All of man is inwardly power and outwardly wisdom. If what is in harmony with wisdom emerges from power, it is a luminous reality and it is a sign of the future happiness of the slave. If what is opposed to wisdom emerges from power, it is a dark reality and it is a sign of the future punishment of the slave, unless Allah's forbearance dominates. Success is by Allah.

Beside him all creatures are incapable

Since all realities are combined in our Prophet ﷺ, along with the knowledge of Divine legislation and all the other knowledges of the first and the last, the rest of mankind are unable to encompass that. That is why he says, "**all creatures are incapable**" meaning that they are unable to understand what he has and therefore submission and obedience to his judgement is mandatory for them, just as the angels obeyed by prostrating when they were unable to grasp the knowledge granted to Adam.

When the Companions saw sheep prostrate to him ﷺ in the episode of the garden, they said, "Messenger of Allah, we are more entitled to prostrate to you than they are!" The Prophet ﷺ said, "If anyone had been prostrated to," or "If I were to command anyone to prostrate to another, I would have commanded a woman to prostrate to her husband." So prostration is to Allah alone. As for Adam he was a *qibla*. The goal of the prostration is Allah who commanded it.

to him understanding is a trifle

By saying this the Shaykh stresses the incapacity referred to previously and makes it clear. To the Prophet ﷺ all this knowledge "is a trifle", in other words inadequate and paltry, or such that it vanishes and disappears. "Understanding" is in the plural and refers to things that are understood in terms of worship. No one is able to understand the divine secrets and inward gifts, which Allah singled out for him ﷺ, because they only see his outward manifestation. As for the inward, only His Creator knows the one for whom Allah has singled it out. In a *hadith* we find, "By Allah, I have not recognised a truth other than my Lord." How excellent are the words of al-Busiri who said:

How can one perceive his reality in this world?
Sleeping people are distracted from him by dreams.

Not one of us has attained to him, either before or after

No creature has been able to reach him "either before" his physical existence in this world "or after" it. Rather the understanding of all creatures becomes exhausted and their knowledge falls short in their inability to comprehend the Muhammadan reality. It is possible that the word "before" here refers to those in his time ﷺ such as the Companions ﷺ and that the word "after" refers to those who came after them since all are the same in respect of their inability to comprehend him ﷺ. That is why Uways al-Qarni said, "By Allah, the Companions of Muhammad have only seen the outward shell of Muhammad ﷺ! As for the inward, no one knows it." He was asked, "Not even Ibn Abi Quhafa (Abu Bakr)?" He answered, "Not even Ibn Abi Quhafa."

This means that it is impossible for the entirety of his secret 🕌 to be encompassed by any other creature. As for grasping some of it, people have a portion of it according to their different degrees of gnosis of Allah. That is how it is with the *awliya'*, may Allah be pleased with them. Some of them perceive something of the secret of the Prophet 🕌 and some of them perceive his *ruh*. Some perceive his intellect and some perceive his outward self 🕌. The people of firmness and fixity, such as al-Mursi and those like him, perceive his secret 🕌 and he is not absent from them for a single second. As for the people of witnessing and vision among the wayfarers, they perceive his *ruh* 🕌. The people of watchfulness among the people who are moving forward perceive his intellect 🕌. The people of the veil among the people of proof and evidence perceive his outward self and his personal manifestation. They see him as confined to the form which he took in this world 🕌, whether asleep or awake, according to their annihilation in him 🕌. They have different ranks. As for the form which some of them give him, such as Al-Kharubi and those who follow him, by this *hadith* from the Companions 🕌 perhaps that was in his time 🕌. Allah knows best.

I heard the shaykh of our shaykh, Moulay al-'Arabi, say, "I met two of the scholars of Fes in the Qarawiyyin mosque and they said to me, 'What do you say about the words of Abu-l-'Abbas al-Mursi: "The Messenger of Allah 🕌 was not

absent from me for the blink of an eye"? How can that be?'"
He answered them, "How can you ask that! He and those
like him are the masters. Their consciousness inhabits
the world of the *malakut*, which is the world of the spirits.
It contains the wives of the Prophets and others. Their
consciousness is not confined to the world of outward
forms, which is the world of the *mulk*." He continued,
"Then I said to them, 'Do you know where the world of
spirits is? There where the world of the forms is, there also
is the world of the spirits.'" Then he got up and left them.
The place is the same but the capacity of vision varies. The
people of inner sight see the *malakut*, which is the world
of spirits. The people of outward sight see only the *mulk*,
which is the world of forms.

So *malakut* in the usage of the Sufis is what is perceived
by inner sight and knowledge, whereas *mulk* is what is
perceived by eyesight and illusion. You could say that the
malakut is what is perceived by the people of gatheredness
and *mulk* is what is perceived by the people of separation.
Or you could say that *mulk* is what is outward and *malakut*
is what is inward. *Malakut* is the perception of the people
of witnessing and inner sight and *mulk* is the perception of
the people of evidence and proof.

**The meadows of the *malakut* are embellished with the
beauty of his flowers.**

The expression "meadows of the *malakut*" is used to give
the nearest possible description in terms of this world to an
other-worldly experience which resembles it. The word used

for flowers, *zahr*, refers specifically to those flowers which open in the springtime. So the *malakut* is a place where the gnostics walk in meadows which contain flowers, blooms, greenness and beauty whose beauty is only complete and whose flowers only appear by following the *shari'a* of Muhammad. Otherwise it is a dark reality. Phenomenal being, which is the *mulk*, is, in itself, all darkness. It is only illuminated by the manifestation of the Truth in it, in which case it becomes all light. If someone fails to perceive the light of truth in it, it is for him nothing but darkness and *mulk*. It is not possible for the truth to be manifest in it except to someone travelling on the Muhammadan *shari'a* under the guidance of a shaykh who knows its fine points, secrets and outward and inward realities. Otherwise, you will remain trapped in the darkness of phenomenal beings in the prison of illusion.

The basins of the *jabarut* spill over with the flood of his lights.

The word for "basins", *hiyad*, is the plural of *hawd* which means a place where water is collected, such as a reservoir or tank. *Jabarut* is what is perceived by the intellect and understanding, through insight and knowledge, and in a later state, after recognition of the *malakut*. In short, *mulk*, *malakut* and *jabarut* occupy the same space but the name varies according to the difference in perception. The perception varies according to the difference in ascent in gnosis.

If someone looks at phenomenal being and sees it as independent in itself, sustained by the Power of Allah, and perception of its Maker within it is not disclosed to him, it is called *mulk* in respect of him by the manifestation of the disposition and existence of power in it. Neither have any reality with the people of *haqiqa*. That is why the Shaykh does not perceive it. The person with this kind of perception is veiled by his stopping with illusion. When someone has his inner eye opened by Allah and arrives at witnessing the Maker of being, within phenomenal existence or before it, it is called *malakut* in respect of him. The one with this perception is a gnostic with opening. If his insight reaches to the existence of the source of all roots and branches, which is the pre-eternal subtle vastness before it is manifested and recognised, that is called *jabarut*. Ibn al-Farid indicates it in his words:

It is not purity or water or fineness or passion
or light or fire or spirit or body.
It is before all beings, new and old,
with no form and no mark.
All things exist by it and then it is by a wisdom that they
are veiled
from everyone who does not possess understanding.

Whoever perceives the penetration through all things of pre-existent mercy, which is the blessing of existence and the blessing of support, calls that *rahamut*, and in that case there are four worlds: *mulk, malakut, jabarut* and *rahamut*. I composed a poem on this subject, some of which goes:

If a self is held in the prison of passion
in which the intellect is fettered by the power of the
handful,

The knowledge of the protection of wisdom occupies it,
  and it only sees phenomenal being on every side.
That is why the root of the *mulk* is the illusion of its stability.
  The one who looks at it is veiled in a prison of darkness.
If the secret of the spirit of purity penetrates to the perception
  of the secret of the Essence within the container –
And by that we mean the secret of meanings which flows
  through every container for the people of *haqiqa* –
That is the *malakut* of Allah, so named for its vastness.
  The one with gnosis of it obtains the opening of the
    inner eye.
If it swims in the sea of subtleness and delight,
  and the root of roots and branches by reflection,
That is a sea which the youth has not encompassed,
  but he fears it in a gulf.

If you wish to be exact, there are in fact five worlds: *mulk*,
malakut, *jabarut*, *lahut* and *rahamut* in respect of the
branches in relation to the roots. Someone said about that:

If all the branches are connected to their roots
  and plunge into the seas of gatheredness at every instant,
That is something whose secret is called *lahut*
  and its knower truly delights in mastery.
If he looks at the people of heresy with mercy,
  and its movement through things is all a blessing,
That is the *rahamut* in which a gnostic perceives
  character by the Name of the Real in every breath.

The truth is that for anyone for whom the world is the
solidity which appears to his senses, it is called *mulk*. What

is concealed of the secrets of meanings is called *malakut*. What does not enter the world of the formation of secrets and remains with their basic source is called *jabarut*. This is only understood by the one enters the station of *ihsan* and plunges into the seas of meaning. Otherwise, it is enough for him to submit to the masters of this knowledge. Know that witnessing the world of the *malakut* veils one from witnessing the world of the *mulk*, and witnessing the world of the *jabarut* veils one from witnessing the world of the *malakut*. For anyone who rises to a station, the state which preceded it is hidden from him, except in the case of the *rahamut*, and then his witnessing is of all the worlds simultaneously. Allah Almighty knows best.

"**Spilling over**" means flowing out. The ocean of the *jabarut* is likened to basins filled with the water of the unseen which pours out into the visible world little by little according to the will and volition of Allah. Since our Prophet ﷺ is the means for the emergence of those lights, they are ascribed to him with the ascription of the effect to the cause. In short, the sea of the *jabarut* overflows with the lights of the *malakut* and the root of the lights of the *malakut* is the luminous Muhammadan handful. For each of those who emerge from the *jabarut*, the Muhammadan light is the means of their doing so and the source of it. This is the meaning of his words.

All is *jabarut/lahut* because whoever is not thankful for the means, is not thankful for the end result. Whoever is not thankful to people is not thankful to Allah. The people of attraction and annihilation have withdrawn from the means and so they only witness the *jabarut*. The people of going-on witness both the means and end result by their perfection, and give everyone with a right their right. Their separation does not veil them from their gatheredness nor their gatheredness from their separation. May Allah benefit us by them and permit us to proceed in their Path. Amen.

The Shaykh chose the metaphor of basins rather than that of seas in order for there to be a correspondence with the previous metaphor of meadows. Basins water meadows just as the *jabarut* sustains the *malakut*. Indeed, it is its source, as has already been already explained. The wayfarer, however, rises to the *jabarut* and so it must first be affirmed and then obliterated. Beings are firm by its firmness, obliterated by the Oneness of His Essence.

There is nothing, which is not dependent on him

In other words connected and attached to him as the means is to the end result. When anything emerges from the world of the Unseen, our Prophet and Master Muhammad ﷺ is the means by which it happens, as in the report: "If it had not been for Muhammad, I would not have created Throne or Footstool, nor heaven nor earth, nor Garden nor Fire." In the *Burda* of al-Busiri we find, "If it had not been for him, this world not have emerged from non-existence."

for as it has been said, 'without the means the end would have escaped us'.

Then he mentions the reason for the connection of things to him ﷺ by affirming that if it were not for his being the means between Allah and His creation, phenomenal being would have remained in the non-existence which was its original state. So the implication is that the Divine names are connected to him ﷺ because he is the means by which they become manifest.

Bless him with a blessing that comes by You from You to him according to his merits

The main object of this prayer is highlighted here once more in the pronoun "him" ﷺ. The words "according to his merits" mean that the value of this prayer is known to no one but Allah – glory be to Him – and make it clear that the Prophet ﷺ deserves every kind of esteem and veneration. The expression "by You from You to him" means that he receives the blessing directly without the agency of any creature. There is no doubt that gifts and presents which reach a minister directly from the king's hand are greater and more valuable than those they receive through the hands of middlemen.

O Allah, he is Your gathered secret that tells of You, through You

Now the Shaykh mentions the reason why the Prophet ﷺ deserves this honour. The words "O Allah" are not used in this instance prior to a supplication, as they usually are, but rather in vigorous confirmation, in the way you might answer, "O Allah, yes!" to make your reply firm in the mind of the listener. So it is as if he was saying, "I affirm and realise that he ﷺ is Your secret which was hidden and whom You have singled out on account of his gnosis – of Your secret which You lodged him – he ☙ being the secret of all secrets and the fount of all lights, the one 'from whom secrets have broken out and lights have burst forth'."

The adjective "gathered" implies that the secret, which is concentrated in him as an individual, is spread out among other things. So his spirituality ☙ contains all the attributes of perfection manifested anywhere in existence and his humanity contains every variety of good quality shown by all other creatures. His *shari'a* includes all the laws and the Book he brought contains all the Books. He also gathers people to Allah and guides them to gatheredness and cautions them against separation. He makes us aware of Allah through his words and his actions and his states ☙ and so his words and admonitions soften hardened hearts and make dry eyes weep.

The Prophet ☙ was only sent to guide people to Allah and bring them to knowledge of Him. There is no way in which people can have access to Allah, which he did not direct us to and acquaint us with. There is nothing which separates people from Allah, which he did not caution them against. He did not spare any effort in advising people and leading them to the path of guidance. May Allah repay him with the best repayment that a Messenger has received from his people and Prophet from his community.

Your great veil that stands before You

As well as directing people to Allah, he is also a veil concealing the Divine Presence, which no one may penetrate except at his hand. That is why the Shaykh says, "Your veil" to indicate that he stands between Allah and those who enter His presence. Those who take his hand, who esteem him and who follow his *sunna* may be admitted to Allah's Presence with the attribute of awe, gravity and *adab* and, at the same time, he himself will remain in the Divine Presence for ever. Any who try to enter by other than his door 🌼 are cast away and punished. The poet said about that:

You are the door of Allah. Any man who arrives
   at any other door than yours does not enter.

The Prophet 🌼 also veils spirits from destruction, since one characteristic of the spirit is that it desires to dive into the ocean of the *jabarut,* which it is unable to do. So whenever it wants to dive into it, the Prophet chides it and hobbles it with the hobble of the *shari'a.* That is why the Prophet 🌼 said, "Reflect on His Signs, but do not reflect on the quiddity of His Essence", since the core of lordship is veiled from the intellect and there is no way to perceive it. There is no doubt that all the Messengers, peace and blessings be upon them all, are veils for their people, but the Chosen Prophet 🌼 is the greatest of them, as the Shaykh said. So by saying this the Shaykh is describing the Prophet's unparalleled degree of nearness to Allah and explaining how he is a means between Allah and His creation and the way in which His rulings were transmitted.

O Lord, join me to his descendants and let me realise his true worth

Up to this point the Shaykh has been describing the Prophet 🌼. Now he begins to supplicate by asking to be joined to him and follow in his footsteps, which constitutes the greatest *wilaya*. This is asked for in terms of both bodily form and also *deen,* and propounds a desire to follow him 🕌 in every respect. Certainly lineage is of no use without the behaviour to accompany it.

The words "let me realise" here have the meaning of "perfume me with", in other words "let me be soaked in the perfume of his noble character so that that is what people perceive when they meet me." When a human being is said to be of good character what is meant is that he is following in the footsteps of all the Prophets, peace and blessings be upon all of them. Some of the *awliya'* have the character of Nuh, some have the character of Ibrahim, some have the character of Musa, some have the character of 'Isa, and some are Muhammadan. That is the most comprehensive good character of all since it contains all the good qualities of character which were divided up among others.

Allah realised the Shaykh's hope and answered his supplication for he was immersed in the knowledges of the People whose basis is taking on the qualities of the All-Merciful. He obtained an ample portion of that. Some of his words demonstrating that were already mentioned in his biography. May Allah give us the benefit of his love! Amin.

Let me know him with a recognition which will protect me from the watering holes of ignorance

He asks to be able to know him 🕌 in a special way, seeking gnosis of the Prophet before seeking the gnosis of Allah, because the former is the means to the latter. It is only possible to reach Allah through his gate ﷺ. Those who recognise him ﷺ with this special gnosis set out to serve and love him and so he himself ﷺ admits them to the presence of his Lord. This generally comes about at the hand of a shaykh who is able to guide others to him. The result of this recognition of him ﷺ is protection from falling into ignorance of any kind whatsoever. Watering holes are places of drinking and places of gathering, and ignorance is likened to bad water. He asks Allah to keep him safe by means of gnosis of the Prophet ﷺ from falling into such a place of drinking or coming near to it.

and which will let me drink deeply from the watering holes of overflowing favour

Then he mentions their opposite and asks that his gnosis will allow him to drink – the word for "drink" here is the one used for the action of those who are desperately thirsty – directly from these pools of "overflowing favour". That consists of direct knowledges and sovereign secrets, which are granted by bounty and favour, not on account of earning and service. There is no doubt that anyone who truly recognises the Prophet ﷺ and gives him his due will certainly drink from one of his springs and come to one of his watering holes, and take their portion of knowledges which he knows ﷺ by unveiling or inspiration, because "if someone acts by what he knows, Allah will bequeath him a knowledge which he did not know."

The Shaykh likens direct knowledges to sweet waters which people come to drink. He asked Allah to allow him to drink from them without any intermediary other than the the Prophet ﷺ so that his veins and joints will be filled to repletion. Though that will still leave room for more since "contentment with Allah is deprival." There is no limit to knowledge or to the extent that one can be completely quenched by it. *"Say: Lord, increase me in knowledge.'"* (20:114)

Carry me to Your Presence on the back of his way surrounded by Your help

Then he asks to be taken to the presence of purity and the place of intimacy. The Shaykh means that during his journey he should be borne on the Muhammadan Sunna, not in the sense of being a burden, because anyone conveyed by Divine Concern covers, without being aware of it, a distance in one hour which others could not travel in years. Someone who is loved is not the same as someone who loves. Someone who travels by attraction is not the same as someone who makes his own way. *"Allah chooses for Himself anyone He wills and guides to Himself those who turn to Him."* (42:13) As we find in the *Hikam*: "If you could only reach Him after the annihilation of your bad qualities and the eradication of your claims, you would never reach Him. But if He wants to bring you to Him, He veils your attribute with His attribute. So you reach Him by what comes from Him to you, not by what goes from you to Him."

"Presence" here means the presence of the heart with the Lord or the presence of the spirit or secret with the Truth. It has three categories: the presence of the heart for the seekers, the presence of the spirit for the wayfarers, and the presence of the secrets for those who have arrived. Or you could say: the presence of hearts for the people of watchfulness, the presence of spirits for the people of witnessing, and the presence of secrets for the people of direct speech. Or you could say: the presence of hearts for the people of evidence, the presence of spirits for the people of eye-witnessing, and the presence of secrets for the people of fixity.

In short, as long as the *murid* is veiled by witnessing himself, while he is striving for the presence of his heart with his Lord, he is in the presence of hearts. When he has an opening, he withdraws by witnessing his Lord from witnessing himself. Or, you could say that he withdraws by his gathering from his separation, and so he is in the presence of spirits. When he becomes fixed and returns to going-on, so that his gatheredness does not veil him from his separation nor his separation from his gatheredness, then he is in the presence of secrets.

The wisdom of that is that when the spirit continues to be immersed in heedlessness, it is called a *nafs* and it has not entered the presence at all. When the spirit wakes up or is straight and begins to strive with itself in the Presence, it is called *qalb* since it turns (*taqallaba*) from heedlessness to presence and from presence to heedlessness, or it turns from obedience to disobedience and from disobedience to obedience. When it reaches the station of *ihsan* and has an opening in the station of gnosis, it is called *ruh* because of its rest (*raha*) from the toil of the veil and it enters the company of the lovers. When it is taught *adab* and discipline and the rust of the senses is polished away from the source of the inner eye, it called a secret since it is concealed from the perception of intellects, or because its possessor is concealed from the understanding of people, since the reality of the *wali* is only recognised by his Great, All-High Master or the one who has entered *wilaya* with him.

So the Presence is ascribed to the spirit but it has different names at different levels of ascent. It is called the presence of hearts as long as it is a heart, then the presence of spirits as long as it remains a spirit, then the presence of secrets as long as it remains a secret. When it moves to the Presence, it is only complete when it is accompanied by help. The Shaykh asks to be surrounded by help, in other words to be encircled by help on every side. There is no doubt that when the slave is accompanied by help and gnosis on his journey, he will reach the goal and his desire, and delight in the shortest possible time in the Presence of Arrival. How excellent are the lines:

> If Allah's help surrounds a man,
>> any help he desires comes speedily to him.
> If Allah does not help a man,
>> any effort he makes is just a burden for him.

Hurl me against falsehood so that I may cut right through it

Now he mentions the fruit of arrival, which is absence from otherness, asking to be hurled against falsehood which is what is other than the Real. We find in *hadith*, "The most truthful words which a poet has spoken are the words of

Labid: 'Everything except Allah is false and every bliss must vanish.'"

He likens otherness, which is falsehood, to an animal with a brain. When its brain is struck, it dies. That is why he uses a word which means to cut through the skull, meaning to strike through to the brain, so that it shatters and vanishes. When falsehood is removed, the truth appears. *"Say: 'Truth has come and falsehood has vanished. Falsehood is always bound to vanish.'"* (17:81) *"That is Allah, your Lord, the Truth, and what is there after truth except misguidance?"* (10:32)

There is no doubt that what is other than Allah has no place whatsoever for those who have achieved realisation. Those who have realised the truth refuse to witness another with Allah since it is impossible to witness Him and to witness another together with Him. The apparent existence of an existent thing alongside Him does not veil such a person from Allah since there is nothing with Him. It is the illusion of an existent with Him which veils you.

> Since I have recognised the Divine, I do not see other than Him.
> Otherness is forbidden in our eyes
> Since I have gathered together what I feared would separate.
> So today I have arrived gathered.

plunge me into the sea of Oneness

When the witnessing of otherness leaves the heart, it drowns in the sea of Oneness. The poet says:

Love emaciated me so much that if I were to plunge
  into the eye of the sleeper, he would not wake up.
I placed a seal on what happened
  but now, if I wish, I will speak of it.

The word used for Oneness, *ahadiyya,* is an absolute form
of oneness, so the meaning is "admit me into the seas of
the oneness of Your Essence, Attributes and Actions". That
is why it is designated as gatheredness, although each sea
in fact has its own independent existence. Whoever dives
into the sea of the oneness of the Essence, withdraws from
himself and from witnessing otherness and remains with
the existence of his Lord. Whoever dives into the sea of the
oneness of the Attributes, withdraws from the attributes
of himself and the attribute of others, and goes on by the
attributes of His Lord. Whoever dives into the sea of the
oneness of Actions, withdraws from his action and the
actions of others and abandons his management and
choice, since no one is going to take on the management of
what Someone Else is already doing. He employs the term
"absolute oneness" (*ahadiyya*) which is more eloquent than
"simple oneness" (*wahdaniyya*) because the unification
referred to here is that of tasting, state and station, not that
of knowledge and creed, which is part of the business of the
people of the veil, the people of proof and evidence. The
shaykh of our shaykhs, Sidi 'Abdu-r-Rahman al-Majdhub,
said:

O students of the science of *tawhid,*
  here are the seas which lead to my loss.

This is the station of the people of divestment,
who remain with their Lord.

That is because these seas are only known to the people of divestment and presence. As for someone whose outward is attached to many means, he does not desire these doors to be opened for him. I heard our shaykh al-Buzidi say, "The gnosis of the person of means does not approach the gnosis of the one who is divested." He also said, "The imperfect man of divestment is better than the perfect (well-educated) man of means, since the inward of the one with means is never free of turbidity." I heard the shaykh of our shaykh, Moulay al-'Arabi ad-Darqawi, say, "The thought of the man of divestment is purer and deeper than the thought of the man of means, because it grows out of purity, since the purity of the inward comes from the purity of the outward and the turbidity of the inward comes from the turbidity of the outward."

All of this applies to wayfarers who have not yet reached the goal. As for those who have arrived and are fixed, they are not under discussion since all of their business is by Allah. This applies, for instance, to the state of the Companions, may Allah be pleased with them, since some them made use of means like Abu Bakr as- Siddiq, 'Umar al-Faruq and others. There is absolute consensus about their excellence. It is probable that that occurred after the perfection of their state. Furthermore they witnessed the light of Prophethood which kept them from relying on anything other than Allah. One glance from the Messenger of Allah ﷺ removed a person from his distractions and habits in a single hour. Allah is the One who possesses immense favour.

snatch me up from the mires of Unification

When someone is sailing in dangerous waters, he is either kept safe or drowned, and the traveller on the Path is prey at this point to the sea of illusion or the sea of doubts and thoughts or the sea of dualism and heresy. So the Shaykh asks to be rescued "from the mires", *awhal,* which is the plural of *wahl*, meaning swampland. He likens *tawhid* to a swamp in that it can be accompanied by turbidity and confusion. Turbidity is brought about by seeing otherness alongside Allah. This is the *tawhid* of the common people which is made turbid by illusions, doubts and thoughts. Confusion is brought about by belief in incarnation and union. Some ignorant people believe that Divinity can descend into otherness and claim that it has and does. That is the position of the Christians. Others claim the existence of otherness but that it is unified and mixed with Divinity. That is forbidden unbelief. As Shaykh Ibn Ata'allah says in his *Hikam*:

> What a wonder! How can existence be manifest in non-existence? How can the temporal be affirmed with the One who has the attribute of out-of-timeness?

The people of realisation do not affirm the existence of anything else together with the Real. They see that all is from Him and to Him. Everything except Allah, if you are precise, is non-existent both in detail and in general. That was indicated by the speaker when he said:

If someone does not exist by his essence from his essence,
  his existence, if it were not for Him, is absolutely
    impossible.
If you have not tasted what the Men have tasted,
  then lower your head to the feet of the Men
Until they let you drink of the cool pure wine of *tawhid*.
  Otherwise, surrender to the people of perfection.

They have likened someone who sails on the sea of
tawhid to someone who sails on a physical sea. If the
sailor is a skilled mariner, he seeks refuge in the lee of the
Muhammadan *Sunna*, and so he is one of those who are
successful and are saved. If the sailor is ignorant of the sea,
he seeks refuge in the lee of his own intellect and conjecture
and the waves clash over him and he is destroyed.

and let me drown in the source of the sea of Unity

After seeking deliverance from drowning in the sea of
confusion, the Shaykh then asks to be drowned in the
sea of Unity, which is absolute purity. What is meant is
to withdraw into witnessing the Essence alone and to be
absorbed into the Reality, absent in its existence by the
existence of what is witnessed, as al-Junayd said:

  My existence is that I withdraw from existence
    by what appears to me of witnessing.

so that I may not see or hear or find or feel other than by it

When someone withdraws in the Real, his entire affair is by
Him, not by himself. That is why the hoped-for result is to
see only by the Sublime Essence and to hear only by It and

from It, as ash-Shustari said: "We speak by Allah and hear from Allah." It is as Allah says in the *hadith qudsi*: "When I love him, I am his hearing by which he hears, his sight by which he sees, his hand by which he strikes, and his foot by which he walks." In another variant, "When I love him, I am him." The Shaykh further indicates this by continuing, "**or find**" – in my inward any joy or sorrow, contraction or expansion or any other inward state – "**or feel**" – heat or cold or softness or hardness or any other outward physical things – "**except by it**", meaning by the source of the ocean of Unity which is in fact the Sublime Essence.

So all the actions of such a man are by Allah from Allah and to Allah. This is used to designate the station of annihilation. It is possible that by the "**sea of Unity**" the Shaykh means the manifestation of man. In that case the sea of Unity is the encompassing sea, referred to when Allah says, *"When We said to you, 'Surely your Lord encompasses the people with His knowledge.'"* (17:60) The source of that sea is the appearance of the human being because he is the pearl in the shell and the core of existence. When he recognises Allah in himself and drowns in His sea, he then recognises Allah in other than himself as well. Whoever knows himself, knows his Lord, so reflect.

Make the Great Veil the life of my spirit

Then he returns to the station of annihilation. The Great Veil is, of course, the Prophet ﷺ who has already been called "Your great veil" earlier in the *du'a*. The Shaykh asks that his witnessing of the Great Veil may become the source of his life, because whoever drowns in the sea of Unity and denies the means by which he reached it, in other words affirms Wisdom but invalidates the *shari'a*, is a dualist and heretic and his spirit dies. Whoever affirms the means and affirms the Wisdom has a living spirit and remains blessed in the presence of witnessing as a gift and shows proper *adab* towards the worshipped King. His inward witnesses Power and his outward witnesses Wisdom, or you could say, his inward is freedom and his outward is slavehood. Or you could say, that his inward is attraction and his outward is wayfaring. Or you could say that his inward is *haqiqa* and his outward is *shari'a*. He is the one whose *ruh* has an abiding life which will not falter or wear out until it arrives at the Last Day.

Know that denial of the means can occur with some *murids* when they look forward towards annihilation in the Essence and in the first attraction, but that does not continue, except in the case of someone who does not have a shaykh, or who leaves him before being given right guidance. As for the one who continues in the care of the shaykh, he will certainly bring him through to going-on, as the season of winter passes with the arrival of the season of spring and the season of spring passes with the arrival of the season of summer, and so on. The means referred to here is the "luminous handful" which became dense and emerged from the *jabarut* and was called Muhammad ﷺ.

Anyone who joins it to its source and does not look at the Wisdom of its manifestation denies the means and he is imperfect or fails. Anyone who looks at the Wisdom of its manifestation and it is firm by his affirmation, obliterated by the oneness of the Essence, affirms it by Allah and fulfils its rights, which are the rulings of the *shari'a*. They must be affirmed in respect of existence even though they are invisible in respect of witnessing. The means comes from the end itself. Anyone who stops with the means and is veiled from the end is ignorant of Allah without recognising it. If anyone is veiled by the means from the end, if he is attracted and absent, he is imperfect, if he is sober, he fails. Whoever joins the two of them has perfect realisation. Success is by Allah.

and its spirit the secret of my reality

He is here asking for his witnessing of the spirit of the Messenger of Allah to become the means to the secret of his own reality, in other words the means to the transformation of his own spirit into a secret. So the reality of the human being is the spirit of the Prophet ﷺ. In short, looking at the outward of the Prophet ﷺ brings about realisation of the *shari'a* and is the reason for the life of the *ruh*. Looking at his inward ﷺ brings about realisation of the *tariqa*. By it the *ruh* is purified until it becomes a secret. So it was first *nafs*, then intellect, then heart and then spirit and when it is completely refined, it becomes a secret.

and its reality the integrator of my worlds

This refers to witnessing his totality ﷺ, both his outward and inward, which brings realisation of the Truth, through which the secret is purified by joining together the inner worlds of knowledge, understanding, reflection, intellect, investigation and consideration. So all the worlds are contained in the Muhammadan reality, and it is the *jabarutian* handful or the *jabaruti* manifestation while witnessing the primal *jabarut*. The result is that the outward of the Prophet ﷺ is *mulk* and his inward is *malakut* and joining the two of them is *jabarut*. The Shaykh seeks first to look at the *mulk* of his outward ﷺ to realise his *shari'a*. He seeks secondly to look at the *malakut* of his inward ﷺ to realise his *tariqa* and so it is a means of ascent to enable the light of his reality to shine. He seeks thirdly to look at the *jabarut* of his totality ﷺ to complete his reality.

If you wish, you could say, he seeks firstly by his words, "Make the Great Veil the life of my spirit", to obey the outward of the Prophet ﷺ, since he is the cause of the life of the *ruh*, both sensory and meaning. The outward is the locus of legislation. He seeks secondly by his words, "his spirit the secret of my reality," to correspond to the inward of the Prophet ﷺ. It is the locus of the purification of the spirit, since whoever looks at his inward ﷺ, and sees the perfect character he possessed, is drawn to follow him ﷺ. That is the action of the *tariqa*. He seeks thirdly by his words "its reality the integrator of my universe," to join the outward and the inward. By that the reality is illuminated and its secret appears.

Or you could say that he seeks firstly to realise the station of Islam by witnessing his outward ﷺ; he seeks secondly to realise the station of Iman by witnessing his inward

🕋 and he seeks thirdly to realise the station of Ihsan by witnessing his reality 🕋. Or you could say he seeks firstly to witness him 🕋 in respect of his *mulk*, and secondly to witness him in respect of his *malakut*, and thirdly to witness him from the aspect of his *jabarut*. In fact it is even more than that because when the Shaykh seeks to return to going-on by witnessing the means, he seeks to have hunger for it by witnessing its *mulk*, *malakut* and *jabarut* and in that way the *jabarut* of the means is added to the *jabarut* of the goal.

through the realisation of the first Truth

The first Truth is the prior witnessing in the world of the spirits on the day of *"Am I not your Lord,"* (7:172), so realising it means recalling that and using it to help in constant witnessing. Or the first Truth is the witnessing of Lordship and drowning in Oneness. Or the first Truth is Allah Almighty since He is the One who precedes every truth and every right is from Him. Or the first Truth is the basic *jabarut*. He desires his worlds to be transferred to the *jabarut* of the means while continuing to see the *jabarut* of the goal since it is the basic source and first Truth.

The difference between the *jabarut* of the means and the *jabarut* of the goal is that the *jabarut* of the means is veiled with Wisdom and covered with the cloak of Might and Power. So its outward is Wisdom and its inward is Power. Whoever adds the secondary *jabarut* to the primal *jabarut* absolutely without taking Wisdom into consideration falls into heresy because he invalidates Divine legislation and

Wisdom and rends the cloak of Power and Might. Whoever adds it taking Wisdom into consideration and with the cloak of Pride and Power is a perfect comprehensive imam who is fit for teaching and ascent. May Allah place us among them, by His grace.

O First! O Last! O Outwardly Manifest! O Inwardly Hidden!

"**First**" before everything, "**Last**" after everything, "**Outwardly Manifest**" above everything, "**Inwardly Hidden**" beneath everything. That is how the Prophet ﷺ explained it in the *hadith* which Malik reported in the *Muwatta'*. It states: "O Allah, you are the First, and there is nothing before You. You are the Last, and there is nothing after You. You are the Outwardly Manifest, and there is nothing above You. You are the Inwardly Hidden and there is nothing beneath you. Settle my debt for me." Firstness designates pre-eternity and lastness designates going-on for ever, outwardness designates manifestation and inwardness designates veiling by Wisdom beyond Power. He is outward in His inwardness and inward in His outwardness. The name Outwardly Manifest obliterates the manifestation of otherness and conceals it since there is no outward with Him, glory be to Him and may He be exalted! His name the Inwardly Hidden demands the manifestation of His created beings so that He is inward in respect of their outward sensory. If He were to remain with His attribute of inwardness, He would not be recognised or worshipped.

We read in the *Hikam*: "He manifests everything because He is the Inwardly Hidden. He conceals everything because He is the Outwardly Manifest." He said at the end of the *Intimate Conversation*: "How can You be hidden when You are manifest? How can You be absent when You are One who is present, watching?" In short, the limitation inherent in His words: *"He is the First and the Last, the Outward and the Inward."* (57:3) demands that He alone has manifestation and not any other because that is what is implied by them. All that is manifest is Him. All that is hidden is Him. Or you could say: He manifests all that is hidden and conceals all that is manifest, since there is nothing with Him. Or you could say that He is Outward in respect of definition and Inward in respect of underlying solidity, since there is no how to the essence of Lordship. Or you could say, that He is Outward by His Power and Inward by His Wisdom, meaning because of His Wisdom. So he manifests Wisdom and conceals Power. This was indicated by one of the gnostics when he said:

> She appeared and was not hidden to anyone
> except for the blind who cannot see the moon.
> But she was concealed by what she manifested as a veil,
> and how can someone who is veiled by might be seen?

Know that Wisdom is the source of Power and Power is the source of Wisdom since the Doer is one. I will mention to you something of the Sea of Power and something of the Sea of Wisdom to show you the difference between them despite their being unified in place. Success is by Allah.

The Sea of Power is an overflowing sea and its business is force. It has no firstness and no lastness. It is manifest and concealed. It moves and is still. It contains and repels. It gives and withholds. It preserves and elevates. It controls decreed matters. Around its axis revolve the root of the branches and branches of the root. Arrival occurs at it and the hearts of those with yearning fly to it and the spirits of the wayfarers swim on the edge of its gulf and the secrets of those who have arrived dive into the depths of its gulf. The hearts of the gnostics cannot know the Essence of His immensity. The end of it is astonishment and bewilderment and then devotion and so it is the Presence.

As for the Sea of Wisdom, it is also an overflowing sea. Its business is outward. It manifests the means and lowers the veil. It connects judgements to causes and affirms evils and inclinations. It covers what emerges from the element of Power with its cloak and veils what appears of the secrets of lordship with the might of His pride. It illuminates the *tariqa* and protects the *haqiqa*. It manifests slavehood and conceals freedom. Whoever stops with it is veiled. Whoever pierces through to the Sea of Power is attracted and arrives. Whoever witnesses the two of them together, is perfect and beloved and accompanied by Divine concern.

Know that in the case of Power and Wisdom, each one calls for its people by the tongue of its state. As for Power, it says to Wisdom, "You are subject to my force and my will. You only do what I wish. Nothing will issue from you but what I will. If you wish to oppose me, I will turn you back. If you get ahead of me, I will catch you up." Wisdom says to Power, "You are subject to my rule and my command and prohibition. If you disobey me, I will discipline you and perhaps execute you." If Power emerges in harmony with Wisdom, that is a sign of Beauty, sooner or later. If Power emerges contrary to Wisdom, it is a sign of Majesty, sooner or later. Because Wisdom is dependent on *shari'a* and Power is the locus of *haqiqa*. When *haqiqa* is in opposition to *shari'a*, it is disobedience, and it is the reason for Majesty. A man alternates between Power and Wisdom, as he alternates between *haqiqa* and *shari'a*, and Allah knows best.

Hear my cry as you heard the cry of Your slave, our master Zakariyya, peace be upon him

This is requesting a swift answer in the form of a miracle. Zakariyya, peace be upon him, was given a child from his loins when his wife had despaired of bearing a child and he was an old man. This indicates that the Shaykh was seeking a spiritual heir. It is as if he feared that the path would be cut off after his death since he had not left an heir to his secret. And so Allah answered his supplication with Abu-l-Hasan ash-Shadhili, who took his secret and spread it in the east and west. The Shadhiliyya *tariqa* spread like the sun on the horizon and had many followers in the east and the west. All of that is recorded in the biography of the Shaykh, may Allah be pleased with him. A man has his followers placed in his balance, so by that measure how vast is the worth of the Prophet Muhammad ﷺ!

Help me through You – for You

Then he completes his request and asks for Allah's help, seeking to be strengthened and helped outwardly directly by Him, not by means of anything else, so that he is truly a sincere slave of Allah. This is because sometimes, when help arrives through means, the soul will incline to love those means and thereby be veiled from the goal, which is not the case when there are no visible means. The person concerned is then a true slave because he has love for the true Helper.

Support me through You – for You

This is asking to be strengthened inwardly by not seeing other than Allah, so that the supplicant is a sincere slave to Him. The Shaykh affirms that "**help**" in the outward corresponds to means and "**support**" inwardly arrives by lifting the veil and is in harmony with what is correct. It is said that "**help**" and "**support**" alternate. Joining the two of them is expressed in various ways, the first of which is "**realisation**". This happens when "**help**", which is guidance, is accompanied by "**support**" in the form of success.

In short, the locus of "**help**", guidance, "**support**" and success is the heart. But most "**help**", in the form of guidance, appears outwardly on the limbs, so that they are guided to purity and going straight. They are thereby strengthened to persevere in worship. The effect of "**support**" in the form of success appears in the inner worlds and strips away vices and adorns the inward with virtuous qualities, such as noble character, pleasure, submission, love, gnosis and other such characteristics. Allah Almighty knows best.

Join me to You

Then he mentions the fruit of **"help"** and **"support"**, which is being gathered to Allah and absence from what is other than Him through drowning and continuance. Otherwise, the gatheredness he obtains is that indicated by the words of the Almighty: *"O Prophet, fear Allah."* (33:1) Gatheredness is witnessing lordship in a state of constant connection. Separation is witnessing slavehood in a state of constant disconnection. Or you could say that gatheredness is witnessing Power alone and separation is witnessing Wisdom alone. The people of attraction and annihilation only witness gatheredness and the people of wayfaring, before the removal of the veil, only witness separation. The people of going-on witness gatheredness in the source of separation and separation in the source of gatheredness. They are gathered in their separation and separated in their gatheredness. Their gatheredness does not veil them from their separation and their separation does not veil them from their gatheredness, may Allah be pleased with them.

Come between me and other than You

In seeking constant gatheredness, the Shaykh also seeks the negation of its opposite, which is separation. Witnessing other than Allah is heedlessness of gnosis. Otherwise, not. It is as if he seeks to have a barrier placed a between himself and any heedlessness which affirms otherness or have a barrier set up between himself and illusion since that is what establishes otherness. I heard our shaykh al-Buzidi often say, "By Allah, only illusion veils people from

Allah. Illusion is a non-existent matter which has no reality. People imagine the existence of otherness but otherness has no existence."

Allah. Allah. Allah.

This is realisation of the gatheredness which is sought. The vocative particle is elided since it indicates distance and there is no distance with gatheredness. "Allah" is repeated three times for the number of the three worlds: *mulk*, *malakut*, and *jabarut*. Each time a world is annihilated by it the seeker rises to another until he is firm in the third, in the world of *jabarut*. When he says, "Allah" the first time, he annihilates the world of the *mulk*. When he says it the second time, he annihilates the world of the *malakut*. When he says it the third time, he reaches the *jabarut* and remains in it. I heard our shaykh say, "When a man says 'Allah', by it he shatters all phenomenal being provided he has received it from the Shaykh. Shattering is destruction and removal." The shaykh of our shaykhs, Sidi 'Ali, used to say, "No one thinks that phenomenal being dissolves when the name of Allah is mentioned over it." I say, "What the two shaykhs said is sound. When you say, 'Allah' and turn with your heart to phenomenal being from the Throne to the earth, it dissolves and disappears and not a trace of it remains. So may Allah repay them well from us."

The Shaykh's repetition of this Immense Name is permission to repeat it and confine oneself to it in *dhikr*. It is true, as opposed to what al-Hattab mentioned from 'Izzu-d-din ibn 'Abdu-s-Salam. Perhaps it was before he met the Shaykh. There are three views regarding this question: absolute permission for both beginning and end; general prohibition; and a distinction whereby it is permitted at the end and not at the beginning. The well-known view is the first. It says in *Lata'if al-Minan*, "Shaykh Abu-l-'Abbas al-Mursi used to encourage it a lot. He said, 'It is the Sultan of the Names.' Al-Yusi said, 'The fruit of this Name is recognition of the Essence.' Abu-l-Hasan an-Nuri did it and he continued for some days saying, 'Allah Allah Allah' without stopping. He did not eat or drink. He mentioned that to al-Junayd and he said to him, 'If you say it by yourself, you are an idolater. If you say it by Allah, you are not the speaker, so what is this intoxication?' He was silent for a time and then said, 'You are an excellent doctor!'"

"He who has imposed the Qur'an upon you will most certainly bring you back home again." (28:85)

When there is real gatheredness accompanied by help and delight, heedlessness and slackness will not mar it. This will occur definitively after the Resurrection and the Gathering. So this *ayat* is recited over the *ruh* to console it, meaning: "He who has imposed the rulings of the Qur'an on you, and acting by them, will bring you back to a magnificent Hereafter." So always be connected to your Beloved. As for the abode of this world, it is the abode of terrors and the place of separation and movement. It is not strange that turbidity should occur as long as you are in this abode. It produces what deserves to be described by it and must be described.

"Our Lord give us mercy directly from You and open the way for us to right guidance in our situation." **(18:10)**

Then he mentions the supplication of the People of the Cave in order to be like them in self-denial, devotion to Allah and fleeing from what is other than Him. He said, **"Our Lord, give us,"** i.e. grant us and bestow on us immense **"mercy"** from the treasures of Your handful, which will envelop us and alienate us from other than You, **"directly from You"**, i.e. from Your hidden commands because the word *ladun* indicates greater connection and nearness than the word *'inda*. **"Open the way,"** i.e. appoint, **"for us in our situation,"** all of it, **"right guidance"**, i.e. what is correct. The meaning is: Make all of our business guidance and correctness so that it accords with Your love and Your pleasure.

This is the end of the prayer in the old text. Some people add, *"Allah and His angels call down blessings on the Prophet. You who believe, call down blessings on him and ask for complete peace and safety for him."* (33:56) This *ayat* indicates the immensity of the business of the prayer on the Messenger of Allah ﷺ, since Allah – glory be to Him and may He be exalted – began with Himself, and then second with the angels of His purity and thirdly with the believers from *jinn* and men. So it is greater than the command to prostrate to Adam, peace be upon him. The prayer on him ﷺ contains many benefits and it has numerous fruits. Ibn Farhun and others have spoken of them, and so we will not go on at length about them. The *faqir* must not neglect it. If he is travelling, he ends by mentioning it and begins with it. If he is firm, he immerses his moments in it.

Then he obeyed the command of the Creator and said:

"May Allah bless him and his family and Companions and grant them peace."

There is disagreement about whether the prayer on the Prophet ﷺ is mandatory or recommended, the latter being contrary to the well-known position. The well-known position is that is mandatory once in a lifetime, and then the recommendation remains. Only someone who is deprived neglects it.

Then he ends the prayer by mentioning what has come from our master 'Ali who said, "Whoever wants to have an ample measure, should finish his supplication with, '*Glory be to your Lord, the Lord of might, above that which they describe, and peace be upon the Messengers and praise be to Allah, the Lord of the worlds.*' (37:180-182) i.e. proclaim the absolute purity of your Lord, the Lord of Might, uncontaminated by anything that the unbelievers ascribe to Him in terms of partners or children.

Peace, in other words, goodness and greeting and honour, be upon the Messengers chosen for the secret of His revelation. Praise belongs to Allah, the Lord of the worlds, for helping His lovers and His troops. May Allah place us among His supported troops, the people of experience and happiness. Amin. Peace be upon the Messengers, and praise belongs to Allah, the Lord of the worlds. May Allah bless our master Muhammad, the Seal of the Prophets and Imam of the Messengers, and his family and Companions, and grant them peace.

THE KHAMRIYYA OF IBN AL-FARID

Praise belongs to Allah who lets the hearts of those He loves drink from the wine of His love so that they become among those who are enraptured and intoxicated by His love. He makes them withdraw from witnessing other than Him by witnessing His secret and they walk in the meadows of His *malakut* while their spirits are attracted to the Presence of His purity, so they are familiar with Him in their retreats. He prepares their secrets to bear the burdens of His gnosis and they dive into the seas of His *jabarut*, sailing with the ships of their reflection. Blessing and peace be upon the one who helped beings by the secret of his *nasut* while the realities of gnosis shone from the light of His *lahut*. May Allah be pleased with his Companions and the noble people of his house!

Before and after everything is the knowledge of *tawhid*, which is the most majestic of knowledges and the most true of the fruits of understanding gained from it. How could that not be the case when its subject is the Sublime Essence and its radiant Attributes and pure Names. By it one will be forever in the bliss of the Garden and be granted nearness to the Generous Giver. It is divided into two categories: the *tawhid* of proof and evidence, which is for the common people of belief; and the *tawhid* of witnessing and seeing, which is for the elite of the people of *ihsan* among the people of tasting and ecstasy. They drink the cups of love and are intoxicated and withdraw from existence. Then they become sober after their intoxication. They enjoy the sweetness of the vision and witnessing. How sweet a drink and how excellent a path! Offering one's life to achieve it is an insignificant sacrifice and expending one's spirit and lifeblood to obtain it is a mere trifle. How excellent is what the speaker said:

If my blood is spilled to achieve my heart's desire,
  a mere glance from You makes shedding my blood as nothing.

Among those who have obtained precedence in this area, and who had a portion and importance in respect of this secret, were the Prophets and the Messengers, peace and blessing be upon them. The greatest of them with respect to that was the Master of Mankind, our Master, the best blessing and purest peace be upon him, since the secrets overflowed from the sea of his secret and their lights split off from the sun of his light. All of them took a handful from the sea of the Messenger of Allah or a drink of his refreshing rain.

Then the elite *awliya'* and pure friends inherited that from him. They strove against their lower selves with various forms of discipline and exerted themselves to the utmost in seeking their Beloved. They were true to their Lord in their behaviour and turned away from their portions and appetites and so they obtained the greatest legacy after realising their spiritual kinship, clear evidence of witnessing the contract of love and the rulings connected to good company. They experienced the emergence of the sperm drop of concern from the loins of *wilaya*, whose veins are in the placenta of the will. Then came the manifestation of the foetus of happiness, which grows in the womb of the people of gnosis and is cared for by its parents who are watchfulness and striving. Then it is nourished by the milk of the Knowledge of Certainty up until the time of its weaning through witnessing the Lord of the Worlds. This is the knowledge inherited from the Prophets, peace be upon them. It is not the *tawhid*, which is a result of proof and evidence and subject to increase and decrease, since doubts and illusions occur to him which are impossible in respect of the Prophets, peace be upon them.

One of those who took hold of this high legacy and splendid secret was the sultan of the lovers and imam of the intelligent, the sovereign gnostic and eternal sage, the honour of the *deen*, Abu Ja'far 'Umar ibn 'Ali in al-Mursid known as Ibn al-Farid as-Sa'di, Egyptian by residence, birth and death. He was the wonder of his time and unique in his age and among his contemporaries. He was born in 576 AH in Cairo and he died there in 632 AH. He is buried at the foot of the Muqattam outside of Cairo. There is an immense tomb built over him and it is a well-known site for people to visit. May Allah give us the benefit of his blessings.

We read in the *Diwan,* quoting from the Shaykh's son:

"The shaykh was of medium height with a handsome face and reddish complexion. When he listened in *sama'* and experienced ecstasy and the state overcame him, his face increased in beauty and luminosity. The sweat poured from his body until it flowed to the earth. He had light, majesty and inspired awe. When he attended a gathering, tranquillity appeared in that gathering. His gathering was attended by the great men of the state – amirs, wazirs, judges and leaders of people. They had the utmost *adab* and humility towards him. When they spoke to him, it was as if they were speaking to a great king. When he walked in the city, people crowded to him to seek his blessing and supplication. They wanted to kiss his hand, but he would not allow anyone to do that. Rather he shook hands with them. His clothes were good and his scent fragrant. He used to spend amply on all who came to him and would give generously. He did not seek to obtain anything of this world and did not accept anything from anyone. The sultan sent him a thousand dinars and he returned them to him. The sultan then asked if he could prepare a grave for him alongside his mother under the dome of Imam ash-Shafi'i. He did not give permission for that. Then he asked him to prepare for him a place which could be visited and which would be known as his, but he was unhappy about that."

He said:

"At the beginning of my divestment (*tajrid*), I used to ask permission of my father and then go to the Valley of the Wretched at the second mountain of Muqattam and would stay there. I would wander night and day and then I would return to my father to be dutiful to him and his feelings. At that time, my father was the deputy of the judge, al-'Aziz, in Cairo and Egypt. He was one of the great people of knowledge and action. He experienced joy at my return to him and made me sit with him in the gatherings of judgement and the schools of knowledge. Then I yearned again for *tajrid* and once more asked his permission and returned to wandering. I continued to do that time after time until my father was asked to be the Chief Qadi. He refused and retired from judgeship and then left people and travelled, following the path of Truth.

"Yet I experienced no opening. One day I returned from wandering to the city and went to the Suyufiyya Madrasa. I found an old man, who was a greengrocer, at the door of the madrasa performing *wudu'* in an incorrect order. He washed his hands and then his feet, then wiped his head and then washed his face. I said to him, 'Shaykh, you are this old and are in the Abode of Islam and among the *fuqaha'* of the Muslims and yet you do not perform *wudu'* the right order?' He looked at me and said, "Umar, you will not have an opening in Egypt. You will have opening the Hijaz in Makka – may Allah honour it! – so go there. The moment of opening is near for you.' I knew then that the man was one of the *awliya'* of Allah and that he was concealing himself by making a show of ignorance. I sat down before him and said, 'Sir, where am I in relation to Makka? I will not find a mount or companions outside of the months of *hajj*.' He looked at me and pointed and said, 'Here is Makka right in front of you.' I looked and saw Makka – may

Allah ennoble it! – I left him and sought it. It remained in front of me until I entered it at that moment. Opening came to me when I entered it and continued in waves and did not stop.

"Then I began to travel in its valleys and I stayed in the wilderness night and day. I stayed in a valley located a ten days ride from Makka with a good mount and I used to come from it every night and day and pray the five prayers in the noble Haram. There was a huge beast with me who accompanied me coming and going and knelt for me like a camel kneels. It would say, 'Sir, ride!' But I never rode it.

"Then after fifteen years. I heard the greengrocer shaykh calling, "Umar! Come to Cairo. Attend my death.' I went to him swiftly and found him dying. I greeted him and he greeted me and he gave me some gold dinars and said, 'Use this to prepare me and do such-and-such. Give those who bear my bier to Qarafa a dinar each. Leave me on the earth in this place.' He indicated it with his hand and it was continuously before my eyes. It was Qarafa where the stream passes under the mosque known in the land by its nearness to Maraki' Musa at the foot of Mt Muqattam. He added, 'Wait for the coming of a man who will descend to you from the mountain and then you and he will pray over me. Wait to see what Allah will do about my business.'

"When he died, I prepared him as he had requested and then I put him in that blessed place as he had commanded. Then a man came down from the mountain as a swift bird swoops down. I did not see him walking on his feet. I recognised this person. I used to see him slapping the back of his neck in the markets. He said, "Umar, come forward and lead us in prayer over the shaykh.' I went forward and prayed as imam. I saw green and white birds in rows between the heaven and the earth praying with us. I saw that one of them was a green bird of immense size. It landed at his feet and swallowed him. Then it rose to them and they all flew off, raising their voices in supplication until they vanished from our sight.

"He said, "Umar, haven't you heard that the souls of the martyrs are inside the stomachs of green birds that fly in the Garden wherever they wish? They are the martyrs of the sword. As for the martyrs of love, all of them, body and soul, are inside the stomachs of the green birds. This man is one of them, 'Umar, and I was one of them, but I slipped and was excluded from them. I slap the back of my neck in regret and chastisement for that slip.' Then the man went back to the mountain like a bird until he disappeared from my sight."

His son said, "The Shaykh was buried in this blessed place according to his instruction. His tomb there is well-known." That was already mentioned. His grandson said, "I wrote some verses about that:

Pass through Qarafa under the tail of al-'Arid.
   Say, 'Peace be upon you, Ibn al-Farid.'

You produced wonders in the *Nazm as-Suluk*
and unveiled that deep hidden secret.
You drank from the sea of love and fidelity
and had your fill of a deep encompassing sea.

The Shaykh said, "I saw the Messenger of Allah ﷺ in a dream and he said to me, "Umar what is your lineage?' I answered, 'Messenger of Allah, the Banu Sa'd, the tribe of Halima as-Sa'diyya, your nursemaid.' The Messenger of Allah ﷺ said, 'You must be from me. Your lineage is connected to me.' I said, 'Messenger of Allah, I recorded my lineage from my father and my grandfather back to the tribe of Sa'd.' 'No,' he said, raising his voice, 'rather you are from me and your lineage is connected to me.' I said, 'You have spoken the truth, Messenger of Allah,' repeating that. Lineage to him is either that of family or that of love, and that of love is nobler than that of parentage. It is that which made Bilal, Suhayb and Salman al-Farisi People of the House and put Abu Talib and Abu Jahl far away."

This was indicated by the Shaykh in his *qasida* in *ya'*:

In the law of passion, the ascription between us
is closer than an ascription on account of parentage.

Shaykh Ibn al-Farid was accused of what other people of realisation, such as ash-Shushtari and Ibn Sab'un, were accused of: *hulul* (claim of incarnation) and *ittihad* (claim of unification), so that some of the people of the outward forbade reading his poem in *ta'* which he called *The Breaths of the Heart and Gems of the Garden*. Then he saw the Messenger of Allah ﷺ who told him, "Call it *'Nazm as-*

Suluk (*The Poem of the Way*)'" and he renamed it that. Then the one who forbade it was put to the test with an affliction and repented and retracted what he had said. His grandson said, "How could it be imagined that in his *qasida* the Shaykh would incline to *hulul* when his creed was far from it as he says in it:

When I realise the Name of Allah
   why should I fear the rumours of misguidance?
Here is the Dihya who came to the trusty one, our Prophet,
   in his form at the beginning of the revelation of
      Prophethood.
Is it Jibril? Tell me me if he was Dihya when he appeared
   to the guide of true guidance in a noble form?
He alone among those present, was privileged with
   knowledge
   of the true nature of who it was without doubt?
He saw an angel giving him revelation while others
   saw a man who was his Companion.
In the more perfect of the two visions, I have an indication
   which removed the idea of *hulul* from my creed.

The meaning of the words of the Shaykh is that all being is like the form of Jibril when he took on the form of Dihya. His outward was Dihya and inward was Jibril. If you realise the truth, you will only find Jibril and there is neither *hulul* nor *ittihad* since there is nothing with him. That is how being is with the light of the Real. Allah is the Light of the heavens and the earth, so understand that.

The Shaykh has many *qasida*s, which were compiled by his grandson into a *diwan*. The most famous and precious of them is the poem in *ta'*, *The Poem of the Way*, which was already mentioned. He used to say about it: "This splendid radiant unique *qasida* has not been imitated nor has it been allowed for anyone to come up with its like. It is almost outside of the capacity of a mortal."

A group of scholars, who used to keep the company of the Shaykh and were close to him, related that he did not compose his verse in the way poets normally do. He experienced periods of divine attraction in which he left his senses for days, sometimes for a week or ten days. When he recovered, he dictated what had been opened to him: thirty, forty or fifty verses. Then he left it until that state recurred.

Similar to that is his *qasida* in *mim* known as *al-Khamriyya* (the Wine Ode), which we want to discuss here. Indeed its words are sweeter and it has a more fluid style. Only a *malakuti* tongue and a *jabaruti* heart could articulate it. In it the poet goes to great lengths to praise the pre-eternal wine and in it he revealed the secrets of the unseen reality and removed the cover of protection from the secrets of the *jabarut* and the lights of the *malakut*. May Allah repay him with the best repayment! He made perceptions easier to understand and clarified the paths to them, using the most succinct expressions and most eloquent indication.

We desired, by Allah's help, to briefly explain its words and unpack its meanings after doing the *Istikhara* of the Prophet and receiving a spiritual indication to go ahead with it. This is the time to begin this composition relying on the strength and power of Allah and what Allah has opened of the gifts of His grace. I start by Him. The shaykh said:

$$شَرِبْنا عَلى ذِكْرِ الحَبيبِ مُدامةً$$

$$سَكِرْنا بِها مِن قَبْلِ أَن يُخْلَقَ الكَرْمُ$$

After remembering the Beloved, we drank a wine
  by which we were intoxicated before the vine was
  created.

Mudâma and *mudâm* – from the verbal root *dâma*, meaning to last – are both names for wine because the Arabs used to like to have it constantly with them and so they called it that for good luck. The word *karm* is used both for the vine and the grapes themselves. He is saying: "After remembering the Beloved with our hearts and spirits we drank a pure wine in the station of purity by which we were intoxicated, and so we were absent to sensation and saw the lights of the Beloved in everything. He is with everything and before everything and after everything. Intoxication made us absent to the darkness of temporal beings and we saw the lights of enduring timelessness." I indicated this meaning in my poem in *'ayn* in which I said:

We were intoxicated and wandered in the radiance of His beauty
  and withdrew from sensation while the light was shining.
The sun of the day appeared to us and shone:
  the light of a star does not remain when the sun is shining.

He said that this intoxication, induced by the pre-eternal spiritual wine, occurred before the existence of the vine from which physical wine comes. Ash-Shustari indicated this meaning when he said:

Not the drink of past cups passed around. They are terrestrial.

Their wine is other than my wine: my wine is pre-eternal.

His words: "By which we were intoxicated before the vine was created" can mean that this intoxication occurred after the appearance of the world of forms and that the spirit became intoxicated, at the mention of the Beloved, with pre-eternal wine before the manifestation of the vine from which the terrestrial sensory wine comes. What is meant is that he was intoxicated with the spiritual wine before the manifestation of the physical reality of earthly wine. It is also possible that this intoxication was experienced by the spirit before time, in the world of spirits, before the manifestation of the world of the forms, and so his words, "before the vine was created" refer to its physical appearance, i.e. before the manifestation of the physical reality of earthly wine. That is supported by his words which come later, "I had rapture from it before I was formed." This will be discussed later, Allah willing. The first interpretation is more apparent, and Allah knows best.

Absence in Allah is called intoxication because it shares with physical intoxication in being absent from sensation. As the light of the intellect is veiled by the darkness of clay in the intoxication which results from physical wine, it is similarly veiled by the brightness of the lights of meaning which come suddenly from the pre-eternal wine and render the subject absent from sensation. That is why that absence is called "intoxication", and Allah knows best.

There are a number of technical terms which are used by the People of Sufism. We will mention some of them upon which the understanding of the words of the poet depend. They include: *dhawq* (tasting), *shurb* (drinking), *sukr* (intoxication), and *sahw* (sobriety), as well as *hiss* (sensory), *ma'na* (meaning), *qudra* (power), *hikma* (wisdom), *wajd*, *wijdan* and *wujud* (three degrees of ecstasy), and *jam'* (gatheredness) and *tafriqa* (separation).

As for *dhawq* (tasting), it is the shining of the lights of the timeless Essence on the intellect so that it withdraws from seeing temporality in the lights of timelessness; but that does not last. It sometimes shines and flashes and at other times is hidden. When it flashes, the person concerned withdraws from his senses. When it is hidden, he returns to his senses and to seeing himself. They call this *dhawq*.

If that light lasts for an hour or two, it is called *shurb* (drinking). When it continues and lasts beyond that, then it is called *sukr* (intoxication). It derives from the annihilation of forms in the witnessing of the Living, Self-Sustaining and withdrawing from effects in the witnessing of the Effector. It is also called *fana'* (annihilation).

If the person concerned returns to experiencing the establishment of things by Allah and their being sustained by Him, and sees them as being one of His lights, having no existence apart from Him, that is called *sahw* (sobriety). It is also called *baqa'* (going-on) since things are seen through the faculty of inner sight to go on by Allah after they have been annihilated by His light. The author of the *Hikam*, Ibn 'Ata'allah, indicated this when he said: "The light of the inner eye lets you see His nearness to you. The source of the inner eye lets you see your non-existence by your existence. The truth of the inner eye lets you see His existence, not your own non-existence or existence. 'Allah was and there was nothing with Him. He is now as He was.'"

He also says in explanation of intoxication and sobriety and clarification of the nature of the *shari'a* and the Reality: "Then there is the one who possesses inner reality. He has withdrawn from creation by seeing the Real King. He is annihilated to causes by seeing the Maker of causes. This is the slave who is face-to-face with the reality and its radiance is manifest on him. He has travelled the Path and has mastered its dimensions. However, he is drowned in the lights and created traces have been wiped out. His intoxication dominates his sobriety. His gatheredness dominates his separation. His annihilation dominates his going-on. His absence dominates his presence. More perfect than him is the slave who drinks and is increased in sobriety. He withdraws and it increases him in presence. His gatheredness does not veil him from his separation and his separation does not veil him from his gatheredness. His annihilation does not keep him from his going-on and his going-on does not divert him from his annihilation. He gives everything with a due its due and he gives everyone with a portion his full portion."

Wajd (ecstasy) is a *warid* which descends and moves the heart and unsettles it. It is either an exhilarating feeling, which provokes expansion and joy, or a disquieting fear, which provokes contraction and sorrow. *Wujdan* is the enduring of the sweetness of witnessing and its connection to the one experiencing it, while intoxication and astonishment predominate. This is the true reality of *wujud* (existence). Al-Junayd indicated this when he said, "My existence is that I withdraw from existence by what appears to me of witnessing." Know that what causes *wajd* is listening to the words of the Beloved and the cause of *wijdan* is witnessing the beauty of the Beloved. The state may dominate a person, in which case they may feel compelled to dance, following the agitation of the heart. Their state is similar to that of a baby in the cradle. The baby is made tranquil when the cradle moves and weeps when it is still. That is how it is with such hearts, which are made tranquil when the body is moved. Otherwise they remains unsettled. That state might be very short-lived.

Someone in a true state of ecstasy, however, is firm and settled, intimate with the Divine Presence, and so astonishment and confusion depart and the person concerned is like a firm mountain. Al-Junayd was asked. "What is it with you? You used to show your ecstasy when listening and then you changed so that now you make no movement at all?" He recited the words of the Almighty, *"You will see the mountains you reckoned to be solid going past like clouds,"* (27:88)

Evidence for that is found in the women who saw Yusuf. When he appeared to them suddenly with his radiant beauty, they lost their senses and *"they cut their hands and said, 'Allah preserve us! This is no man."* (12:31), whereas Zulaykha, who was constantly in that state, did not do any of that. That is the case with the masters of *wijdan*. When they first looked towards the light of the Presence, they were astonished and lost their senses. Once they were firm in witnessing it and at home in it, not one of its lights moved them. The witnessing of beauty may dominate the gnostic so that he dances and delights in it, but that is rare, and Allah Almighty knows best.

As for *jam'* (gatheredness) and *tafriqa* (separation), *jam'* designates the disappearance of the temporal into the affirmation of the timeless, or you could say that it designates the amalgamation of the branches with their roots, and so what is not is annihilated and what goes on continues. *Tafriqa* is a term which designates the affirmation of rulings and wisdom, establishing the form or slavehood and *adab* with lordship. The locus of *jam'* is the inward and the locus of *tafriqa* is the outward, since Lordship without slavehood is imperfect and slavehood without lordship is impossible. That is why it is said, "Gatheredness without separation is heresy, since it invalidates rulings and wisdom, and separation without gathering is deviance, since it removes the person from the definition of perfection. Combining them is the source of perfection."

I heard the shaykh of our shaykh say, "Some people have *shari'a* and no *tasawwuf*, some people have *tasawwuf* and no *shari'a* and some people make the *shari'a* one door and the *haqiqa* several doors. *'Such people are the party of Allah. Truly it is the party of Allah who are successful.'* (58:22)" These are the first words I heard from him when I met him. He said to me, "You are one of the third category." May Allah make us realise their love and provide is with *adab* with them. Amin.

The term *hiss* (sensory) designates what is dense and appears among phenomenal beings whereas the term *ma'na* (meaning) designates the subtle internal light in them. As for the secret by which things are established, it is that the sensory is a container for the meaning. Phenomenal beings are vessels which bear the meaning. Allah knows best.

The term *qudra* (power) designates actions which issue from the Sublime Essence, whether they are according to norms or outside of the way things normally occur. The term *hikma* (wisdom), on the other hand, designates the connection of causes to effects. The word "custom" is used for those things which occur in the normal course of events. They are the cloak of "power" and its covering. Whoever stops at the cloak of "wisdom" is veiled to the witnessing of "power". Whoever is veiled from the attribute is veiled from what is described since the existence of both is necessary. Allah knows best. Recognition of these things is essential to the understanding of the people of knowledge. Allah knows best. Then he says:

لَهَا البَدرُ كَأسٌ وهي شمسٌ يُديرها

هلالٌ وكَم يبدو إذا مُزِجتْ نَجمُ

It has the full moon for a goblet, being a sun encircled by a crescent.

When it is mixed, how many stars appear!

He says that this pre-eternal wine has a goblet, which is the moon of special *tawhid*. Anyone who is a *mushrik* by affirming otherness, or by seeing things along with the Master, does not drink from the wine of passion. You could say that whoever has a heart which is filled with love of things, or is tempted by the goods of this world, does not taste anything of this wine, which is the sun of gnosis. When it shines on the horizons of the heaven of the heart, it covers up the existence of phenomenal beings and unobscured eye-witnessing occurs. The crescent of happiness passes it around to the drinkers in the upsurge of the happiness of will. If it is drunk pure, then intoxication causes forms to disappear and only the lights of the Living, the Self-Sustaining remain. If, however, it is amalgamated with sobriety and *suluk*, the drinker becomes perfect perfected and then how many stars of knowledge will appear, how many of the treasures of multiple understandings will be opened to such a one! When he has permission to give expression to that state, then hearts can hear his words and his indications are made plain to them.

Shaykh Abu-l-Hasan ash-Shadhili said when speaking about love: "The drink is radiant light from the beauty of the

Lover. The cup is the subtle kindness bringing that to the lips of the hearts. The cupbearer is the one who undertakes that task on behalf the elite of the great and righteous among His slaves. He is Allah who knows the destinies and best interests of His slaves. Whoever has that beauty unveiled to him or is given something of it – just a glimpse or two – and then has the veil lowered in front of him, tastes and yearns. Someone for whom it continues for an hour or two is truly a drinker. Someone for whom it persists, who drinks on until his veins and joints are filled with the hidden lights of Allah, that is called quenching. Such people may withdraw from the sensory and from the intellect and not know what is said nor what they say. That is intoxication. Then they are returned to *dhikr* and acts of obedience and are not veiled from attributes so that matters decreed conflict with one another. That is the time of their sobriety, expansion of their sight and increase of their knowledge. They are guided by the stars of knowledge, illuminated by the moon of *tawhid* in their night and by the sun of their gnoses in their day. *'Such people are the party of Allah. Truly it is the party of Allah who are successful.'* (58:22)"

Then the poet says:

$$\text{ولو لا شَذاها ما اهتديتُ لِحانِها}$$

$$\text{ولولا سناها ما تصوّرها الوَهْمُ}$$

Were it not for its sweet fragrance, I would not have been guided to its tavern.

Were it not for its radiance, imagination would not have conceived it.

Shadha is a perfumed breeze. It says in the dictionary that *shadha* means a strong scent. The tavern is the place in which wine is sold or drunk. The dictionary says that word *han* refers to both the shop and its owner. The *han* is the merchant and the radiance is luminescence and light.

He is saying: "This pre-eternal wine has a high value and is sublime, subtle and hidden. It is not obtained by any device or means, only through its fragrant breeze which wafts into the heart. So the spirits pick up its scent and are attracted to the presence of the Knower of hearts. If it were not for that, we would not have been guided to its source or directed ourselves to seeking it. But when the crescent moon of guidance shone out to us from the rising of prior Divine Concern, the breeze of election blew into our hearts from the vastness of the presence of Lordship. Then we continued to follow its trail and inhale what diffuses from it until it brought us to witnessing of the lights of the Beloved and intimate conversation with the One who is Near in the place of witnessing, direct communication, peace and face to face contact. We said about that state:

Time obeys you and people are slaves.

Live every day of your lives as an *'id*.

Shaykh Abu-l-Hasan said, "The metaphor of the beginning of love is like a man who catches the scent of musk at a distance. He continues to follow that scent and it intensifies for him until he enters the house where the musk is located. When he enters it, the scent floods through him and so he ceases to perceive it. That is like what happens with the seeker of the truth. His heart continues to be attracted to the presence and to thirst for it and to turn to it with the lights of turning, which is the sweetness of the process, until he is drowning in the lights of turning towards it. That is the presence of witnessing and his state is still and his thirst is removed by his arrival at Presence the Beloved. There only remains *adab* and rising through the stations. This is the meaning of the first line.

His words: "If it had not been for its radiance, imagination would not have conceived it," means this wine is hidden from inadequate thoughts and beyond the perception of intellects and understanding. If it had not been for its lights which shine on the hearts after they are freed from all otherness and purified from every turbidity, the intellect could not conceive of it nor could understanding grasp it, since it is beyond intellectual perception and is not obtained through verbal transmission. It is perceived only by keeping the company of Men, the people of realisation and perfection, because it is direct tasting which cannot proceed from written pages. As Ibn al-Banna says in *al-Mabahith*:

> Beware of desiring to obtain it from a notebook, poem or
> verse.

He also said:

> The one with cash and coins does not obtain it.
> It is only purchased by payment of the self.

If someone sells himself to a perfect shaykh to whom he gives authority over his self, the lights of gnoses shine on him and he obtains favours from Allah that no one can describe. Otherwise he merely exhausts himself and those connected to him. This happens all too often and the rare exception has no ruling. Success is by Allah. Then he said:

$$\text{وَلَمْ يُبْقِ مِنْهَا الدَّهْرُ غَيْرَ حُشَاشَةٍ}$$

$$\text{كَأَنَّ خَفَاهَا فِي صُدُورِ النُّهَى كَتْمُ}$$

**There is nothing left of its time but its final gasp;
 as if it was a secret hidden in the breasts of the
 intelligent.**

Hushasha is the final breath of the spirit of someone in their final illness. *Nuha* is the plural of *nuhya* meaning intelligence and here it refers to the people of intelligence.

He is saying that this wine has left the hearts of people and vanished with the departure of its people and died with the death of its masters. It has slipped from the hearts of people as the *ruh* slips from the dying body. In this time nothing remains of it except a tiny drop, like what is left of the spirit of the dead person in his last breath. This wine, which the Shaykh mentioned earlier, is the leavening of the hearts by the lights of the Beloved so they are veiled from others by their vision of the All-Conquering One.

At first the lights of this wine are outwardly manifest and its secrets are shown to its masters and so they pass it around between themselves and speak about it using subtle words and different types of indications and they are effaced. I have said elsewhere, "Its lights were hidden and its secrets concealed and it is as if it its concealment and hiding

162

were Allah's concealment of it from other than its people. That is because heedlessness has overpowered people and their *himma* has been directed to this world. When Allah saw people turning away from His door and taking refuge in other than His Presence, He hid that secret in the hearts of His *awliya'* and hid His *awliya'* among His slaves."

What the Shaykh says about the rarity of this knowledge and its disappearance has been said by more than one, both before him and after him. That is only because of its rareness and inaccessibility. Al-Junayd said, "The carpet of this knowledge of ours has been spread out and we have spoken about it for twenty years and yet only spoken about its fringes." He used to say, "I have sat with people for two years while they were conversing about knowledges which I did not understand nor know what they are. I was not concerned by my lack of knowledge at all. I used to accept it and love it without knowing it." He used to say, "We were conversing with our brothers of old about various knowledges which we do not know in this time of ours and no one asks me about them. This is a subject which is as if it is locked and barred."

It says in *al-Qut*, "One of our scholars said, 'I know that those before had seventy knowledges. They used to come to together and discuss them and acquaint one another with them. Today all we have left is one knowledge. I discern many knowledges in this time of which consist of falsehood, delusion and claims which have appeared and are called 'knowledges'." Then he said, "Our imam Sahl used to say after 369 AH, 'It is not lawful now to speak of this knowledge

163

of ours, due to the scarcity of its people, because there are people who listen to others and then innovate and dress up things with words. They clothe themselves in artificial ecstasies, their wellspring is their stomachs and their words are mere devices.'" Abu-l-Qasim al-Qushayri said at the beginning of his *Risala*, "Know, may Allah have mercy on you, that most of those who had true realisation among this group have passed on and only their trace remains in this time of ours." One of them said regarding this:

> No, by the One to whose House Quraysh make hajj,
> > facing the corner of its cube,
> My eye has not seen the tents of a tribe
> > but that I weep for those I love in its courtyard.
> As for the tents, they are like their tents,
> > but I see the women of the quarter are not its women.

Ibn al-'Arabi al-Hatimi said of these lines, "The author said this in his time when he met those who still wore the clothing of such people but were different from them inwardly. As for today, there are neither tents nor women." Shaykh Abu Madyan said in his *qasida*:

> Know that the Path of the People is no more
> > and today the state of those who claim it is as you see.

And it says in *al-Mabahith*:

> O you who ask about the customs of the *faqir*,
> > You ask about something that is rarely clearly explained.
> What you ask about has died
> > and become bones crumbled to dust.

There are only some traces which perhaps haven't been
effaced.

That is what we follow and understand.

Your gift is to win lands.

The secret and meaning are just inhabitants.

The Shaykh of our Shaykhs, Sidi 'Ali al-'Imrani said, "From
Tunis to Wadi Nun you will not find anyone speaking of
this knowledge except for one or two men," alluding to the
scarcity of the existence of those who possess realisation.
This does not indicate that the Men, by whom Allah shows
mercy to His slaves, are cut off in any time. The known
number will not cease to exist until the *deen* ceases to exist.
We read in *Lata'if al-Minan*, "One of the gnostics was asked
about the numbered *awliya'* and whether their number
reduces over time. He said, 'If their number was reduced
by even one, the sky would not release its rain nor would
the earth allow its plants to grow. The corruption of time is
not due to the lessening of their number nor the decrease
of their support. When the time is corrupt, however, Allah
desires to conceal them. When the people of the time
turn away from Allah, preferring what is other than Allah,
admonition does not avail them and reminder does not
make then incline towards Allah. Then they are not worthy
to have the *awliya'* appear among them. That is why it is
said, "The *awliya'* of Allah are brides and criminals do not
get to see any brides."'"

The Prophet ﷺ said, "When you see the impulse to avarice
being obeyed, passions being followed, this world being

preferred and everyone admiring his own opinion, then you must guard your own soul." They paid heed to the words of the Messenger of Allah ﷺ and preferred concealment. Rather Allah preferred it for them because some of them were in the time of the early imams, establishing the proof, referred to by the words of the Messenger of Allah ﷺ: "A group of my community will continue to openly support truth. They will not be harmed by those who oppose them until the Day of Rising." 'Ali said, "O Allah, the earth will never be deprived of those who afford proof of You for You. They are few in number but great in worth with Allah. Their hearts are connected to the highest place. Those are the khalifs of Allah among His slaves and His land. O! O! O! How I yearn to see them!"

These imams exist in our community now. They appear as the sun appears on the horizon in the beings who enjoy prior divine attention. Then Allah bestowed on us recognition of them and the honour of keeping their company. We find them to be among the people of Prophetic instruction, travelling the Path, recognising the Source of realisation. They have travelled through the lands of *tajrid* and dived into the seas of *tawhid*, calling to Allah by *himma* and to what is lawful, acknowledging the terminology and expressions of the Path, rising to Allah in their states, and directing to Allah by their words. They have progressed through the stations of attraction and annihilation and returned to the station of going-on. Allah has guided a large number at their hands and taught many people by them. However, as the sun is covered by clouds and beautiful women concealed by veils, so Allah has masked their secret by dark states and shaytanic actions on the part of some of their companions, although they themselves are innocent of any such thing. In fact they warn constantly against that. The command of Allah is decreed and success is by Allah, and there is no strength nor power except by Allah, the High, the Immense. Then he said:

وَمِن بينِ أَحشاء الدّنانِ تصاعدتْ

وَلَمْ يبقَ منها في الحقيقة إلّا اسمُ

It rises from the insides of the wine jars,

  while in reality nothing but its name remains of it.

This is correct in connecting this verse to what is before it since it corresponds to it. Perhaps the transcriber removed it from its proper place (since it refers directly to the verse before last). *Ahshsa'* is the plural of *hushwa*, which are the intestines. *Danan* is the plural of *dann*, which is a great earthenware wine jar with a narrow bottom. As soon as it is put down, it automatically pours. It is also called a *raqud*. Both wine and vinegar are stored in it. Here it is applies to the hearts or the bodies because they are the vessels for the divine wine. "Rising" is used for a thing ascending. The poet says: "This wine rises and ascends inside people, and inside their breasts, while nothing remains of it in reality except for its name without what is named and a trace without a locus." That is how it is with the knowledge of true *tasawwuf*: all that remains is bragging with the tongue while the hearts are in ruins. Someone said about that:

The people of *tasawwuf* have passed. *Tasawwuf* has
become prattle.

Tasawwuf has become comfort and a showy prayer mat.

Tasawwuf has become a *tasbih*, feigned ecstasy and a belt.

Your self says you are lying. It is not the proper customs
of the path.

What has already been mentioned about this is enough.
The blessing does not end and success is by Allah. Then he
says:

$$ فإِن ذُكِرْتْ فِي الحيِّ أصبحَ أهلُهُ $$

$$ نشاوَى ولا عارٌ عليهم ولا إثمُ $$

**If it is mentioned in the quarter, its people become
drunk**

and there is no shame nor wrong action for them.

The 'quarter' means the tribe, as the dictionary says.
Nashawa is the plural of *nashwan* and is like *sukran*
(intoxicated) in measure and meaning. He says, "If this
wine were to be mentioned with real recollection, in terms
of both knowledge and state, in a tribe, village or town, the
people of that tribe would become drunk and enraptured
by the mere mention of the Beloved and be dominated by
attraction to the pre-eternal Presence." There is, however,
a precondition: that the one who mentions it is himself
dominated by intoxication and attraction while having
some sobriety and that he mentions it among its People. If
he is as I said, there is no doubt about the intoxication of the

people of that town, their attraction to the Presence and the shining of the lights on them.

I myself witnessed the truth of this when we went to the tribe of Anjara and al-Fahs in the first year after meeting the shaykh, when intoxication dominated us. When we spent the night in a house, most of the household were intoxicated in the morning, constantly mentioning Allah. I found children, shepherds, and bath-keepers following me, weeping. We did not reply to them except with grave seriousness. In the Fahs of Tangier I saw the people of the Makhzan and government leaders wearing tasbihs, and they repented and left what they were doing. We verified this matter, which the Shaykh mentioned, with our own eyes. Praise is to Allah.

His words: "There is no shame for them..." are elicited by a comparison with the wine of this world, which involves blame and wrong action in the judgement of the *shari'a*, because by it the intellect is blotted out and destroyed in darkness. It debars people from remembering Allah and from the prayer. It is different from this wine, through which the intellect withdraws into the light, radiance and beauty of the Beloved. There is blame and wrong action in leaving it, not in drinking it, as he says:

$$وقالوا شربتَ الإثمَ كَلا وإنما$$
$$شربتُ التي في تركها عندي الإثمُ$$

They said, "You drank wrong action." No!
I drank that which I consider it to be a sin to leave!

Success is by Allah. Then he said:

وإن خَطرتْ يوما على خاطر امرِئٍ

أقامتْ به الأفراحُ وارتحلَ الهمُّ

**If it occurs one day to the thought of man,
joy remains with him and worry departs.**

He says, "When this pre-eternal wine, which is true gnosis, is imbibed by the heart of a unifying man, who is purified of other-than-Allah and free of the imagination of the forms of effects, and that state remains continuously in it, that heart becomes still. What that means is that joy, happiness, delight and rapture dwell in it from the presence of that wine. Sorrow and care are removed from it by witnessing the Living, Self-Sustaining, because that wine is nothing other than the gnosis of the pre-eternal essence, as we will see from its definition, Allah willing.

The gnostics consider the Garden of Gnosis to be higher than the Garden of Adornments, because no one who enters the Garden of Gnosis yearns for the Garden of Adornments. The Almighty says: *"Yes, the friends of Allah will feel no fear and will know no sorrow."* (10:62) This means in both abodes. The Almighty also says in a *hadith* qudsi: "I have prepared for My righteous slaves what the eye has not seen nor the ear heard nor has ever occurred to the heart of man." That is not limited to this world or to the Next World. They obtain it in both abodes. It is also the case that fear and sorrow only occur because of the separate existence of the human being. Someone who has actually vanished from his own existence only sees ultimate perfection.

When the heart experiences sorrow, it is denied witnessing and vision. As the author of the *Hikam* said: "Allah revealed to Da'ud, 'Da'ud! Say to the truthful: "Let them rejoice in Me! Let them enjoy My invocation!"'" This means that joy is only pure and bliss perfected by looking at His Noble Face. The Almighty says: "*Say: 'It is the favour of Allah and His mercy that should be the cause of their rejoicing.'*" (10:58), indicating that nothing else can be. The favour of Allah is His gnosis and His mercy is His guidance. The poet said about this meaning:

> You are my happiness and You are Him to whom I complain
>> of my pain.
> You are my moon in the darkness of the night.
> If I speak, I do not speak by other than You.
>> If I am deaf, you are the bond of my concealment.

Another said:

> Gnosis of the One with Majesty embodies
>> might and radiance, delight and joy.
> The gnostics also have splendour
>> and the light of love.
> Congratulations to the one who knows You, O my God!
>> He, by Allah, is always full of joy.

I said in my *Khamriyya* in *ta'*:

> Intoxication by it comprises happiness and delight,
>> and the very best of lives in bliss and joy.

And I said in my poem in *'Ayn*:

I am enraptured by the Crusher since it brings with it
my rest,

My spirit and my joy, and His beneficence is vast.

We confined the words of the Shaykh to the persistence
of the intake of that wine because simple drinking and
passage do not necessarily bring about continual happiness,
being like a flash of lightning, the effect of which rapidly
disappears. As the veil drops on the removal of that light,
then joy and happiness also depart, because the person
who has this station is in a state of constant change (*talwin*).
Someone in constant change is also travelling with the
travellers, and travel is a "portion of punishment". He has no
rest from toil and is not free of fatigue until he reaches the
station of stability (*tamkin*). Then he has rest and the heart
moves freely and cares and sorrows vanish from it as has
already been made clear. Success is by Allah. Then he says:

$$ \text{ولو نَظَرِ النّدمانُ خَتمَ إنائِها،} $$
$$ \text{لأَسكَرَهم مِن دونِها ذلك الخَتمُ} $$

**If the drinking companions just looked at its vessel's
stopper,**

**they would be become drunk from seeing the
outside of it.**

Nadman can be singular or plural according to the
dictionary. What is meant here is the plural by the evidence
of the plural pronoun in his words, "their intoxication". They
are the group who speak about the wine in their gathering.

The stopper of the vessel is what seals it. He likens the pre-eternal wine to physical wine or to the sealed nectar in the Garden. This pre-eternal wine is stored in its vessel which is sealed with the seal of preservation and protection. If those who intend to drink it were to look at that seal, they would become intoxicated even before drinking, so what about when they actually drink it? And what do you think about the one whose thirst is then completely quenched?

The vessels containing this wine are the inward of the gnostics and the seal referred to is the outward aspect of their humanness. All who direct themselves to them with respect and *adab* and look at their outward with humility and contrition, abasement and need, being certain of their elite station, become intoxicated by merely seeing them before taking anything from them or keeping their company. We have witnessed this secret in ourselves and in our shaykhs. Many of the *murid*s experienced attraction and intoxication before even receiving the *wird*. It happened merely by seeing. I saw some Christians in the port of Ceuta when we went there. When we held the circle of *dhikr*, they were attracted and followed us to the end of the limit of what is possible for them. They remained bewildered, standing behind us, since some of the light of the wine shone on them. Allah knows best.

The *Qutb*, Mawlana Ibn Mashish said about this when he spoke about love: "Some of them are intoxicated by merely witnessing the cup, even if they have not yet tasted any of its contents. How do you think it will be after they have held it to their lips, after they have drunk from it, after their thirst has been quenched, after they have become intoxicated, after they have become sober following their drunkenness, and after that in the various stages they have reached? The Cup is the recognition of the Truth, by which anyone Allah wishes among the sincere of His creation scoops up some of that pure, unadulterated undiluted drink. Sometimes the drink is witnessed as a form for that cup, sometimes it is witnessed as a meaning and sometimes it is witnessed as knowledge. The form is the portion of bodies and selves. The meaning is the portion of hearts and intellects. The knowledge is the portion of spirits and secrets. What sweet a drink it is! Bliss to the one who drinks it and continues in it, not being cut off from it! We ask Allah for His bounty. *'That is Allah's favour which He gives to whoever He wills. Allah's favour is indeed immense.'* (62:4) A group of lovers may gather and all drink from one cup. They may drink from many cups. The drink may differ according to the cups that contain it. The drink from the same cup may be different for each when many lovers drink from it."

He further said, "When the drinker witnesses that cup as a form, it is the state of beginners at the time of their first attraction. My brother told me that he actually tasted actual wine in his mouth and smelt its scent in his first attraction. When the drinker witnesses it in meaning, tasting the sweetness of the transaction and the pleasure of obedience, his heart disappears into the state of *dhikr*, even though it may be obstructed by the Veil. When the drinker witnesses it as knowledge, meaning the knowledge of unity gained through the removal of the Veil, he becomes intoxicated by witnessing the lights of the Beloved and then becomes sober after his intoxication."

The "form" is the portion of bodies and lower selves because this is what people experience at the beginning of the Path when their bodies are opaque and their lower selves are strong. Only something sensory has an effect on them or some type of physical miracle. The beginner is strengthened by this means but not people advanced on the Path. The "meaning" is the portion of hearts and intellects because this is what travellers who are in the middle of the journey experience. Their activity is no longer confined to the body but has been transformed to that of the heart and intellect. They drink from the subtle meanings because, even if they are veiled from actual vision of them, they are on the way to seeing them. They have glimpsed its lights and its secrets have shone on them. The "knowledge" is the portion of the spirits and secrets because the spirit and the secret are the locus of direct witnessing and knowledge of the Divine Unity. They are drowned in the source of the sea of unity. The terms spirit or secret are applied to them when the veil is lifted from them and they enter with the lovers. Otherwise they are referred to as 'self', 'intellect' and 'heart'. The locus of all these is one and the same. I said about this in my *qasida* in *ra'* which was composed about the spirit and its transformation through stages:

It is first the self and then the intellect then afterwards
   the heart.
   It then becomes the spirit and then the secret in
      pure gold.

175

When the self inclines to the earth and is dark
  at the beginning of the affair it is called the self.
When the limbs of passion are hobbled with halter ropes,
  then intellect takes responsibility for obeying the
  command.
Even if it settles on good, it still experiences thoughts,
  which veer the heart as ships veer on the sea.
Then the heart becomes the master of the command
  and makes the limbs safe both secretly and publicly.
When it spies the haven of arrival, it heads straight for it
  and, in *dhikr*, the weariness of the senses disappears.
It is called spirit in its attainment of its source,
  but the sensory remainder shines from pure goodness.
When the mirror is polished and free of all sensory rust,
  then the secret of Allah is added to the secret.

That is the end of what is desired of it.

In the words above, "A group of lovers may gather" the word "group" indicates that their intoxication has come about at the hand of one particular shaykh and he is 'the cup' that is referred to. The words "They may drink from many cups" mean that that someone may be intoxicated at first by the cup of one shaykh and then by other shaykhs whom his first shaykh has given him permission to meet. The one who is divinely attracted may have about forty shaykhs and drink from all of them. However, that is rare. The words, "The drink may differ" means that some of it is mixed with sobriety, which is the perfect drink, some of it is pure attraction followed by sobriety, some of it predominantly attraction, and so on, according to what is drunk and according to the number of cups. The words, "The drink from the same cup may be different" means what is drunk from the hand of the same Shaykh, and so the water is one but the flowers many. The wine is one and the vessels many. Some are hard, strong and wide and not overpowered by intoxication. Some are fine and subtle or narrow, and the least thing affects them. The water is one, which is the sobriety of the perfection of the one who gives the drink. Allah Almighty knows best and success is by Allah. There is no strength nor power except by Allah, the All-High, Immense.

Then he says:

ولو نَضَحوا منها ثرى قبر ميّتٍ

لعادتْ إليه الروحُ وانتعشَ الجسمُ

If they were to sprinkle the earth of a dead person with it,

the spirit would return to him and the body would be revived.

Nadh is splashing and *thara* is earth. To "revive" is to get up and rise. He says that this pre-eternal wine, which is the Divine Reality, is immensely strong and has a powerful effect on the heart and brings about the breaking of physical and spiritual norms. If its people were to sprinkle some of it on the grave of a dead person, he would rise and come out his grave by the permission of his Lord. Its effect is strengthened according to the extent of its realisation in the heart of the person concerned, in making his command accord with the command of Allah. That is why, in the case of the Prophets and Messengers, things reacted for them and normal patterns were broken more than was the case with others.

Sayyiduna 'Isa brought the dead to life, healed the blind and lepers by the permission of Allah. Our Prophet ﷺ used to feed large numbers of people from a *sa'* of food and would give water to an army from his noble fingers. He brought to life the girl baby who had been buried alive and gave her a choice between returning or remaining and she choose to return to her Lord. According to one view, he brought his parents to life so that they would become Muslim. He replaced the eye of Qatada after it fell into his hand and it was the better of his two eyes. There are other things which are too many to mention.

Similar miracles at the hands of the *awliya'* are reported by multiple transmission and are beyond number. It is also possible, however, that the words of the Shaykh are a metaphor and indication. By the earth of the grave of the dead he means the ordinary human nature of the ignorant or heedless person. The return of his spirit and revival then means his coming to life and rebirth with gnosis and knowledge. In other words the meaning is: "If the gnostics sprinkled some of the wine of their *himma* on the outward of the one whose spirit is dead through ignorance and heedlessness, it would become alive and rise to the presence of the Truth, and rise with knowledge and *dhikr* immediately." This has been experienced by the people of truthfulness.

We read in a tradition, "Allah has some men who are such that when they look at someone that person is happy with a happiness after which he will never be wretched." Shaykh Abu-l-'Abbas al-Mursi said, "By Allah, there is nothing between me and a man but that I look at him and free him from need." His shaykh attested to that for him. He said about him, "An excellent man is Abu-l-'Abbas! A desert man came to him and urinated on his leg and then did not leave until he was one of the *awliya'* of Allah." I heard our shaykh, al-Buzidi say, "As Shaykh Abu-l-'Abbas sufficed others with a glance, there remain in this time of ours those who also suffice others by a glance in the same way he did, or even more so." I heard our shaykh Moulay al-'Arabi say, "There are still gnostics in this time of ours, like ash-Shadhili and those like him (indicating himself), and this is a well-known matter with the people of experience and the people of true sincerity. Anyone who goes to them with true sincerity profits immediately and is revived after his (spiritual) death."

I consider this possibility – that of bringing people's hearts to life – much more likely to occur at the hands of the gnostics than the first type of miracle, the physical one. They do not resort to them and they do not often appear at their hands. How many a perfect gnostic there is at whose hands Allah brought to life a large number of dead selves and hearts, while very few physical miracles, such as giving life to the dead which the Shaykh mentioned, appeared at their hands! Also nearly all of our knowledge lies in indication and metaphor. It is not taken literally except by someone who does not know what is meant. Allah knows best. Then he said:

$$وَلَوْ طَرَحُوا فِي فِيءِ حَائِطِ كَرْمِهَا$$
$$عَلِيلاً وَقَدْ أَشْقَى لَفَارَقَهُ السَّقَمُ$$

**If someone terminally ill was put in the shadow
of a wall with the vine on it, the illness would
leave him.**

Fay' is the shadow of something cast by the sun. The wall is that of a garden. "Terminally ill" is being right on the verge of death. He is saying: "By the strength of its effect, this pre-eternal wine can heal all illnesses and diseases, to the extent that if an ill person on the point of death were to be placed in the shadow of the wall of a garden where this vine is growing, even before its grapes have been harvested – no, even before its grapes appear – Allah would take care of him and his illness would leave him immediately." This would be the height of exaggeration of praise for it were it physical wine. However the fact is that it is as he says. He is referring to sicknesses of the heart and the garden is the Garden of the gnostics. Allah heals the illnesses in the hearts of all of those who enter into the shadow of their company and love, even if they are on the point of spiritual death because of their doubts and thoughts, wrong actions and crimes. This is also an established fact since "a person is on the religion of his close friend".

If someone has direct experience of the Divine Majesty, those present with him are also affected by it. The tradition says: "Learn certainty by sitting with the people of certainty." By Allah, those who have success only have success by keeping the company of someone who has had success. The benefit of company and the fruits that come from it is something that is so well-known that it does not require any corroboration. The knowledge of realities is gained through experience. Ibn 'Abbad writes in his Poem of Wisdoms:

The benefits of brotherhood cannot be denied.
  But if its conditions are not met it has no merit.
Those conditions are the brotherhood of a gnostic
  And abandoning personal gain and sideways looks.
His words and state are such that
  They only call us to the All-Merciful.
His constantly flowing lights flood through you
  And loving care envelops you.

Sidi Ibrahim at-Tazi said, "Visit the lords of *taqwa*. Passing by them will bring healing and is the key to the doors of guidance and good. It happens according to the amount that the will is abandoned."

Our breast is expanded beyond the load that weighed us down:
  you help the wronged and elevate the obscure.
You give to the one who lacks and mend the broken
  and how many a killer is delivered from the depths of sin!

and the poem continues in this vein until it says:

There is no difference in their judgements between an
instructed *salik*

and a *majdhub*, between a living man and an inhabitant
of the grave,

Between those who do without and worshippers, all are
blessed,

but the blazing sun is very different from the pale full
moon.

Then he says, may Allah have mercy on him:

$$ ولو قرّبوا مِن حانِها مُقعدا مَشَى $$

$$ وتنطقُ مِن ذِكرى مذاقتِها البُكُم $$

**If they brought bedridden people near its tavern,
they would walk,**

**and the mere mention of its taste would cause the
dumb to speak.**

As has already been mentioned that the word *han*
denotes a wine shop or the place where it is drunk. He is
saying, "If they were to drink in the vicinity of someone
unable to walk to the place of this pre-eternal wine,
then his feet would be released to walk swiftly before
arriving at it. What then do you think would happen
if he were to enter among its drinkers or drink from it
himself? The same thing happens if the sweetness of its
taste is mentioned in the presence of a dumb person.
The blessing of its mention will immediately make him
speak. So what then you do think would happen if he

were actually to taste it with his tongue?" What he says has really taken place. There are *karamat* of the *awliya'* that bear out these things or even greater occurrences, such as the case of the girl who was an invalid for years. When a righteous man spent the night with her family, she asked him to intercede with Allah on her behalf and then immediately rose from her sick bed. Other such physical *karamat* have taken place at the hands of the *awliya'*. However, it is possible that the meaning here is metaphorical, and that what is intended by the bedridden are those held back from good deeds and who fail out of laziness to perform acts of obedience and whose appetites keep them from rising through the stations. When such people draw near the people of this wine, who are the gnostics, their chains are loosened and they hasten to progress outwardly and inwardly.

What is meant by the dumb in this understanding are those rendered dumb by heedlessness and whose tongues are tied by ignorance and innovation and so they only speak of things which do not matter. They only talk about the sensory. When such people keep the company of the gnostics, they speak out clearly and their tongues are released to utter wisdoms and direct knowledges. It says in the *Khamar*, "Whoever does without this world for forty days speaks words of wisdom" or words to that effect. Abu Sulayman ad-Darani said, "When people avoid contaminating themselves with sins, they wander in the *malakut* and then return bearing rare knowledges without any scholar having taught them." Then he says:

$$ولو عبقتْ في الشّرق أنفاسُ طيبها$$
$$وفي الغرب مزكومٌ لعادَله الشمُّ$$

**If the breaths of its perfume were exhaled in the east,
someone in the west with a cold would smell it easily.**

The wind exhales (*'abiqa*) when it blows. The dictionary says: *'abiqa* with *'abqan* and *'ibaqa* means lightning but that meaning is not appropriate here. *Anfas* is the plural of *nafas* (breath) with movement like the wind. He is saying, "If the breaths of the fragrance of this pre-eternal wine were to blow from the east and there was someone ill with a cold in the west, in other words someone whose nose was blocked preventing them from smelling anything, and then the breaths, the sweet breeze, of that wine were to reach him, his power of smell would return to him and he would become well again by the blessing of its fragrance and the strength of its scent." This can be taken literally as generous praise for the scent of this wine were it be manifest to the physical senses but it is probable that what is meant here by someone with a cold is a person who does not smell anything of the scent of election and is ill on account of his denial of its people. If their *himma* were to be directed to him and the scented breaths of their wine wafted towards him, his denial would be revoked, even if he were far from them in distance. He would smell the scent of *wilaya* on them and hurry to keep their company and serve them until he joined their path and sat on the carpet of nearness and intimacy with them. Allah Almighty knows best. Then he says:

$$\text{ولو خُضِبتْ مِن كأسِها كفُّ لامسٍ}$$

$$\text{لَمَا ضلَّ في ليل وفي يده النجمُ}$$

If the hand of a man who held it were to be stained from its cup,

he would not be lost at night due to the starlight flowing from it.

A hand is dyed and stained with dye. *Lamis* refers to touching with the hand. *Dalla* means to be lost and destroyed according to the dictionary. He is saying, "If someone's hand were dyed from contact with the cup of this pre-eternal wine, his hand would shine and become a star by which one is guided in the darkness of land and sea. So his hand becomes like the hand of Sayyiduna Musa when he clasped it to him. When he travels at night, he is guided and is not misguided from the Path, like someone who has a star in his hand lighting up the path ahead of him. Another possible meaning is an exaggerated emphasis on its effect with respect the breaking of physical norms. It is also possible that by the dyeing of the palm he means something which directly touches his heart and is connected to it. If his heart were to rely on it, a light would shine in it by which he would be guided in solving problems in the realm of the *shari'a* and decode the conundrums of the oceans of the realities. With this dazzling light in his heart he will never lose his way on his journey to the source of reality. The Almighty says: *"You who believe! if you have taqwa of Allah, He will give you discrimination"* (8:29) in other words a light which differentiates between the truth and the veil that covers it.

Shaykh Abu-l-Hasan ash-Shadhili said something which accords with this – the application of a sensory metaphor to the arrival in the heart of the knowledge of the reality. He says, 'Love is Allah detaching the heart of His slave from everything other than Him, so that the person sees angels encircling his knowledge of Allah with protection, and the *ruh* being taking to His Presence and the secret being immersed in its witnessing of Him. And the slave seeks to increase in his love of Him and so he is given increase and experiences unbearable sweetness from the pleasure of his intimate conversation with Him. He dons the robes of nearness on the carpet of proximity and caresses the virgins of the realities and the matrons of knowledge." What is desired of you is for knowledge to reach the heart. He likens the knowledge of realities to virgins and the knowledge of the *shari'a* to matrons because of the much greater difficulty of gaining access to the former than the latter, since there are sinners and unjust judges with no portion of good who also have that kind of knowledge. Allah Almighty knows best. Then he says:

$$\text{ولو جُليت سِرّا على أكمِهِ غدا}$$

$$\text{بصيرا ومن راووقها تسمع الصمُّ}$$

If it were disclosed secretly to a blind man, he would see;

just from the sound of its filter the deaf would hear.

The disclosure referred to here is a passive usage, meaning something being unveiled and disclosed. *Akma* is someone who is born blind. *Ra'uq* (filter) is not mentioned in the dictionary with a *hamza*. It is mentioned with a *waw*. *Rawuq* is used for filter, i.e. the wine is filtered and inward. The wine is the drink which is filtered and the cup containing it. It is permitted to change a *hamza* into a *waw*, as in *u'qqatat* and *waqqatat*. He also said that *rawq* is admiration for a thing and its potency. *Summ* is the plural of *asamm* (deaf).

He is saying that if this pre-eternal wine were to be disclosed and appear secretly to a man born blind, he would immediately see, as indeed happened at the hand of 'Isa and other *awliya'*. If you say that the word 'disclosure' demands manifestation and openness and therefore contradicts the word, 'secretly', I say in answer that this pre-eternal wine is the embodiment of subtle, unseen meanings and so the manifestation of its effects in the visible world is the unveiling and disclosure of their secret nature. There is no doubt that its emergence in the visible world can take a secret or open form. The poet designated it secret to emphasise it, since it is more likely to have been an open occurrence, meaning that if it were only to emerge from the world of the unseen to the world of the visible secretly, then a blind man would still become sighted, enabling him to see its lights and witness its secrets, so how much more would that be the case if it were to emerge openly?

Another aspect of the beauty of the purity of this wine and the excellence of its essential nature is that it makes deaf ears hear, so that they become hearing after they were deaf. Or one of the astonishing things about its beauty and the beauty of its vesture is that deaf ears hear and listen to its beautiful resonances in spite of being deaf. This is better. It is possible that he means by the one born blind, someone with a blind inner eye. When he accompanies the people of this wine and they disclose to him something of its beauty and radiance, then his inner eye is opened and he has a clear sign from his Lord. And equally by the deaf, he means people whom admonition does not profit and who do not benefit from being reminded. When they hear the purity of admonition and good warning from some of the people of this wine, they restrain themselves and are curbed. It is said that they were not able to hear but then became among *"those who listen well to what is said and follow the best of it."* (39:18) Allah Almighty knows best and success is by Allah. He is the One who guides to the straight road. Then he says:

$$\text{ولو أنّ ركْبًا يمّموا تُربَ أرضِها}$$
$$\text{وفي الرّكب ملسوعٌ لَما ضَرّهُ السّمُ}$$

> If riders were to head for the soil it grows in, and
> among the riders
> was someone who had been stung, the venom
> would not harm him.

Rakb is the plural of *rakib*, like *sahb*, of *sahib*. It is also said that it has no singular. *Tayammama* means "to head for". The one stung is someone who has been bitten by a snake or stung by scorpion. *Samm* (poison, venom) is something whose effect is fatal. He is saying: If a group of riders were simply heading for the soil in which the grapes grow from which this wine is produced, and among them there was a person who had been bitten by a snake or stung by a scorpion, the venom of that sting would not harm him. What do you think, then, would be the case if that person were to actually reach that soil, or to pick up a handful of that earth, or if that soil were laid onto the place he had been stung?

It is possible that what is meant by the person stung is someone stung by their own appetites and acts of disobedience. When he is with the people who are heading towards arrival at it or to the place where it is evoked, falling into any of those things will not harm him, since the blessing of their companionship will remove the harm of them from him and move him to abstain from them. The benefits of good company have already been discussed. As has been said by people of knowledge, "If someone aims to visit a righteous person, the angel on his left does not record anything as long as he is visiting him." Perhaps he came across the *hadith* on that. Allah knows best. Then he says:

$$\text{ولو رسمَ الرَّاقي حروفَ اسمِها على} \\ \text{جَبينِ مُصابٍ جنَّ أبرأهُ الرَّسمُ}$$

If a talisman maker were to write out its letters on the brow
of someone afflicted by *jinn*, the inscription would cure him.

A talisman maker is the one who makes amulets for protection. The dictionary says *ruqya* is seeking protection and the plural of is *ruqa*. The verb is *raqa* with *riqya*, *raqya*, *ruqya*. The *raqqa'* spits into his amulet. *Jabayn* according to the dictionary, are the two clear patches on either side of the eyebrows, rising to the short hair or the limits of the forehead between the temples and front hairline. All of that is the brow. *Junn* is also *jinn* and *junun*. Form X is the passive form, meaning "to be struck by madness". It is one of the verbs which must have an object. These verbs do not have an active form. *Abra'a* means to heal.

He is saying that if the amulet-maker were to write the letters spelling out this pre-eternal wine on the brow of a person who is ill, afflicted by insanity, that writing would cure him immediately. The letters of this pre-eternal wine are the letters of the Name of Majesty. If a gnostic writes it on a mad person in the presence of someone who desires it, that person would be cured immediately, Allah willing. The same applies to someone whose heart is beset by shaytanic thoughts and illusory doubts. When a gnostic instructs him in this name and writes it in his heart, he is cured immediately and becomes one of the people of complete certainty and great tranquillity. Allah knows best. Then he says:

$$ \text{وفوقَ لِواءِ الجيشِ لو رُقِمَ اسمُها} $$
$$ \text{لأَسكَرَ مَن تحت اللّوا ذلك الرّقمُ} $$

If its name were to be written on the banner of an army,

those under the banner would be made drunk by that inscription.

Liwa' is an identifying banner. The plural is *alwiya*. The plural of plurals is *aluwiyat. Jaysh* is an army or those travelling to war or something else. *Raqama* is means "to write" and *mirqam* is the pen and *raqm* is writing and inscription.

He is saying that if the name of this pre-eternal wine were written on an army's banner, that writing would intoxicate all of those under that banner. All of them would become intoxicated by the wine of love and would voluntarily totally devote themselves to the pleasure of their Beloved. All of this extols this wine and yearning for it. I indicated something of that in my poem in *ta'* when I said:

What an intoxication! If its breeze blows over the graves of the dead!
They are immediately brought to life.
If its breezes were to diffuse its scent to all mankind,
everyone would become intoxicated in a single instant.
If people's spirits were on sale in the grave of its tavern,
that exchange would be a cheap transaction.
So be ecstatic and roam in the perfection of its beauty,
and do not be prodigal and look at other than the Beloved.

Success is by Allah. Then he mentioned the fruits of this wine, and what develops from it inwardly and says:

تُهَذِّبُ أَخْلاقَ النَّدامى فيهتدي

بها لطريق العزمِ مَن لا لَهُ عَزْمُ

ويكرُمُ مَن لَمْ يَعرفِ الجودَ كفَّهُ

ويَحْلُمُ عند الغيظ مَن لا لَهُ حِلْمُ

It refines the character of the drinking companions and by it

those who lack resolve are guided to resolve.

Someone whose hand did not know how to give becomes magnanimous,

and someone unforgiving becomes forbearing when enraged.

To refine something is to cleanse, purify, rectify and put it right, as it says in the dictionary. *Akhlaq* is the plural of *khuluq*, which a person's innate character, good or ugly. *Nadama* is the plural of *nadim*, who is a man's intimate in the drinking gathering or another gathering. Here it is applied to the drinker himself. *Yukrimu* is the present tense of *akrama*. *Hilm* is forbearance and intelligence as stated in the dictionary. *Haluma* and *hulum* means to pardon and overlook and not be impetuous.

He is saying that this wine protects and purifies the character of those who drink it. Then evil character is replaced with good character and laziness is replaced with energy and vigour, so that someone who had been lacking in resolve is guided to the path of resolve with respect to piety and *taqwa*. Avarice and miserliness are replaced by generosity and magnanimity, so that the one who did not know generosity at all becomes the most generous and most magnanimous of people. Anger, rancour, haste, and violence are transformed into forbearance, sound heartedness, tranquillity, deliberateness and gravity. Fear, anxiety and dismay are changed to courage, certainty and independence in Allah. Doubt and confusion are transformed into tranquillity and stillness. Excessive management and choice are changed to contentment, submission and serenity under the blows of fate. Pride and love of elevation, rank and leadership are replaced by humility, peace of mind, obscurity and love of humble things rather than high things. Love of this world, avarice and cupidity are replaced by doing without, contentment and scrupulousness. Wealth is with Allah rather than anything other than Him. Esteem for the wealthy and forming alliances with them are replaced by turning away from them and making do without them; and boasting about connection with them is replaced by being satisfied by one's knowledge of Allah. Disdain and disparagement of the poor is replaced by exalting and elevating them, and being near to them and love for them.

There is much more of this which is too much to express here, to the extent that some have said, "The lower self has as many imperfections as Allah has perfections." The majority of those imperfections are transformed into perfections under the influence of this wine. It is not obliged to establish election by praising the quality of mankind since, as Shaykh Ibn 'Ata'allah says in the *Hikam*: "If you could only reach Him after the annihilation of your evil qualities and the eradication of your claims, you would never reach Him. But if He wants to bring you to Him, He veils your attribute with His attribute and your quality with His quality. So He makes you reach Him by what comes from Him to you, not by what goes from you to Him." Success is by Allah. He is the Guide to the Straight path. Then he says:

$$\text{ولو نالَ قرمُ القومِ لَثْمَ قِدامِها}$$
$$\text{لَأَكسبهُ مَعنى شَمائِلها اللَّثْمُ}$$

If the master of the people managed to kiss what covers it,

    that kiss would imbue him with the meaning of its qualities.

Qarm is a master. The master of the people is their leader. *Lathm* is a kiss. *Lathama* is grammatically like *daraba* and *sami'a* and *litham* is like *kitab*. *Shama'il* (qualities) is the plural of *shamal*, meaning nature.

He is saying that if the master and great man of the people were to manage to kiss the veil of this wine and inhale something of its scent, he would be garbed in that veil, meaning its good nature. So his character would be refined and his form adorned, and he would become forbearing, generous, merciful, interceding and humble, easy and gentle, and other such qualities. The transformation is that which is obtained by the one who realises it. The wine refines character and transforms the sources because it is the fruit of *dhikru-llah*. There is no doubt that real *dhikr* of Allah refines and purifies the person who does it. The Almighty says: *"The prayer precludes indecency and wrongdoing. And remembrance of Allah is greater still"* (29:45), i.e. greater than the prayer in forbidding indecency and wrongdoing.

This is something which has been tested. We have experienced it and seen it, and praise belongs to Allah. Hearing about something is not like actually seeing it. The leader of the people is singled out for this business because he has greater need of discipline than others. Only people of forbearance, steadfastness, deliberateness and tranquillity are truly fitted for leadership, otherwise those under them will be corrupted or exhausted. Success is by Allah. Then he says:

يقولون لي صِفها فأنت بوصفها

خبيرٌ أَجَلْ عندي بأوصافها علمُ

They say to me, "Describe it. You know what it is like."
Yes, I have knowledge of its qualities.

Those who listen to him say, "Describe to us this wine for which we yearn and which you praise extensively." He says to them, "Yes, I have knowledge of its attributes and qualities and direct experience of it. Then he says:

صفاءٌ ولا ماء ولطفٌ ولا هوا

ونورٌ ولا نارٌ وروحٌ ولا جسمُ

تَقَدَّمَ كلَّ الكائناتِ حديثُها،

قديماً ولا شكلٍ هناك، ولا رسمُ

وقامت بها الأشياءُ ثَمَّ لحكمةٍ

بها احتجبت عن كلِّ مَن لا له فهمُ

It is pure but not like water; insubstantial but not
  like air;

  Luminous but not like fire; spiritual without
  embodiment.

It comes to all beings, temporal and timeless,

  but there is no form there nor any trace of it.

Things subsist by it but then through wisdom it is
  veiled

  from all who possess no understanding of it.

He says regarding the description of the pre-eternal
wine and the Pure Essential Essence that it is a hidden, all-
penetrating, existing Essence, subtle like the subtleness
of the air but not air, pure like the purity of water but not
water, luminous like the luminosity of fire but not fire,
spiritual like the spirit of bodies but without a body, in other
words described with timeless, essential life. It preceded
the temporal attributes and existence of all beings because

its existence is timeless and pre-eternal. Then there were no bodies whatsoever, small or large. Large bodies like the Throne, Footstool, the heavens and the earth are like the writing, in other words the letters. Small bodies, like angels, *jinn* and human beings and all other creatures are like the details and forms of those letters. There is no doubt that the use of benefit of writing and letters lies in taking meanings from them and understanding them. When the meaning is grasped, there is no need for the writing and it is erased. That is the nature of phenomenal beings. They are only set up so that their Master may be seen in them. When you recognise Him, then those traces and forms are cast aside and there only remains the Great, the Exalted. It says in a poem:

My station flung its words at the writing
and I did not see either nearness or distance in the
moment.
By it I was annihilated to myself and by it my withdrawal
was clear.
This is the manifestation of the Real intended in annihilation.
Esteem encircles us on every side and the attributes of the
Real
become part of what is close to the slave.

We read in the sound *hadith*, "Allah was and there was nothing with Him." One of those with realisation added, "And He is now as He was." In the *hadith* of at-Tirmidhi from Abu Ruzayn al-'Uqayli we find: "I asked, 'Messenger of Allah, where was our Lord before He created His creation?' He answered, 'He was in a hiddenness above which was air and below which was air.'" The word *amad* means concealment. The Almighty says: "*That Day the facts will be unclear to them,*" (28:66) in other words hidden. Allah was in concealment and subtleness and so He was neither perceived nor recognised. Rather His immensity encompassed every 'above' and every 'below' and every 'air' so there was no above and no below and no air. Existence belongs to the High, Most High before time and in what continues.

'Ali, may Allah honour his face, was asked, "Cousin of the Messenger of Allah, where is our Lord? Or does He have a place?" His colour changed and he was silent for a time. Then he said, "Your words, 'Where is Allah?' is a question about place and Allah has no place. He created time and place. He is now as He was, without time and without place." Abu-l-Hasan an-Nuri was asked at the time of the persecution of the Sufis, "Where is Allah among His creatures?" He answered, "Allah was when there was no 'where' and creatures were in non-existence. He is where He was where He is and He is now where He was since there is no where and no place." One report says, "I was a treasure and was not known. I wanted to be known, so I created creation and made them recognise Me."

His words: "Things subsist by it" mean that pre-eternal wine manifested its lights and brought forth its beauty in the manifestation of things as the author of the *'Ayniyya* said:

The beauty of my Beloved appeared to my sight,
    and there are precursors in every sight of the Beloved.

When its beauty appears variegated,
  it is given names for that in which it appears.

I said in my *Khamriyya* in *ta'*:

A bride appeared as a bride my sight
  and she lowered the veils of pride over might.
All things are sustained by the pre-eternal wine. There is
  no existence without it, rather there is no ascription to it:
Since I recognised God I do not see other than Him.
  That is how other with us is forbidden.

One of those with realisation said, "If someone tried to force me to see other than Him, I would not be able to. There is nothing with Him so that I should witness it."

So this wine was veiled after its manifestation on account of a pre-eternal wisdom. It concealed the secrets of lordship and lowered the veil of pride over its innate magnificence. Thus that wine was concealed after its manifestation and it was veiled after its emergence. It was veiled from those with no understanding and no insight – if their inner eyes were opened, they would not see other than it. We read in the *Hikam*, "The light of the inner eye lets you see the nearness of the Real to you. The source of the inner eye lets you see your non-existence by your existence. The truth of the inner eye lets you see His existence, not your own non-existence or existence. 'Allah was and there was nothing with Him. He is now as He was.'"

Al-Majdhub said:

Whoever witnesses being by being,
  has might while the inner eye is blind.

Whoever witnesses being by the Maker of being,
    that is the one who finds the cure for the secret.

In my *Khamriyya* in *ta'*, I indicated this meaning alluded to
by the Shaykh:

If you ask me about the attributes of its perfection,
    I know them by witnessing and report.
The light of its radiance preceded every being,
    subtle, aware in purity and power.
Things were established by it so that they are revealed,
    and it is hidden by wisdom from all the ignorant.

Know that you will not understand this wine through
tasting and knowledge unless you accompany its people.
They are the people with direct knowledge of that, the
people of attraction and wayfaring. If you do not accompany
them, then do not desire to understand it, even if you read
a thousand books and keep the company of a thousand
scholars or worshippers. Success is by Allah.

Then he says:

$$وهامتْ بها روحي بحيث تمازجا اتِّ$$
$$حَادًا ولا جِرمُ تخَلّلهُ جِرمُ$$

My spirit was besotted by it when they mixed
    in unification, but there is no body which penetrates
    another.

The dictionary says that *huyam* is like insanity which
arises from passionate love. He also said that the verb
hama, yahimu with the nouns *him* and *hayman* means

to love a woman. A man who is *ha'im* is bewildered. *Tamajaza* means to be mixed. *Ittihad* is applied to two things. One is the mixture of two bodies so that that they become one body. This is impossible in respect of Allah Almighty. It constitutes disbelief on the part of anyone who believes it. It is also applied to the actual unity of the thing when it becomes one. It is what is meant here. Concerning this the Qutb Ibn Mashish said "The drink of love is the mixture of attributes with attributes, qualities with qualities, lights with lights, names with names, descriptions with descriptions and actions with actions." *Jirm* is the body. The plural is *ajram*, *jurum*, and *jirm*, as in the dictionary.

The poet is saying, "My spirit was mad with love – in other words light-headed and attracted in love and passion because of this wine – and it continues to thirst for it and to seek to reach it by relinquishment and purification. When it becomes refined and purified of the remains of the senses, it connects to it and mixes with it so that it finds itself in the Presence without awareness. Ignorance and illusion veil it from the Presence. When ignorance is removed and knowledge is firm, it finds itself in the Presence, and it drowns in the source of the Sea of Oneness, and hidden and open *shirk* are removed from it." That is the meaning. One of the easterners said:

Before today I was veiled by illusion,
    bound by the limitations of separation,
Single, alone, and I reckoned it to be two.
    When beauty appeared and the rust was removed,

201

The eye fell on the source,

and I became the source of the source.

We read in the *Hikam*, "It is not the existence of anything with Him that veils you from Allah – since there is nothing with Him – what veils you is the illusion that something exists with Him." He also said, "To reach Allah is to reach knowledge of Him since our Lord is too great to be joined to anything or that anything be joined to Him." This is the meaning of *ittihad* when it is used by the Sufis. It means the constancy of the knowledge of oneness after ignorance of it or the constancy of knowledge after obtaining separation. Part of that is what the author of the *'Ayniyya* said:

Dive into the seas of unification

freed of mixture with others if you truly pursue the goal.

Beware of *tanzih*: it limits;

and also beware of *tashbih*, it deceives.

He also said in another eulogy:

You are I, and she was I,

and she has no single contending existence.

I was annihilated by her in her and there is nothing between us.

I arrived by her and am by her.

He also said:

I annihilated it until it was annihilated and it was not.

But I look with illusion.

An aspect of that is the words of the poet:

I am from the one I love and the one I love is I:
  we are two spirits in two bodies.

He does not understand these words in their literal
meaning of *ittihad* and incarnation because they are
free of that. They are an expression of love and involve
affirmation of both the Beloved and lover, an outpouring
of passion on the part of the lover. When arrival is
achieved, this type of expression is no longer used. That is
why it says in *The Hikam*: "The gnostic is not the one who
makes an indication and then finds Allah nearer to him
than his indication. The gnostic is without indication – by
his annihilation in His existence, and total absorption in
witnessing Him."

Another aspect of this is what the Shaykh guarded against
in his words, "There is no body which penetrates another,"
so that the listener understands that what is being referred
to is not any kind of blameworthy *ittihad*. Many of those
who fail to understand what is meant suspect those who
speak in this way. Perhaps he meant that which cannot
be encompassed by knowledge. It was already mentioned
that the Shaykh freed himself of this concept in his *Ta'iyya*,
Nazm as-Suluk, and the writings of ash-Shushtari, Ibn
Sab'in, and Ibn al-'Arabi are full of such expressions. They
are realised *awliya'*, may Allah be pleased with them and
make them pleased. I indicated this matter of incarnation
and *ittihad* in my *Khamriya* in *ta'*:

It is free of the ruling of *hulul* in its description
  and it has only allowed to alight in its form.

Her beauty appeared as a bride in my sight,
  and the curtains of pride were lowered by might,
Nothing but her radiance appeared in existence
  and she was only veiled by veils of evil.

Allah knows best. Then he said:

خمرٌ ولا كرمٌ وآدمُ لي أبٌ

وكرمٌ ولاخمرٌ، ولي أمُّها أمُّ

ولطف الأواني، في الحقيقة، تابعٌ

للطف المعاني، والمعاني بها تنمُو

Wine without a vine, I have Adam for a father.

A vine and no wine, and I have its origin as a mother.

Separation occurred and all is one.

So our spirits are the wine and our forms are the vine.

The Shaykh likens the *ruh* flowing in the body to the wine concealed in the vine and he likens outward humanity to the vine which brings forth the wine. In the state of his wayfaring towards illumination, the attraction of the *murid* dominates his wayfaring and his intoxication dominates his enlightenment. Thus spirituality dominates his humanness and overcomes it and so his humanness no longer has authority. Sometimes his wayfaring dominates his attraction and his enlightenment his intoxication, and so humanness dominates spirituality and overcomes it. If spirituality dominates humanness, it is like the existence of the wine without the vine. If humanness dominates spirituality, it is like the existence of the vine without the wine because then it is inward.

So the Shaykh made his state clear during the course of his journey. He said, "I am sometimes wine without the vine. That is in my state of intoxication and attraction and then I am the khalif of Allah on His earth, following in the footsteps of our father Adam because attraction is a matter of Divine providence. When the spirit overpowers humanness, it overcomes all existence. Therefore he is like the greatest Adam, the khalif from Allah. This is the meaning of his words, "I have Adam as a father" because the son is the khalif of his father, and so then he is the khalif of Allah in his being.

"Sometimes I am a vine without the wine." The vine is like humanity. It is possible that his words, "Adam is a father to me" is an indication that his attraction is mixed with his wayfaring because the technical term is outside of the human and is connected to spiritual beings or to animals as opposed to the one who is travelling in his attraction. His outward is wayfaring and his inward is attraction, but sometimes attraction dominates and so humanness is held back. This is the meaning of his words, "Adam is a father to me." This means: "I am a human being who is one of the sons of Adam who has not left the level of Adamness." This is the source of perfection. Sometimes wayfaring dominates and attraction is concealed in spirituality. The attributes of humanness appear on the wayfarer and so the spirituality is helped by humanness and drinks from its cup, as at-Tustari said:

My cups revolve from me to me, and so humanity is like
the mother.

Spirituality is a child which suckles from its milk. This is
the meaning of his words, "I have a mother in its mother,"
i.e. then it is the mother of the wine. It is that the vine is a
mother. What is meant by it is humanity which overpowers
spirituality and as the vine overpowers the wine. This
possibility is better and clearer, and Allah knows best.

All of this definition is before reaching realisation.
Otherwise, the sensory is obliterated and the meaning is
firm. All is one. Humanity is only established by spirituality
and spirituality is only manifested by humanity. When the
meanings fall, the vessels fall, and beings are firm by its
firmness and are obliterated by the oneness of his source. So
there is no humanity nor spirituality. Existence belongs to the
One, the Eternal Support who has no partner. They wrote:

Only the truth remains and no being remains,
  and there is no existent and nothing distinct.
That is what proof of eye-vision brings.
  I do not see anything but Him with my eye when I look.

NOTE: What the poet mentioned in these two verses
of the likeness of attraction to wine without the vine and
wayfaring to the vine without the wine is a comparison
which al-Junayd used in his famous poem when he was
asked about *tawhid*. He wrote:

The glass is fine and the wine is fine.
  So the business is similar and alike.

It is as if it were wine and no glass,
   and as if it was a glass without wine.

Humanity is likened to the glass and spirituality to the wine. When spirituality dominates humanity, which is in the state of attraction, it is as if it was wine without a glass. When humanity dominates spirituality, and that is in the state of wayfaring, it is as if it is a glass without wine. I clarified this meaning in my *Khamriyya* in *ta'*:

It is by the fineness of the wine in the vessels, which pervades
   by the subtle meanings of the wine in the root of my formation.
Sometimes the wine disappears into the body of its cup
   and sometimes the cup disappears into the wine of intoxication.
The disappearance of the vessels in the meaning is achieving
   the annihilation of the vessels in the timeless meanings.
So our forms are the cup and our spirits are wine
   whose cupbearer is the attraction of encircling concern.

Allah knows best. Then he said:

ولطف الأواني في الحقيقة، تابع
للطف المعاني والمعاني بها تنمُو

The subtleness of vessels follows in reality
   the subtleness of meanings and meanings rise by that.

Latufa (to be fine) is like *karuma*, whose verbal nouns are *lutf* and *latafa*, meaning smallness and fineness and *latif* is subtle, as it says in the dictionary. *Nama* means "to rise", and vessels here refers to all phenomenal beings. The meanings are the secrets of lordship which are established by it. It is the antecedent wine whose root is subtle and fine. When the outward lights become sensory, they become dense. Whoever stops with the outward of their density is ignorant of Allah and veiled from witnessing Him. Whoever pierces through to their inward, finds that they bear the meanings and are the envelopes for the secrets of lordship, and so he withdraws from vessels by witnessing meanings and becomes a gnostic who is brought near and loved. At-Tustari said about that, "Do not look at the containers. Plunge into the sea of meanings. Perhaps you will see me." We read in the *Hikam*, "The outward of phenomenal beings is deception. Their inward is instruction. The lower self looks at the outward deception, while the heart looks at the inward instruction." He sees the material density of the vessels while their root is immaterial subtleness. So the root of the vessels are meanings but His Name is the Outward. The closest example of its manifestation in the sensory is snow. Its inward is water and outward is snow. Al-Jilani said about that in his poem in *'ayn*:

> The metaphor for phenomenal being is that of snow.
> Water which is its source, becomes it.
> In reality, snow is not other than water,
> although it is other in the judgement of the law.

This is the meaning of the words of the Shaykh. In reality, the subtleness of the vessels follows the subtleness of the meanings and, in reality, the root of the vessels are meanings. The meanings are subtle and the subtleness of the vessels follows their subtleness. They become dense and physical in respect of the one who stops with them and is deceived by the appearance of their outward and is preoccupied with their physicality so that the forms of their outward are imprinted on the mirror of his heart. So he becomes blind and veiled to seeing the subtle meanings. That is why the people of meaning say that all that decreases the sensory increases the meaning, and all that increases the sensory decreases the meaning. This is the meaning of his words, "meanings rise by that," i.e. by the subtleness of the vessels. He returns them to their source and the meanings rise and ascend.

The containers are subtle when their sensory remains unseen and one turns away from their distractions and their attachments. "Free your heart of others and you will be filled with gnoses and secrets," wrote the shaykh of our shaykh, Moulay al-'Arabi and then, "Say also to them, 'Remove the lump of this world from your hearts and your meanings will be strengthened.' Or you might say, 'When your luminousness is strengthened by light, then certainty becomes strong. When certainty becomes strong, *himma* rises. When *himma* rises, there is arrival and success is by Allah.'" The lump (*dabla*) is the wick of the candle when it is ashy. When you trim it, then its light shines. That is how it is with care for this world. It extinguishes light of certainty in the heart. When you trim it, then its light shines.

I said to one of the *fuqara'*, "Three matters strengthen grasp of the meanings. The first is mutual reminding with the people of the art and staying with them. The second is reflection and the heart moving through the stages of *tawhid* until beings disappear from the inner eye. The third is *dhikr* of the tongue in a group or alone. It is the weakest of them in respect of support and strengthening meanings. Although it is the door of entering and reaching them, once the *dhikr* of the heart is obtained, there is no need for it. In comparison with reflection, its effect is weak."

I said to them, "Three matters strengthen the grasp of the senses. The first is the occupation of the limbs with the sensory in seeking its portions. The second is lack of caution with the tongue regarding the sensory with its people. The third is reflection on the sensory and the occupation of the heart with anxiety regarding it. By these three matters the sensory is strengthened and the meanings weakened until their light is extinguished. We seek refuge with Allah from that."

I also said to them, "The pillars of *wilaya* are three: the freeing of the heart from the sensory, esteem for the shaykh and *adab* with him, and constant *dhikr* with presence. Each of them can apply to the tongue or the heart or the secret." I wrote some verses about that:

O you who desire the ranks of the Men,
  be annihilated to the sensory in every state.
Free the heart of otherness
  and it will be filled with lights and secrets

Esteem the shaykh with ample truthfulness
  and do a lot of *dhikr* with an attentive heart.
These are the rules of *wilaya*
  and the place of manifestation of gnosis and concern.

I heard our companion, the divine gnostic, Sidi ‘Abdu-r-Rahman ar-Rahmani, say, “The sensory is all that strengthens the materiality of your existence. The meaning is all that annihilates you to your existence and makes you stop seeing yourself. Preoccupation with the sensory can be a means to strengthening the meanings, as is the case in serving the shaykhs and the brethren and everything that leads to purification of the meaning.” It is as Sidi ‘Abdu-l-Warith said, “Serving the Men is a means to reaching the Master of masters.” There is no god but Allah. Allah knows best. Then he says:

ولا قبلها قبلٌ، ولا بعدَ بَعْدَها

وقبليّة الأبعاد، فهي لها ختمُ

وعصرُ المدى من قبله كان عصرها

وعهدُ أبينا بعدَها ولها اليتمُ

There is no ‘before’ before it and no ‘after’ after it.
  The beforeness of afterness has a seal.
The confinement of the extent from before it is its time
  and the age of our father after it, so it is an orphan.

He said that this pre-eternal wine is timeless and lasts for ever. There was no time before it in which there was a time before it, nor after it in which there was a time after it. The beforeness, which is established for it before the manifestation of creation, is a firstness without beginning. It has a seal after the manifestation of things, which is a lastness without end. So it precedes the manifestation of sequential time and it will remain after it. This is the meaning of his words, "The beforeness of afterness has a seal," i.e. the lack of prior end for phenomenal beings is their seal after the manifestation of beings. Allah says, "*He is the First and the Last, the Outward and the Inward.*" (57:3) So the names are many while the Named is one. It is the Holy Essence. The First is the source of the Last and the Last is the source of the First. The Outward is the source of the Inward and the Inward is the source of the Outward. The author of the *'Ayniyya* indicated that when he said:

> There emerged from Him in Him the effects of His description.
> He guided you by what He makes of effects.
> So His attributes, the Name and the effect, which is existence,
> is the source of the Essence, and Allah is all.
> There is nothing other than Allah in mankind,
> and there is nothing heard and no listener.

His words: "The confinement of the extent" means that the existence of this wine is timeless, existing before the confinement of time and its number and organisation. The time of the existence of our father Adam and the time of his life was after it because its manifestation was in time while its existence is timeless. Therefore orphanhood is confirmed for it, i.e. isolation and having no need of the matter of beforeness and afterness. It does not have a prior father nor a child connected after it. The Almighty says: *"He has not given birth and was not born. And no one is comparable to Him."* (112:3-4) Then he says:

محاسنٌ، تهدي المادحينَ لوصفِها

فيحسُنُ فيها منهُم النثرُ والنّظمُ

ويطربُ من لم يَدْرِها، عند ذكْرها

كمشتاق نعم، كلّما ذكرتْ نُعْمُ

Beauties guide those who praise to describe them,
  and prose and poetry are both excellent means
    to this.
The one who did not know her is rapturous when she
  is mentioned,
    like someone who yearns for Nu'm whenever Nu'm
      is named.

Tarb is joy, which can also applied to sorrow as in the dictionary. *Tarab* is used for great joy in the present tense as *taraba*. *Nu'm* is a woman's name, as in the dictionary. Here it means the name of the beloved.

He says, "The enumerated attributes of this wine are her beauties. She guides those who praise to her description and they praise her as much as they can. So all the praise of her they utter is good from them, whether in verse or prose, because she is above what can be said about her. If the people of this world had remained praising her for the whole span the life of this world and the Next, they would not reach one tenth of her beauty and radiance. Those who do not know her are joyous when mentioning these emanations out of yearning and love. So how much more is that the case for the one who actually knows her? He is the father of the one who does not yet know her directly but yearns for her with the yearning of a lover for his beloved whose name is Nu'm. When this beloved is mentioned, his body shakes out of desire for her and he yearns to see her. As for the one who actually knows her and is connected to her and is firm in witnessing her, hearing her praise does not cause him to shake because of his strength and firmness and so he is the master of states and they do not master him. He is like the firmly rooted mountain. Allah Almighty knows best. Then he says:

$$ وقالوا: شربتَ الإثمَ! كلّا، وإنّما شربتُ الّتي في تركها عنديَ الإثمُ $$

They said, "Your drinking was wrong action."

No, I drank what it would be a wrong action not to drink.

Grammarians says that "no" (*kalla*) is the particle of rebuke and disapproval. He says, "The blamers and critics said to me, 'You drank what made wrong action inevitable for you because you brought about the rending of your honour, the ruin of your outward and destruction of your property.' I said to them, 'No, on the contrary, I drank what it would be a wrong action not to drink, because it disciplines the character of the drinking companions. It is those who do not drink who are not free of wrong action and not purified of fault.'" That is why al-Ghazali said, "The knowledge of *tasawwuf* is an obligation for every individual since no human being is free from faults." Shaykh Abu-l-Hasan said, "Anyone who dies not knowing this knowledge of ours, dies persisting is wrong actions while he is unaware of it." Someone else said, "Whoever has the *shari'a* and not *tasawwuf* has deviated," and so forth about what is reported in praise of *tasawwuf* and its masters. Success if by Allah. Then he said:

هنيئا لأهلِ الدير كم سكروا بها
وما شربوا منها ولكنّهم هموا

> Cheers to the people of the monastery! How often they are intoxicated
> by it when they have not drunk it, but only aspired to do so.

Hana and *hana'* (well-being, congratulations) are what He gives you without hardship, and which is easy and agreeable. It says in the dictionary, "It is declined as an adverbial *hal* whose regent must be elided, i.e. "Good is confirmed in enjoyment," i.e. ease without hardship. *Dayr* is the monastery in which monks worship. It is possible that he means the people of the monastery. Here worshippers are the ascetics who are devoted to Allah in the deserts and mountains.

They see themselves as belonging to Allah, as monks reckon themselves to be seeking the love of Allah in monasteries. They have not obtained any of it since they have abandoned the *shari'a* which is the Door of Allah. The Almighty says: *"Come to houses by their doors."* (2:189) This is not the case with the servants, worshippers and those who are truly devoted to Allah. They have entered the business through its door.

The shaykh said to give them good news and delight in their state, "Cheers to the people of the monastery!" i.e. immense good is confirmed for them easily without hardship. How many have been intoxicated by this wine until they wandered and became lost, rejected family and children, and left their homelands and towns! Moreover they have not yet drunk of it since they have not reached its masters who are the gnostics, the people of Prophetic instruction. If such people were to make them reach the pre-eternal wine, they would become intoxicated where they are among their children, but they aspired to drink it and so they wandered in its quest and are intoxicated before drinking. What do you think would be case if they were actually to drink it? And what do you think they would be like if they were to be fully quenched by it?

So the intoxication of worshippers and ascetics is flight from things since they are absent from seeing the One who made them. If they had witnessed the One who made them, they would not have fled from them. We read in the *Hikam*, "The worshippers and those who do without are alienated from everything since they have withdrawn from Allah in everything. Had they seen Him in everything, they would not be alienated from anything." Their intoxication is imperfect as opposed to the one who is connected to the people of the wine who have let him drink of it.

The intoxication of such a one is mixed with sobriety and each time he drinks, his sobriety is increased. Whenever he is absent, he increases in presence. Sobriety does not veil him from his intoxication nor his intoxication from his sobriety. He gives each of them its full share. It is possible that by the people of the monastery he means the Christian monks who are cloistered there, i.e. if it had not been for the love in their hearts, they would not endure these hardships of hunger and cold. If it had not been for the wine of love which their souls had caught scent of beyond the veil, they would not have devoted themselves in this way.

If you were to say that it is not proper to say "Cheers" to them since they are without good, I would say that the gnostics have fine sight. They witness the inward lights and withdraw from the outward darkness. They witness Power and recognise Wisdom. They are like the bee, which goes to every flower, sweet or bitter, and only sweet honey emerges from it. That is why the shaykh of our shaykhs, 'Abdu-r-Rahman al-Majdhub, said:

Creation is light and I observe in them that
> They are the greatest veil while the entrance is in them.

In this vein ar-Rifa'i says:

Show *adab* at the door of the monastery. Remove your sandals
> greet the monks and line up the sandals for them.

Esteem the priest if you wish for a portion,
  and say the *takbir* over the deacon if you wish to rise.
Beware of the dead deacons. Listen to their tunes.
  Beware lest they strip away the intellect.
The moons appeared as rising suns in them
  and the crosses did *tawaf* of it. Beware lest you be tested.
Beware lest you listen to them with friendship.
  Beware of that joining you to them.

Until he said in the *qasida*:

When I came to the monastery, I became a master,
  by my asceticism, I began to drag the tail of the garment.
I asked about where the winehouse was.
  Do I have a way to reach it or not?
The priest said to me,"What do you want?"
  I said, "Do I want wind from you or not?"
He said, "My head and the Messiah son of Maryam
  and my *deen* and there is no substitute for blood."

And so on to the end of his words. So the gnostics have a
strange manner and wondrous view. Only those who keep
them company experience it. It grows from submission.
When someone opposes them, he becomes one of the
deaf and dumb who do not understand. There is no doubt
that there is more likely and apparent to be appetite in the
divested reality beyond the *shari'a*. That is why he said:

وعندي منها نَشوةٌ قبلَ نشأتي

معي أبدا تبقى وإن بَلِيَ العظمُ

I was intoxicated by it before I was born,

    **and it will abide with me forever, even when my
bones are decayed.**

Nashwa means drunkenness. The verb is *nasha* meaning
"he became drunk". He is saying, "By this wine my spirit was
intoxicated before time, before the formation of humanity.
So what appeared in the visible world only preceded in
the world of the unseen. So the spirit has intoxication
since it knew of prior happiness and divine concern before
the manifestation of mankind. Then that intoxication
remained for it after it left this subtle humanity. Even if its
greatness remains, its trace has disappeared. The *ruh* has
no annihilation. When it leaves this corporeal existence,
it remains with what it had of gnosis and knowledge. It
continues to rise in stations as in this world for ever. "A man
dies on what he lived and he will be resurrected on what he
died." I indicated this meaning which the Shaykh said in
my *Khamriyya* in *ta'*:

We were intoxicated by it before time and after my formation

    and my joy continues in another formation.

Then he says:

عليكَ بها صِرفا وإن شئتَ مزجَها

فعدلكَ عن ظَلم الحبيب هوالظُلمُ

You should have it pure, but if you wish, it can be mixed.
Avoiding the Beloved's lustrous teeth is wrongdoing.

Sirf is purity in wine and in other things, as it says in the dictionary. *Mazj* is mixture. Turning away from that is to go away from it. *Zalm* is more precise than *zulm*. It is illustrated by the saliva. It says in the dictionary that *zulm* is putting a thing into other than in its proper place. The true verbal noun is *zalm*. The verb is *zalama*, and from it comes *zalim* and *mazlum*. Then he said that the *zulm* is snow in Hudhayl ath-Tha'alabi, and 'the saliva on the teeth'. If he means the water of the teeth, it is saliva which agrees with what some said. Then it is an allusion to the wine of love but it is unlikely due to the contrast of moving from saliva to wine. What is clear is that it is known wrongdoing to turn away from the manifestations of majestic force, since there is no way to drink the wine of love in fidelity and purity except after the passage of those Divine outpourings on him. Otherwise, it is as Abu-l-Mawahib said, "If someone claims to witness beauty before being disciplined by majesty, reject him. He is a charlatan." It is like the words of the poet:

Love is is my religion, and so I do not desire any re-
   placement for it.
   Beauty is an obeyed king, unjust or just.
The self is precious, but I spend it for You.
   Abasement is bitter, but it is lawful in Your pleasure.
O You for whose love my punishment is sweet,
   I do not complain of You and there is no reluctance nor
      weariness.

He says that you, O drinker of this pre-eternal wine, must have it pure, i.e. pure, free of travelling (*suluk*). Immerse yourself in pursuing the sources of this drink until you entirely depart from the sensory. If you wish, then mix it with something of wayfaring, giving slavehood its right, which is perfection. If drinking this pre-eternal wine allows you to recognise the Truth in the dispositions of force which are the means to attaining to the drink, then your turning away from it and relinquishing its lights is the great wrongdoing. The Almighty says to you, "Come and We will let you drink Our wine for the price of Our manifestations of Majesty and yet you flee from that." The Almighty means that the distance will be rolled up and shortened for you and yet you flee from it and choose distance. We read in the *Hikam*, "When He opens a way for you and makes Himself known to you, then do not worry about your lack of deeds. He only opened the way for you because He desired to make Himself known to you."

The shaykh of our shaykh, said, "The utter wonder is that a *faqir* says, 'O Lord! Let me know You!' Then, when the Almighty makes Himself known to him, he flees from Him and denies Him." In short, the Garden of gnoses, which is where the drink of pre-eternal wine comes from, is encircled by disliked things: "*Or did you imagine that you were going to enter the Garden ...*" (3:143) "*Do people imagine that they will be left to say, 'We believe,' and will not be tested?*" (29:2) The Shaykh's calling this disposition "wrongdoing" is metaphorical. "*Your Lord does not wrong anyone...*" But here the Beloved is mentioned to facilitate this application since all that issues from the Beloved is sweet and pleasant. If its outward is wrongdoing, its inward is correct and drawing near. Allah Almighty knows best. Then he says:

$$\text{فدونَكَها في الحانِ واستجلها به}$$

$$\text{على نغم الألحان فهي بها غُنمُ}$$

**Look for it in the tavern and seek to obtain it
in tunes of the songs by which the prize is obtained.**

Dunaka is a noun-like adverb meaning "Take". *Lahn* are articulated sounds on the measure of poetry. The plural is *alhan* and *luhun*. *Ghumn* is obtaining something without difficulty, as it says in the dictionary.

He says, "If you want to obtain this wine, then go to the place it belongs and seek it in its tavern. That is meeting with its masters, keeping their company, showing *adab* to them, esteeming them, discussing it with them, and composing poems which talk of it in good tunes and good songs. They are a means to success in obtaining it and winning intoxication by it. They include the poems of ash-Shustari and the author and other *Khamriyyas* or *Bahriyyas*. That is why the Sufis compose them to recite them in the circle of *dhikr* and after it because they inspire love and bring about intoxication. It is a precondition that the poet be of good repute and know the art of composition and speak in every context of what is appropriate, beginning and end, attraction and wayfaring. Success is by Allah. Then he says:

$$\text{فما سكنت والهَمَّ يوما بموضعٍ}$$

$$\text{كذلك لم يسكُن، مع النغم الغمُّ}$$

It never stays with worry at any time in any place,
just as sorrow does not remain with song.

He says "If anyone drinks this pre-eternal wine, and is intoxicated by it and its gnosis remains in his heart and its lights shine on his secret, no care remains for him because reaching this wine is reaching the Beloved and sitting on the carpet of His Presence and witnessing the lights of His Rising. Whoever is with the Beloved is not affected by cares nor do worries afflict him, as the speaker says:

Congratulations to the one who obtains the love of his
  Beloved
  and dives to the noblest source by leaving others.
Bliss without a renewer
  for the number of breaths in every witnessing.

Also cares and sorrows only result from the continued existence of humanness. As for the one who as achieved his vanishing, his entire affair is by Allah, "*Say, 'The truth has come and falsehood has vanished.*" (17:81) The Truth is free of imperfections. If you wish, you could say, "Care and sorrow are only conceivable by the loss of the thing or its departure. What could be lost for the one who finds Allah?" Rather for someone who finds Allah, all his moments are festivals and *'id*s as the poet said:

Time is a sin for me if I am absent, my hope,
  and the *'id* lies in what I had of sight and hearing.

Another said:

She said, "They are the *'id* because of good news." I said
to her,

"The *'id* and good news for me is the day when I meet
you.

Allah knows that people are happy with it

but my joy lies only in seeing you."

If you wish, you could say that this wine is not accompanied
by any care or sorrow because this wine only abides in the
heart of someone who is godfearing. The Almighty says:
"*Whoever has taqwa of Allah – He will give him a way out
and provide for him from where he does not expect*" (65:3),
in other words He will appoint for him a way out of every
care. It also only abides in the heart of a good-doer. The
Almighty says: "*Allah is with those who have taqwa of Him
and with those who are good-doers.*" (16:128) It only abides
in a steadfast heart. The Almighty says: "*Allah is with the
steadfast.*" (8:66) If someone has Allah with him, what could
he possibly lack?

If you wish, you could say that cares and sorrows arise
from lack of trust in the Living, the Self-Sustaining. As
for the one whose reliance on Allah is sound, Allah will
be enough for him and protect him. The Almighty says:
"*Whoever trusts in Allah, He will be enough for him.*" (65:3) If
Allah is enough for him, how could any cares disturb him?

If you wish, you could say that these sorrows arise from
lack of realisation of the decree. As for the one who truly
realises the prior decree and determination, he gives
himself rest from toil and turbidity. Allah says: "*Nothing
occurs, either in the earth or in yourselves, without its being*

in a Book." (57:22) Then He says: *"That is so that you will not be grieved about the things that pass you by or exult about the things that come to you."* (57:23) It is related that a man was overpowered by his state and his way was hindered, so he went out bewildered as to his direction and went into the desert. He found a ruined derelict castle from which the wind had removed the sand. In the garden of that castle was a marble table on which was written this poem by the pen of power:

> When I saw you sitting leaning forward,
>   I was certain that you are accompanied by cares
> What was not decreed will never come about by any means
>   and what is decreed will certainly always occur.
> What will be will happen in its time
>   and the brother of ignorance is sad and tired.
> The eager person runs and does not obtain anything by
>   his desire
>   and becomes powerless and abased.
> Abandon cares and divest yourself of its apparel
>   if you are certain of the decree.
> It is easy for you. And trust in your Lord.
>   The business of the brother of the reality is to make
>   things easy.
> He casts off harm from himself regarding his provision
>   since he is certain that it is guaranteed.

If you wish, you could say that cares and sorrows are darknesses and the pre-eternal wine is shining lights, so how can darkness and light be combined? Or how can grief and joy be combined? The shaykh interprets 'remaining' to demand the advance of care on the heart and its passing over it. The existence of wine is not denied. That is how it is. The Almighty says: *"As for those who have taqwa, when they are bothered by visitors from Shaytan, they remember and immediately see clearly."* (7:201) This *ayat* is one of judgement for the people of the beginnings and the ends by the words of the Almighty before that which is addressed to the Master of the gnostics: *"If an evil impulse from Shaytan provokes you, seek refuge in Allah."* (7:200) Or it is an indication that no one is free from the visitation, even if though the Messenger is protected from its persisting. That, however, contains a notification for others. Allah knows best. Then he says:

وفي سكرة منها ولو عمر ساعةٍ

ترى الدّهر َعبدا طائعا ولك الحكمُ

If you are intoxicated by it, even for the duration of an hour,

> **you will see time become your obedient slave and you will have judgement.**

He says: When you are intoxicated by this pre-eternal wine, even for an hour in a lifetime, you will see that time obeys you and all things are subject to your command and prohibition. You rule them as long as you are in this state of intoxication because you are free of them and independent of them by witnessing their Maker. Whenever things yearn for you, you are their master. You are with created beings as long as you do not witness the Maker. When you witness Him, created beings are with you. We read in a *hadith*, "The Garden yearns for 'Ali and 'Ammar, Suhayb and Bilal."

Anyone whose *himma* rises above created things is free. All things are his slaves and he disposes of them at will and what he desires is what his Lord desires. He does not desire anything except what His Lord decides. He only wants what He wants. For him withholding is the same as giving, abasement the same as might, poverty the same as wealth, contraction the same as expansion, and so on with all the opposites. No difficulty the gnostic experiences in respect of matters of this world affects him detrimentally because he is with his Master, whether He denies him or gives to him. We limit the words of the Shaykh to the time that the effect of the wine is present and that must be the case. As for the one who returns to himself and witnesses his sensory, he does not continue to have this prerogative since the judgements of slavehood then dominate him. The poet says regarding that:

> If we are enticed by it, we wander away from other free
> men and slaves
>> If we return to ourselves, our abasement outdoes the
>> humility of the Jews.

Whoever continues to be intoxicated, inwardly realises his going on and annihilation, and is still with his Master, is constantly free, constantly a master, and all things constantly belong to him. He disposes of them by Allah and he is a *khalifa* from Allah in his judgement and imposition, withdrawn from seeing himself and his own existence, strengthened by the eye of insight which sees the prior decree by which he judges. The sight of phenomenal being is removed from his vision and so he only witnesses its Maker. There is no doubt that if anyone is like that, time serves him and people are his slaves. So every day is an *'id* for him. May Allah make us realise this immense business by the rank of the master of creation ﷺ. Then he says:

فلا عيشَ في الدنيا لِمن عاشَ صاحيا
ومن لم يَمُتْ سكرا بها فاته الحزمُ

There is no life in this word for the one who lives sober,

    and whoever does not die intoxicated by it lacks resolve.

I said that sobriety is etymologically the removal of cloud, and *sukr* (intoxication) is said to be sobriety of intoxication (*sukran*), like *rida*. His intoxication departs, as stated in the dictionary. He says that whoever fails to be intoxicated by this wine and lives as a pure wayfarer, only sees created beings and his thought only deals with them, and so he really only lives the life of an animal. Consequently, in the view the people of knowledge, he has no life because his life is turbid and his provision of knowledge is scanty. He is trapped within the confines of created being and imprisoned in the shape of his essence. The arenas of the unseen are not opened to him. He does not go forth to the space of witnessing and direct vision. His stupidity is clear and his sorrow continues. I said in my poem in *ta'* on this theme:

O the stupidity of the one who does not satisfy his thirst
  for it!
Deprival clothes you in the garb of abasement.
O the success of the one is conversant with it,
  according the number of his breaths in every direction.
Congratulations to him! The business is according to
  his will
and time becomes completely subservient to him.
If someone lives and does not become intoxicated by it
  before he dies,
resolve has escaped him and his portion is regret.

It is as the poet says:

If someone fails to reach You and is misguided, his
  portion is regret.
If someone has firm *himma*, *himma* carries him
  upwards.

Know that there are two categories of sobriety: sobriety after intoxication, which is the source of perfection, and sobriety before intoxication, and this is blameworthy because such a person is veiled from Allah. He is the one whom the poet means here. In the same way, intoxication has two categories: intoxication which accompanies wayfaring and intoxication after it, which is perfection. And intoxication which does not accompany wayfaring nor come after it and this is imperfect, as it does not conform to prophetic teaching. If someone is intoxicated and then becomes sober, he is a perfect, completed Shaykh of instruction. This will continue to be the case as long as existence remains. The only person who says the opposite of this is someone whose heart has been sealed by Allah. We ask Allah for security by His favour and generosity. Then he says:

$$ عَلَى نَفْسِهِ فَلْيَبْكِ مَنْ ضَاعَ عُمْرُهُ $$

$$ وَلَيْسَ لَهُ فِيهَا نَصِيبٌ وَلَا سَهْمُ $$

Let him who has wasted his life weep for himself:
he who does not have either portion or share in it.

He says, "Whoever wastes his life in falsehood, falling short, confusion and turbidity and tastes nothing of the wine of joy, either a little or a lot, should weep for himself in the night and at the ends of the day and should seek refuge in the pure gnostics and people of true right action. Perhaps some of the breezes of the Ever-Generous, Most-Forgiving will waft to him. Perhaps he will join them and enter their path. Otherwise he will remain deluded by his acts of worship, for even if they are a lot in a sensory sense, they are little in meaning, when the goal of the action of limbs is to bring their fruit to the heart. That is the wine of love. If someone does not attain to this wine, his worship is a means without an end. That is why the *Qutb* Ibn Mashish – may Allah benefit us by his mention – said, "Whoever guides you to this world has cheated you. Whoever guides you to action has tired you out. Whoever guides you to Allah has given you good counsel."

Guiding to Allah means that the slave withdraws from other than Him, forgetting himself and his own whims and desires. This is the longed for wine. The worship of the people of this wine is great in meaning, even if it is physically little. Worship imbued with this wine is all multiplied many times over because it includes reflection and insight, witnessing and instruction. The report says, "An hour of reflection is better than seventy years of worship." The poet says:

Every moment with my Beloved is like a hundred years.

Shaykh Abu-l-'Abbas al-Mursi said, confirming this idea: "All our moments are the Night of Power," in other words for us every moment is better than a thousand months. Al-Junayd said, "The noblest and highest of gatherings is sitting with reflection in the arenas of *tawhid* with the breeze of gnosis and drinking the cup of love from the sea of love and looking with a good opinion of Allah Almighty." Then he said, "O what a gathering! How majestic! What a wonderful drink! Bliss to the one provided with it."

Ibn 'Atiyya said, "My father reported to me that one of the scholars of the East said, 'I was in the mosque of al-Aqdam in Egypt. I prayed *'Isha'* and saw a man who was lying down covered by a cloak. He remained wrapped in his cloak until morning. We prayed during the night and remained awake throughout it. When the *iqama* for *Subh* was given, that man got up, faced *qibla* and prayed with the people. I was appalled by his boldness in praying without *wudu'*. When the prayer was over, he left and I followed him to admonish him. When I followed him, I heard him reciting:

An enwrapped body is absent/present,
  an aware heart, a silent invoker.
Constricted in the unseen worlds, expanded
  that is the state of the unknown gnostic.

Then I knew that he was one of those who worship by reflection.'"

Abu-l-Hajjaj ad-Darir said in his poem:

Reflection on the wonders of creation is in truth
  one of the best acts of obedience
Because gnosis exists by it.
  He who truly knows Him fears Him.

Ash-Shushtari said:

Abandon the sword and the prayer beads and the prayer mat
  and become intoxicated with the wine of isolation.

In other words abandon physical striving and physical worship. Occupy yourself with inner worship in the heart. That is why one of the gnostics said, "An atom's weight of the actions of the heart is better than mountains of the actions of limbs." Imam Abu-l-Qasim al-Qushayri said, "Reflection is the attribute of every seeker and the fruit of arrival with the precondition that there is knowledge. When thought is free of defects, then the one who reflects reaches the springs of realisation." Encouragement to reflect and envy of it is found in the Book of Allah and the Sunna of the Messenger of Allah ﷺ to such an extent that volumes are not enough for it. And the same can be said about the reports of the righteous *Salaf*. The Almighty says: *"Those who remember Allah, standing, sitting and lying on their sides, and reflect on the creation of the heavens and the earth*" (3:191); the Almighty says: "*Look at what there is in the heavens and on the earth*" (10:101); and the Almighty says: "*Have they not reflected? Their companion is not mad.*" (7:184) He says: "*Have they not looked into the dominions of the heavens and the earth.*" (7:185) And there are other examples which are too numerous to mention.

When the *ayat "In the creation of the heavens and earth, and the alternation of the night and day..."* (2:164) was revealed to the Messenger of Allah ﷺ, he said, "Woe to the one who recites it and does not reflect on it!" The Prophet ﷺ also said, "There is no worship like reflection." The wife of Abu Bakr was asked about her husband's worship. She said, "His night consisted of reflecting in a corner." 'Isa said, "Bliss for the one whose words are remembrance, whose silence is reflection and whose look is a lesson. The cleverest of people is the one who lends himself and works for what is after death." Ka'b said, "Whoever desires the honour of the Next World should reflect a lot." It was said to Ibrahim, "You reflect a long time." He said. "Reflection is the core of the intellect."

Sufyan ibn 'Uyayna used to often reflect and say, "When a man reflects, then he finds a lesson in everything." Al-Hasan said, "If someone has words which do not contain wisdom, his speech is nothing but prattle. If someone has silence which is not filled with reflection, it is nothing but forgetfulness. If someone has a glance which is not concerned with consideration, it is nothing but idle diversion." It is said about Allah's words, *"I will divert from*

My Signs all those who are arrogant in the earth," (7:146) that the meaning is "deprive their hearts of reflection about Me". Luqman used to sit for a long time alone. His master passed by him and said, "Luqman, you spend a long time sitting alone. Why don't you sit with people? It will be company for you." Luqman said, "I sit often alone for complete reflection."

Ibn 'Ata'allah says in the *Hikam*, "Withdraw the heart into the arena of reflection – nothing helps the heart more than that!" He also said, "Reflection is the lamp of the heart. When it goes, the heart is without light." And he said, "There are two sorts of reflection: 1. Reflection of confirmation and faith. 2. Reflection of eye-witnessing and seeing. The first is for the masters who weigh and determine. The second is for the masters who witness and use their inner sight." The reflection of the people of eye-witnessing and seeing is what produces the wine. It is the goal of the gnostics and it is that which is equal to a thousand years. Indeed a single moment of it is better than a thousand months. Whoever lacks it has no life in this world and should weep over himself. Whoever obtains it and wins it has true happiness. Someone said about the like of it:

> They are the men of Allah and it is oppression for someone who is said
>
> not to be described by meanings which describe a Man.

May Allah make us realise what they have realised and obtained what they have obtained. Amen. Peace and blessing be upon the Messengers and Praise be to Allah, the Lord of the Worlds.

This is the end of what we intended to collect on the *Khamriyya* Ode by Ibn Farid at the hand of the slave of his Lord, the least of his slaves, Ahmad ibn Muhammad ibn 'Ajiba al-Ansi.

The String of Pearls
Concerning Fate and the Decree

In the Name of Allah, the All-Merciful, Most Merciful
May Allah bless our master Muhammad and his family
and Companions and grant them peace.

The Shaykh and Imam, scholar and gnostic of his Lord, the perfect Sufi and righteous, arrived *wali*, Abu-l-'Abbas, Ahmad ibn Muhammad Ibn 'Ajiba al-Hasani says:

P raise belongs to Allah, the All-Powerful King Who alone possesses the capacity of perfect bringing into existence and management, Who originates things and perfects them according to His prior knowledge of what they are decreed to be. Peace and blessings be upon our master Sayyidina Muhammad the bringer of good news and warning, the light-giving lamp, and the pleasure of Allah be with his noble Companions who confirmed His pure *Shari'a*.

The vast ocean of destiny and the decree is a sea of great depth into which only the people of realisation dive and to which only one with success is led. This is a brief treatise delving into it in a manner which will put hearts at ease. I was moved to compose it because I saw many people who showed by their lack of knowledge and mistaken action their need for it. Many are misguided about it and have misguided others. People try to resist destiny by whatever means and devices they can. It is said that the slip of a scholar can misguide the world. I have seen many scholars, in a time of plague, order the doors of a city to be shut and then shy away from visiting the sick out of fear of death. This has moved me to write this book.

There is no educational benefit in book knowledge if it is not supported by direct perception and experience. Beneficial knowledge is knowledge that lifts the veil from the heart, spreads light rays of certainty in the breast and removes doubt and agitation from the heart. True peace of mind is only gained by having access to the masters of knowledge. Only those with certainty and realisation can give either guidance or success. The proof of knowledge is action. The proof of sound action is the existence of the state from which it springs. The proof of the state is direct tasting. And the proof of direct tasting is true gratitude, whose reality is withdrawal from other than the Real.

True gratitude brings a sobriety which consists of witnessing everything as proceeding from the Real. It is being at peace with the course of the decrees of destiny, not delving into management and choice, being content with what issues from the consequences of the Divine decrees and submitting to the judgements of the All-Compelling. Five chapters are needed to accomplish my aim in writing this treatise.

1. The reality of the decree and what it is connected to.
2. Evidence for it from the Book and *Sunna* and the words of the righteous *Salaf* and by way of unveiling.

3.   Clarification of the wisdom which is, as it were, the cloak for fate and the decree, and clarification of the decree by which manifestation and concealment occurs.

4.   The falsity of contagion and omens.

5.   Acquiring certainty and its sources and places.

I have named it *"The Necklace of Pearls Concerning Fate and the Decree."* We ask Allah, our Lord, by His grace and generosity, to make it prove of benefit to those who copy it or learn it or hear it or read it and that He shines the lights of certainty into our hearts and makes the suns of the gnostics shine in the heaven of our secrets by the rank of the Seal of the Prophets, Imam of the Messengers and Model of the courteous, our master Muhammad, the trusty truthful one ﷺ and his family and the pure people of his house.

1. EXPLANATION OF FATE AND THE DECREE
AND WHAT IS CONNECTED TO THAT

Qadar (decree) is a verbal noun. You have power over a thing when you fully encompass its measure. It designates the connection of the source of Allah's knowledge to beings before they exist. No creature appears in the visible world without it being already known by Him and previously decreed, and no word, action, movement nor stillness issues from His creation without him having foreknowledge of it and having decreed how it would be. So the lifespan of the slave is foreordained, his breaths are numbered and his footsteps are already written. The poet says about that:

We walked the steps which were written for us
  and whoever has steps written for him must walk them.
When it is decreed that someone will die in a place,
  he does not die in any other place.

The metaphor of the slave of Allah with regard to the prior decree is that of a child who follows the curriculum which the *faqih* has set out for him. When what has been set out for him by pre-eternal knowledge is complete according to the prior decree and determination, he returns to his Master. So it is incumbent on the slave to be calm under the course of decreed events and to look for what the All-Conquering One does. So fate and the decree, and Divine will and volition are all the same thing according to the people of the *Sunna*. Their source is the prior pre-eternal knowledge of things before they appear and that knowledge persists after their manifestation. The Almighty says: *"We know those of you who have gone ahead and those who are still to come."* (15:24) According to this, when we say that Allah decrees something, decides it, wills it and wishes it, all these mean the same thing. As for His pleasure and His love, they are more specific than will and volition since pleasure and love are singled out for obedience rather than disobedience. He decreed obedience and willed it and is pleased with it. He decreed disobedience and willed it but is not pleased with it and does not love it in respect of the *Shari'a*. This is demanded by proper *adab*. Allah knows best.

2. EVIDENCE FOR THE DECREE FROM THE BOOK AND THE SUNNA AND THE WORDS OF THE RIGHTEOUS SALAF

As for evidence for it from the Mighty Book, Allah says: *"We have created all things in due measure."* (54:49) in other words brought them forth by a prior decree. The Almighty says: *"We have listed everything in a clear register"* (36:12) which is the Preserved Tablet. Allah says: *"Everything has its measure with Him"* (13:8) and the Almighty says: *"Allah's command is a pre-ordained decree"* (33:38) and He says: *"So that Allah could settle a matter whose result was preordained"* (8:42). The Almighty says: *"Nothing occurs, either in the earth or in yourselves, without its being in a Book before We make it happen. That is something easy for Allah."* (57:22) That means that whatever afflicts people in the earth, be it good or evil, by way of drought or famine or drowning, or in themselves by death or killing, is in a Book, the Preserved Tablet, before Allah manifests it.

Then the Almighty says: *"That is so that you will not be grieved about the things that pass you by..."* (57:23) because it was something that was decreed before time that would not come about or would not continue. So you should not be sad about something which was not for you or which would end with you. *"...or exult about the things that come to you,"* because even before it appeared, it was destined for you and it was inevitable that it would come to you. What is desired is balance in withholding and giving, contraction and expansion, lack and occurrence, abasement and might, poverty and wealth, health and illness, and other different states and stages of life, since all these things are the result of preordained decrees. So do not display sorrow about anything you have missed out on nor rejoice over anything that comes to you. The Almighty says: *"Allah has appointed a measure for all things,"* (65:3) in other words a known period of occurrence and predetermined moment of arrival. Nothing can be brought forward by a single instant or delayed for a moment.

The Almighty says about the time of death: *"No self can die except with Allah's permission, at a predetermined time."* (3:145) In other words the time of everyone's death is determined and defined before He brings them into existence. The Almighty says: *"It is He who created you from clay and then decreed a fixed term, and another fixed term is specified with Him."* (6:2) The first refers to your death and the second to your resurrection. The Almighty says: *"It is He who takes you back to Himself at night, while knowing the things you perpetrate by day, and then wakes you up again, so that a specified term may be fulfilled."* (6:60) So a person may be absolutely certain that the end of his life was determined by Allah before time. Then He will return to his Lord. He says: *"Then when death comes to one of you, Our messengers take him, and they do not fail in their task,"* (6:61), meaning that no one can alter the lifespan preordained for them by making it either longer or shorter. The Almighty says: *"Every nation has an appointed time. When their appointed time comes, they cannot delay it a single hour or bring it forward"* (10:49). When their destruction arrives, through punishment or any other cause, they cannot delay it at all nor bring it forward. The Almighty says: *"And no living thing lives long or has its life cut short without that being in a Book."* (35:11) The meaning of the *ayat* is that no one is given a long life or has his life cut short without that being in a Book, the Book being the Preserved Tablet. The *ayat* deals with two sorts of people: one is granted a long life and the other has his life curtailed and so his life is short. All of that is in a clear Book. It is said that the decrease in lifespan is according to the knowledge of the angels. When he maintains ties of kinship, for instance, the increase which is already known to Allah appears. The slave only has one life with Allah which is neither increased nor decreased.

As for His words: *"Allah erases whatever He wills or endorses it,"* (13:39) they mean that He obliterates what is with the angels and confirms what is with Him, which is the Mother of the Book. The Almighty says: *"Though some of you may die before that time – so that you may reach a predetermined age and so that hopefully you will use your intellect. It is He who gives life and causes to die."* (40:67-68) Among you are those who die before becoming old men and He may defer you so that you reach a specified term which was already known before time. The angels record it at the time when the spirit is breathed into a person. Hopefully you will understand and recognise that both death and life are entirely in the hand of Allah.

This means that no secondary cause, such as the plague or other similar things, has any effect where death is concerned. Rather the entire affair belongs to Allah. That is why He says: *"It is He who gives life and causes to die,"*

(40:68) meaning that He alone is responsible for it. *"When He decides on something,"* (19:35) whether that be death or anything else, *"He just says to it, 'Be!' and it is."* (19:35) He says: *"When Allah's time comes it cannot be deferred, if you only knew."* (71:4) These *ayats* are clear in defining the life-span. It was determined before time. It cannot be deferred nor can it be brought forward, either by the plague or anything else. So people should be calm before their Lord and wait to see what Allah will do with them. They should not fear and be cautious in this respect, since caution is of no use with the One who decrees.

As for evidence in the *Sunna*, the Prophet ﷺ said to Ibn 'Abbas, "Ibn 'Abbas, I will teach you some words. Be careful regarding Allah and He will take care of you. Be careful regarding Allah and you will find Him in front of you. Recognise Allah in ease and He will recognise you in hardship. Know that whatever misses you could never have hit you and what hits you could never have missed you." He added in another transmission, "The pens have been lifted and the pages are dry," in other words what missed you was decreed before time. Because it was not written for you it will never come to you, be that good or evil, life or death. The Prophet ﷺ said to Abu Hurayra, "The pen is dry regarding what you will meet, Abu Hurayra."

The Prophet ﷺ said. "Everything is by a decree, even incapacity and cleverness." Malik transmitted it in the *Muwatta'*. The Prophet ﷺ said, "A man can do the actions of someone destined for the Garden until there is only an armspan between him and it, and then what is written will overtake him and he does the actions of someone destined for the Fire and enters it. A man can do the actions of someone destined for the Fire until there is only an armspan between him and it, and then what is written will overtake him and he does the actions of someone destined for the Garden and enters it." Al-Bukhari and others related it.

The Prophet ﷺ said, "Provision seeks out a man as his term seeks him." The Prophet ﷺ said, "Allah entrusts an angel to the womb who says, 'O Lord, a drop! O Lord, a clot! O Lord, a piece of flesh!' When the *ruh* is breathed into it, he says, 'O Lord, what is its provision? What is its life-span? Wretched or happy?' All of that is decreed in his mother's womb," in what al-Bukhari and Muslim related.

The Prophet ﷺ said in explaining the reality of faith: "It is that you believe in Allah, his angels, His Books, His Messenger, and the Last Day and that you believe in the Decree, both its good and its evil." He added in some transmissions: "Both its sweet and its bitter." Good is obeying Allah and doing good. Evil is unbelief. Sweetness refers to things that are in harmony with the human being, such as wealth and well-being and types of beauty. Bitterness is what pains a human being, like illness and poverty, abasement and all types of majesty. All of that has already been decreed and decided. Whoever doubts that is an unbeliever by consensus. Whoever believes in terms of knowledge but is not content with things when they actually occur is a deviant by consensus. That is why Malik said, "Whoever has the *shari'a* without *tasawwuf* deviates." Shaykh Abu-l-Hasan said, "Whoever does not breathe his final breath believing experientially in this knowledge of ours, dies persisting in great wrong action without being aware of it. Whoever does not admire the people of purity does not desire to be described with purity. Purity is contentment and submission to all that emerges from the All-Wise, All-Knowing."

The Prophet ﷺ said, "The Spirit of Purity conveyed to my spirit: 'A soul will not die until it has received its full provision.' So fear Allah and be temperate in seeking it." The Prophet ﷺ said, "Your Lord has decided four things: physique, character, provision and life-span." At-Tabarani related this in *al-Awsat*. In the transmission of Ahmad we find: "Allah Almighty has decided five things for each slave: his lifespan, his provision, his steps, where he will die, and whether he is wretched or happy." What is meant by steps are the steps which he will walk. That is foreordained as we already stated.

So provision, both physical and spiritual, was allotted before time, just as lifespans and steps are allotted. It is the same with ranks and stations. The Pen has dried having written all of that. The Companions asked, "Messenger of Allah, then what is action for?" The Prophet ﷺ said, "Act. Everyone is eased to that for which he was created. If he is one of the people of happiness, the actions of the people of happiness are made easy for him. If he is one of people of wretchedness, the actions of the people of wretchedness are made easy for him." Then he recited: *"As for him who gives out and has taqwa and confirms the Good, We will pave his way to Ease. But as for him who is stingy and self-satisfied,*

246

and denies the Good, We will pave his way to Difficulty."
(92:5-10)

If you were to say, "If the decree has already preceded with what will be and so the slave cannot avoid it, for what is the slave called to account and punished?" the answer is that, by His radiant wisdom, Allah assigns earning to the slave with respect to what he does according to whether he intends good or evil by his action. In reality he is pulled by a chain but the *shari'a* ascribes action to him because of that earning and so the proof against him is established. The Almighty says: *"Say: 'Allah's is the conclusive argument. If He had willed He could have guided every one of you.'"* (6:149) So the kingdom is His kingdom and slaves are His slaves. *"He will not be questioned about what He does, but they will be questioned."* (21:23)

That is also how it is with provision. It is allotted before time and guaranteed by the surety of Allah Almighty. However, His Wisdom demands that the secrets of lordship be concealed. Provision is, therefore, accompanied by the means by which it comes but it does not come about through them. As the saying goes: "Causation must exist but its absence is evident." Yes, whoever really has *taqwa* and devotes himself to Allah is provided for without any means being involved. The Almighty says: *"Whoever has taqwa of Allah – He will give him a way out and provide for him from where he does not expect. Whoever puts his trust in Allah – He will be enough for him."* (65:3) Shaykh Abu-l-Abbas said, "People have means. Our means are *iman* and *taqwa.*" Then he recited: *"If only the people of the cities had believed and had taqwa, We would have opened up to them blessings from heaven and earth."* (7:96) This will be further explained when we discuss Wisdom and Power, Allah willing, and success is by Allah.

As for what the righteous *Salaf* said about the decree, one well-known statement is: "Whatever Allah wills will be. Whatever our Lord did not will will not be." It is also said that this is a *hadith*. 'Umar ibn 'Abdu-l-'Aziz said, "I have no happiness except where the decree lies." One of them was asked, "What do you want?" He answered, "Whatever Allah decrees." Ibn 'Ata'allah said in the *Hikam*. "Every breath you breathe emerges according to a preordained decree." He also said, "How can your subsequent asking be a cause of His prior giving? The decree from Before-time is too majestic to be ascribed to any action. His concern for you did not come from you. Where were you when He directed His concern to you and faced you with His guardianship? There is no sincerity of action in Before-Time. No state exists in Before-Time. There was only pure overflowing favour and immense giving." He means that only what was previously decreed for you in the World of the Unseen can appear for you in the visible world. There was no action on your part in that realm to make you deserving of a gift nor any state to make you deserving of being brought close to Allah or reaching Him. His giving to you is simply a gracious favour and pure generosity from Him. Allah possesses immense favour.

Know that people fall into four categories in the way they look at the prior decree and its concomitant result. One group look at the end result since they know that actions are by their seals. Another group look at the moment and are not distracted by what was before or the end result, only performing what they are obliged to do in the moment, knowing that "the *faqir* is the child of the moment". They only see the moment they are in. Another group look to Allah alone since they know that the past, future and present are turned about in the Hand of the Real and are disposed by His rulings. All moments accept change and the state can change. They see everything as being in His Hand. This category have rest from the turbidity of management since their witnessing of the Manager frees them from concern about the decree. They are different from the others who are dominated by witnessing separation.

The first group is distracted by fear of the decree. The second is dazzled by fear of ends and seals. The third, by being dominated by the moment and witnessing its rulings, fail to witness the Maker of the Moment. When the veil is removed from the fourth group and they witness the Lord of Lords, witnessing the One distracts them from everything but nothing distracts them from Allah. That is why it is said: "The Sufi is the one who does not see other than Allah in either Abode and does not see other-than-Allah together with Allah. Everything is subjected to him and he is not subjected to anything. By it he is free from every kind of turbidity and his purity is not disturbed by anything. The One distracts him from everything and nothing distracts him from the One."

In short, the one who wants constant peace of mind should throw himself down before Allah, look in every moment at what emerges from Allah, and be still under the course of what is decreed for him and so withdraw from his own management and choice. Reflect on what the Qutb Sidi Yaqut al-'Arshi said:

There is only what He wills, so abandon your worries and
prostrate.
Abandon the preoccupations that distract you from that
and let them go.

As for its evidence by means of unveiling and premonition: when people are veiled and overcome by their humanity, Allah may acquaint them with things that are decreed for them before it comes about, either by communicating it to them in a waking state or when they are asleep. The Prophet ﷺ said, "The true dream of the believer is a forty-sixth part of Prophethood. As the end of time approaches, the true dream of the believer is almost never wrong." We realised this matter for ourselves, praise be to Allah! Before a matter of majesty or beauty occurred to us we would often see it before it took place, sometimes a long time and sometimes shortly before it happened. Then we would look out for its arrival in the same way you might look out for someone expected back from a journey. In that case when the event occurs, it finds a heart pre-prepared for it, armed against its assault. Its blows do not unsettle it nor is it fazed by its arrival. So we realised by tasting and unveiling that decreed events really are predestined from before-time and that their time and place is exactly specified and not subject to advancement or deferral.

It is, however, part of the wisdom of the All-Wise that He has concealed this secret with the cloak of wisdom and ensured that everything has a cause. Thus the decree descends in the exact moment singled out for it before time but it is accompanied by the existence of its cause and so it is said, "So-and-so did that," and "This happened to him" and "So-and-so travelled to a place where there was plague and it killed him," or "He carried the plague to another place." Stopping at this without looking into the inward reality of the matter and the true disposal of the decree shows the existence of a dense veil and ugly ignorance. It may even lead to unbelief if the person concerned actually believes in the efficacy of cause and effect and denies the decree. Many a foot of those who lay claim to knowledge slips up here. They only have its outward expression.

Reports about matters before they occur have come down to us by multiple transmissions. Examples of this have come by way of Revelation, as in the words of the Almighty: *"Allah has promised those of you who believe and do right actions that He will make them successors in the land as He made those before them successors."* (24:55) Then Allah established Companions firmly in the East and the West. Another example is found in the words of the Almighty: *"Alif Lam Mim The Romans have been defeated in the land nearby, but after their defeat they will themselves be victorious in a few years' time."* (30:14) Then they defeated the Persians at the time of Hudaybiyya. He also said: *"You will enter the Masjid al-Haram in safety, Allah willing, shaving your heads and cutting your hair without any fear."* (48:27) That occurred on the Day of Conquest.

As for the Prophet ﷺ reporting about unseen future things, there are innumerable instances of that. The Prophet ﷺ warned about the seditions which would occur after him as if he was actually seeing them. All those things took place. Something was found written with the pen of the decree on a short, crumbling wall. Its text is:

What is not decreed will never occur by any device,
and what is will certainly come about.
What is going to be will be in its moment,
and the person with ignorance is sorrowful and tired.
It has been made easy for you, so trust in your Lord.
The affair of the knower of the reality is nothing but ease.

If matters occurred by chance as the Rafidites and Qadarites, the Magians of this community claim, then there would not be reports of things which had not yet happened which then occurred. If you were to say that what I have done is just report something well known since all the Muslims have said this, I would reply that our aim is not merely to impart information. Our aim is to inculcate certainty. There is no doubt that mentioning things that bolster that helps towards that. It is one of the armies of light and success. Allah is the Guide to the Straight Path.

3. ELUCIDATION OF WISDOM AND POWER

May Allah give you understanding of the path of His guidance and make you among the people of His love and affection! Know that the sea of Wisdom is an overflowing sea and a manifest matter, which takes on the outward appearance of causation. The veil has been lowered, protecting the hidden secret and concealing the buried treasure. It connects rulings to their causes and affirms *shari'a*s and religions. It covers with its cloak what emerges from the element of Power and, by the might of His greatness, veils what appears of the secrets of Lordship, concealing the inner reality, making the Path and slavehood manifest, and hiding the secrets of lordship. Whoever halts at it is veiled and whoever pierces through to witnessing the realm of Power beyond it is one of those loved by Allah and destined for success.

The sea of Power is also an overflowing sea. Its business is overwhelming. It has no beginning or end. It manifests and conceals. It moves and makes still. It gives and withholds. It lowers and raises. In its hand are the destinies of things and on the axis of its circumference the spheres of disposal revolve. When Power wants to manifest something from the ocean of pre-ordination, which was before-time, Wisdom covers it with the cloak of cause and effect and it itself remains a buried treasure. The secret of Lordship is protected, the superiority of the knower over the ignorant is made manifest, the one who is far away is distinguished from the one on who has arrived, and the believer from the unbeliever.

The knowers are those who see only the disposal of Power. They recognise the secret of Wisdom but are not veiled by it from witnessing Power. The ignorant are those who halt at witnessing Wisdom and by it are veiled to Power. The knowers attain to witnessing the pure core of existence while the ignorant stops with the dry outward shell of causation. *"Are they the same – those who know and those who do not know?"* (39:9) The knowers look at the Causer of causes and so the veil is removed from them and they enter among the lovers. The ignorant remain with the outer husk of cause and effect and are veiled by stopping before the door. The knowers are characterised by their affirmation of true nature of the arrival of decrees and the ignorant are characterised by their denial of what appears from the presence of the Compeller. The knowers receive what emerges from the element of Power with joy and happiness because of their witnessing the control which the decree has in the disposition of affairs. The ignorant are constantly opposing the Real without being aware of doing it. It is said, "Whoever deals with people by the *shari'a* has long drawn out disputes with them. Whoever deals with them in the light of the inner reality excuses them." It is mandatory to deal with them outwardly by the *shari'a* and remind them, and to deal with them inwardly in the light of the inner reality and to excuse them.

The result of that is that Power emerges and is manifest and Wisdom is covered and concealed. Wisdom is the source of Power and Power is the source of Wisdom since the Doer is one. The Doer of the cause is the Doer of the effect, but the sun must have clouds and a beautiful woman must have a veil. The causes and effects which Power manifests are called Wisdom and what Wisdom conceals of bringing into existence and origination is called Power. The Doer is one. When the slave already has something decreed for him by the Real, majestic or beautiful, and the time arrives for that to occur, Allah moves him to adopt the usual cause of bringing it about and what is decreed by the disposal of the pre-eternal decree takes place, concealed by the cloak of Divine Wisdom. The ignorant person stops with the shell of the cause while the person of knowledge penetrates to witnessing the Causer of that cause. That is how it is when it was decreed before time that a certain affliction would occur in a certain town. Allah moves people to the cause of that despite themselves so that the command of Allah is carried out on them. The Almighty says: *"When We desire to destroy a city, We send a command to the affluent in it and they become deviant in it and the Word is justly carried out against it and We annihilate it completely."* (17:16)

One aspect of that is the plague. When it is already decreed by Allah that it will occur in a town or city at a certain time, by His wisdom the Real appoints a reason and a cause for that, and so the pre-eternal decree occurs at the time which was already known in timeless foreknowledge covered by the Cloak of Wisdom, which is that reason, so that the prerogative of belief in the unseen appears because this world is the Realm of Responsibility, not the Realm of Recognition, as opposed to the Next World. The ignorant man says, "If it were not that so-and-so had made him go, he would not have gone." The knower says, "This was foreordained in the judgement of before time. And so the decree moved him to that place and he died." The ignorant man says, "If he had not gone, he would not have died."

This is the belief of those among the unbelievers whose hearts have been sealed by Allah. Allah forbade the believers to be like them. He says: *"You who believe! do not be like those who disbelieve and say of their brothers, when they are going on journeys or military expeditions, 'If they had only been with us, they would not have died or been killed,' so that Allah can make that anguish for them in their hearts. It is Allah Who gives life and causes to die. Allah sees what you do."* (3:156) The Almighty further says: *"Say, 'Even if you had been inside your homes, those people for whom killing was decreed would have gone out to their place of death.' So that Allah might test what is in your breasts and purge what is in your hearts. Allah knows the contents of your hearts."* (3:153). The plague will be discussed in its proper place, Allah willing. This is the reality Wisdom and Power for the one whose inner eye Allah has opened. Success is by Allah. He is the Guide to the Straight Path

4. On the Fallacy of Contagion and Omens

According to the claim of philosophers and scientists, contagion is the transmission of illness from one place to another. The people of *tawhid* consider that to be a false understanding. The Almighty says: *"Allah is the Creator of everything."* (13:16) He says about magic: *"But they cannot harm anyone by it, except with Allah's permission."* (2:102) The Almighty says: *"But if anything bad happened to them, they would blame their ill fortune on Musa and those with him. No indeed! Their ill fortune will be with Allah."* (7:131) Everything happens according to His judgement and will, or His decree and determination. The Prophet ﷺ said, "There is no such thing as contagion and no bad omens, no bad luck in Safar and no avenging spirit (*hama*)." Anyone who believes that something is contagious by itself is an unbeliever by consensus. Anyone who believes that something is contagious by an intrinsic power in it is a rebel, and there are two positions about his unbelief. Anyone believes that something is contagious by the power and decree of Allah according to wisdom and the process of power is a believer.

The illnesses which they consider to be contagious are mange, plague and leprosy. As for mange, it is found in camels, sheep, dogs, and human beings. All of that is by the power and decree of Allah. It was decreed before time that it would occur to that person at that particular defined moment. It cannot be advanced before it or delayed beyond that moment. However, it is by the Wisdom of the All-wise that things are accompanied by their causes; they are not brought about by them. When the moment arrives in which it was decreed that that illness would occur, Allah brings it about through a cause which covers the secret of His decree and so it is confusing for the one who is affected by it. It may also happen without any cause. It says in *hadith* that when the Prophet ﷺ said, "There is no contagion and no bad omens." They said, "Messenger of Allah, what about camels? They are like gazelles in the sand and then a mangy camel comes and goes in among them and they all get mange." The Prophet asked, "Who infected the first one?" in other words who brought that illness to the first camel? He informed them that everything is by the decree and power of Allah.

As the secret of the decree of the descent of illness is concealed by the apparent cause of it, so the secret of the decree of recovery from it is concealed by medical treatment given. We read in *hadith*: "Allah has not sent down an illness without sending down a cure for it." So medical treatment is not incompatible with reliance on Allah as long as it is seen that healing is from Allah. Medicine is a Wisdom which combines with Power and has absolutely no effect on it. Whoever believes that medicine has a real effect is an idolater, associating others with Allah. The Almighty says: *"When harm touches people they call on their Lord, making tawba to Him. But then, when He gives them a taste of mercy from Him, a group of them immediately associate others with their Lord."* (30:33)

So supplication and treatment are both causes. When relief occurs at the hands of anyone through medicine or something else, sick people believe that it is that which saved them from their illness and so they associate something with Allah, either through the *shirk* of belief in something other than Allah or the *shirk* of reliance on something other than Allah. That happens by the inclination of the heart and its reliance on that means. It detracts from *tawhid* for the elite. That is why the *Qutb* Ibn Mashish said to Abu-l-Hasan, "Flee from the best of people more than you flee from the evil ones, Abu-l-Hasan. Their best will afflict you in your heart while their evil will only afflict you in your body. It is better for your body to be afflicted than for your heart to be afflicted. An enemy who causes you to reach your Lord is better than a loved one who cuts you off from your Lord."

Creation is excluded from the consideration of the people of realisation. They thank people with their tongues but withdraw from them with their hearts, since the Prophet ﷺ said, "Whoever does not thank people does not thank Allah." So causation must exist but its absence is evident. Causation is based on the right of Wisdom and withdrawal from it is based on witnessing Power. Whoever denies causation is ignorant of the Power and Wisdom of Allah. Power and Wisdom are both attributes of the Real. The Almighty says: *"Allah is All-Knowing, All-Wise"* and *"Allah has power over all things."* Allah Almighty knows best.

As for the plague, doctors consider it to be the result of bad air and miasma and the people of the Sunna consider it to be the stabbing of the *jinn*. That is based on an explicit *hadith*. In the Lesser Collection, "The plague is a stabbing by your enemies of the *jinn*. It is martyrdom for you." Al-Hakim related it. In it also, "The plague is a stabbing and a punishment. It was released against a group of the tribe of Israel. When it occurs in a land where you are, do not leave it, fleeing from it. If it arrives in a land where you are, do not advance to it." Al-Bukhari and Muslim and at-Tirmidhi related it. This is how he designated it. We also find: "The plague is martyrdom for every Muslim." Al-Hakim and the two shaykhs related it. Another *hadith* about it is: "It is a punishment which Allah sent to those before you. He made it a mercy for the believers. There is no one who comes into contact with the plague and then remains where he is with fortitude and in expectation of the reward, knowing that only what Allah has written for him will befall him, who will receive any other reward than that of a martyr." Al-Hakim and al-Bukhari related it. Another *hadith* says: "The plague is a virulent disease like the pestilence in camels. The one who stays where it appears is like the martyr. The one who flees from it is like the one who flees from the battlefield." Al-Hakim related it.

The clear *hadith* can be combined with the position of the doctors. When Allah Almighty wants to send it against His slaves, He causes a change in the air and then He sends the *jinn* in it and they are aroused by Allah's permission at the moment when the air has been rendered corrupt by Allah's power. The attack of the *jinn* can be verified by witnessing. Many people have seen them, either while awake or while sleep, in human form, male or female. An army of them may be gathered in one place and then the human being sees them while he is awake or asleep. I heard the drums at the tribe of Anjara between the heaven and the earth at the time of the plague.

The Prophet ﷺ said, "When the plague occurs in a land where you are, do not leave it." It is well known that leaving is unlawful and the well known position is that advancing to it is also disliked. That is why Ibn Rushd said about going to it, "There is a consensus that someone who does so does not commit a wrong action." The reason for the prohibition is that if a human being goes to it and that coincides with the end of his term of life, he will die of it and then it might occur to his imagination or the imagination of someone else that if he had not gone there, he would not have died, and so one falls into the sin of association (*shirk*). As for the people of complete certainty, there is no dislike where they are concerned since they deny the reality of causation. The prohibition applies to those who are weak and does not include those who are strong. This is like the words of the Prophet, peace be upon him, "Flee from the leper as you flee from the lion." Yet it is confirmed that he ate with a leper.

He said, "There is no contagion and no bad omens." So the strong have a ruling that is different from that of the weak. As for Sayyiduna 'Umar turning back from Syria when he heard that the plague was there, the army consisted of a mixture of strong people and others, and 'Umar showed compassion for the weak lest anything creep into their hearts. There were among them people who had not been Companions and were new to Islam.

I have seen many of our companions go forward to wash the dead and to touch the sick in the cities of Tetuan, Tangiers, Sale, Rabat and the camps of the tribes, which no one else would do. They washed and shrouded and touched the sick and no harm came to them. Some of them are still alive. I have seen some who were given the used garments of someone who had died of the plague and put them on immediately and nothing happened to them and they lived for a long time after the plague. I have seen some of our companions from Anjara who came to a place where the plague was raging and stayed there for more than a month washing, shrouding and touching those ill with the plague who then remained healthy and lived for a long time after the plague. So the statement that there is contagion and transmission is false.

We used to say to our companions, "Whoever desires the teaching of certainty and to learn strength and courage should go to where the plague is, putting his trust in Allah, and relying on the view of Ibn Rushd as well as what the other points we already mentioned. As for trying to protect oneself against it by placing guards on the gates and locking them, that is of no use. The Almighty says: *"Wherever you are, death will catch up with you, even if you are in impregnable fortresses."* (4:78) The time may have been deferred before time and so the ignorant person believes that its delay is the result of his eagerness and self-preservation. That is not the case since action is of no use in the face of the Decree. The time demanded the delay. The Almighty says: *"Allah has appointed a measure for all things"*(65:3) and: *"There is nothing that does not have its stores with Us and We only send it down in a known measure."* (15:21)

I heard a nice story from one of our companions, who is an independent *faqih*, that when the plague arrived near Tangiers, they locked the gates to prevent anyone from the place where the plague was from entering. When it became clear that the plague had, in fact, appeared in the city he went to the gatekeepers and said to them, "I am going to go to the *qa'id* about you. Why did you let the plague in?" This was to demonstrate the falsity of the claim that it could be kept out in this way. If you were to say that there were instances when shutting gates at a time of plague had kept people safe from it, I would say that Wisdom is valid for those who hold to it and is not disrupted in their case but they are veiled by it from their Lord and from understanding that it is simply the working of the decree and fate with respect to them. What happened was only what the Pen had written for them. However, they are considered among the weak and have no standing in the Station of the strong. They are among those about whom the Prophet ﷺ said, "Anyone who flees from it is like someone who flees from combat."

As for seeking protection by means of supplication, it does not detract from someone's slavehood as long as they do not believe that by it they can add anything to the length of their life. The benefit of doing it is that it gives comfort and composure and instils patience and acceptance in times of hardship. Al-Qastallani mentioned a particular supplication which can be used when there is a plague outbreak and may also be used as a talisman. Allah may preserve people by its blessing. It is: "O Allah, still the affliction of a blow from the agents of the Jabarut by Your hidden kindness which comes and descends from the door of the *malakut* until we firmly grasp the coat-tails of Your kindness and are protected by You from the descent of Your Power, O You with perfect Power and all-encompassing Mercy, O Master of Majesty and Generosity."

Also beneficial in that situation is the *Hizb* of an-Nawawi recited in the evening after *'Isha'*. It is said that anyone who recites it will not be overpowered by anyone, pious or impious, so that no one will be able to get to him, not by way of *himma*, like the *awliya'*, nor by way of physical actions, like tyrants of mankind and *jinn*. That also applies to the *Wafiza* of Shaykh Zarruq done morning and night. Similar to that is the *Ayat* of Eagerness: *"A Messenger has come to you"* (9:128) to the end of the *sura* repeated seven times. Similar to that is a lot of prayer on the Messenger of Allah ﷺ which removes sorrows, cares and grief.

Something the shaykh of our shaykh, Moulay al-'Arabi ad-Darqawi wrote to us, after saying a lot of other things, was, "If you are confused about something, hasten to purify yourself if you have not already done so. Then pray two *rak'at*s, reciting two short *sura*s, and do the prayer on the Messenger of Allah, even ten times, or three times. Say, "Allah is enough for us, and He is the best Protector!" and "There is no power nor strength except by Allah, the High, the Great" the same number of times. Always give yourself up to your Lord in that way and beware of doing other than that since only returning to your Lord and relying on Him in ease and hardship will benefit you. No one other than Him will be of any help to you at all." We say, "Purify yourself if you are not in a state of purity, strive like that, and recite like that, or do it all. That is what we do. We pray two *rak'at*s (106) and recite two short *sura*s, like *Inshirah* (94) and *Quraysh*, and we say the prayer on the Messenger of Allah ﷺ and say, 'Allah is enough for us and He is the best guardian' ten times and 'There is no power nor strength except by Allah' ten times."

Then he said, "Then evil will leave you and good will come since returning to Allah and relying on Him brings benefits and miracles. By Allah, we used to do as we said until we had pathways in heaven as we have on earth, and more than that and closer. The curse be upon the on who lies. By Allah, if we hold to our Lord as we have stated, we would become His proxy in all our moments and we would be accompanied by His help, excellence, generosity, forbearance, munificence, kindness and gift in our movements and stillness, and Allah will take us by the hand."

Part of what is stressed for a person in the time of plague is contentment, submission and steadfastness when one loses loved ones. "Patience is at the first blow." Allah will replace all that is lost, especially in this difficult time. So no one should rejoice at a birth or be sad over a death. All that remains is the incursions of the Christians and the emergence of the Dajjal, and Ya'juj and Ma'juj. If Allah takes someone to Him, He has delivered him from these terrors. Whoever remains should fortify Himself with the Truly Great, Great. We already mentioned what the Prophet ﷺ said to Ibn 'Abbas ﷺ. "Be careful regarding Allah and He will take care of you. Be careful regarding Allah and you will find Him in front of you. Recognise Allah in ease and He will recognise you in hardship."

One of our companions I trust, the *faqih* and scholar and righteous *wali*, Sidi Muhammad ibn Ma'ruf as-Sahrawi, reported to me, "I saw that in the book of al-Buni, the sun of gnosis, it says: 'When the Christians enter Egypt and the plague appears in the Maghrib, the Christians will go out to the coasts, and Imam al-Mahdi will appear and 'Isa son of Maryam descend. Whoever loses one he loves at this time should not be sad about it. Whoever feels the movement of his soul to Allah should rejoice at meeting Allah and meeting the Messenger of Allah ﷺ and the friends of Allah who died before him. Bilal said when he died, "O joy! Tomorrow I will meet those whom I love, Muhammad and his party.""'

When the *ruh* leaves the prison of the body, it appears in the likeness of the person in perfect shape with all their limbs as a subtle spiritual form like that of the angels. He can be seen and heard and recognised. When it leaves the body, the angels clothe it in garments, which are brought, mellifluously perfumed from the Garden. It ascends like that to heaven with a fragrant scent. The angels say, "This is the spirit of so-and-so, son of so-and-so, may Allah have mercy on him." They bless him and accompany him from heaven to heaven until he reaches the Lote-Tree of the Furthest Limit. The angels then say, "This is your slave, so-and-so, who we have brought to You." Allah will say, "Write his book in 'Illiyun and show him his place in the Garden." They will take him to the Garden and he will see all the good things that Allah has prepared for him. Then he will be returned for the questioning. When the corpse is placed on the bier, the spirit body will be an armspan above it, saying, "Take me forward. Take me forward." When he is placed in his grave and the earth is thrown over him, it will enter the grave and the body will be given a strange kind of life which is like that of the state of sleep. When he is questioned in his grave, Allah will makes him firm with the firm word so that he is able to easily answer the messengers of his Lord. Then his spirit will ascend to the station which Allah has prepared for him.

The Almighty says: *"If he is one of Those Brought Near there is solace and sweetness and a Garden of Delight."* (56:89) Some gnostics have said that the word "solace" refers to arrival and "sweetness" to beauty. When the *ruh* is separated from this body, it is connected to the Pure Presence. It experiences solace and sees only space and the expanse of beauty, which is sweetness. Then it will enter the Garden and will enjoy there the innumerable types of blessing of the Garden. It will be able to go wherever it wishes. In some reports, when the gnostic dies, his *ruh* will be told, "Go wherever you wish. Rest from the toil and terrors of the world." 'Sweetness' is the provision which is connected to its state. The spirits of the martyrs will eat from the fruit of the Garden and drink from its rivers. The spirits of the truly sincere will eat from the fruit of gnostic knowledges and drink from breeze of the pleasure of witnessing and eye-witnessing.

At-Tirmidhi said, "Solace refers to rest in the grave and sweetness to entering the Garden." Bassam ibn 'Abdullah said that solace refers to peace and sweetness to nobility. Sa'd said, "Solace is embracing virgins and sweetness is the company of the pious." According to the literal meaning of the *ayat*, those brought near enjoy marriage with virgins and their provision rushes to them before the Final Hour. Al-Kharraz said, "Solace is the removal of the veil and sweetness is the vision and meeting." It is said solace is compassion and sweetness is deliverance from affliction. It is said that solace is death in martyrdom and sweetness is the beginning of happiness. It is said that solace is the removal of calamities and sweetness is forgiveness, security and peace. It is said that solace is Allah's favour and sweetness is reaching Him. It is said that the solace is pardon without rebuke, and sweetness is provision without reckoning. It is said that solace is for the forerunners and sweetness is for the intermediate and the Garden for the wrongdoers. It is said that solace is for their spirits, sweetness for the hearts, the Garden for their bodies and the Real for their secrets.

Those who are brought near are the forerunners and the forerunners are the people of high *himma* whose spirits rush ahead to the pure Presence. They are the people of annihilation and going on. Death in respect of these people is merely moving from one country to another and from one home to another. Al-Ghazali said about that after his death in something which was found under his turban:

Do not think that death is death.
It is life and it is the end of fate.
Do not fear the attack of death,
and what is but moving on from here.
Remove the bodies from yourselves
and you will see the Real with clear vision.

To the end of the *qasida*.

As for someone who is one of the Companions of the Right, the angels ascend with his spirit as was already stated. Then it will be returned for the questioning. When it has been questioned, it will move with its people in the world of the *barzakh* and they will greet it. They will ask it about the states of those who are still alive. Then it will remain confined in the world of the *barzakh* until the Day of Rising, as opposed to the spirits of those brought near. They are released to go wherever they wish and go as the living go. What is meant by the Companions of the Right are the people of proof and evidence who are confined within the bounds phenomenal being. They have not gone on to the space of witnessing and vision, whether they were scholars, righteous, or worshippers or ascetics.

In short, when someone's reflection ascends from phenomenal beings and is connected to witnessing the Maker of Being, he is one of those brought near. If someone remains imprisoned in phenomenal being and has not been given an opening to the arenas of the unseen worlds, he is one of the People of the Right. Success is by Allah. Normal illnesses remain with them, and leprosy is found with them. It is rare in our region, and so we will not speak about it. Peace.

5. ACQUIRING CERTAINTY AND ITS ELEMENTS AND PLACES

Certainty consists in the stillness of the heart and its being tranquil at the removal of love and in times of trouble. It is derived from the verb, *yaqina*, which refers to the settling of water in a basin when it is still and settled there. Certainty varies according to its different elements and lights. When a person completely relies on Allah Almighty, but from behind the veil of phenomenal beings, taking the effect as evidence of the Effector, this station is called the Knowledge of Certainty and its elements are reflection and contemplation. When this reflection and contemplation are strong, the light of certainty also becomes strong. Then the person looks at these celestial and terrestrial phenomena and reflects on the wonders of their genesis and the diversity of their natures and lights and multiplicity of their individual forms and that all of that is in the hand of the Almighty and from His Power and Will, and that He encompasses that in His Knowledge, Hearing and Sight and that He is not unaware of even a single atom of it in the earth or in the heaven, and they know with the knowledge of certainty of the immensity of their Creator and His amazing power and vast knowledge.

When a person's spirit thirsts for direct knowledge of His Essence and yearns to reach His presence, Allah Almighty gives them the gift of turning to Him, alienates them from His creation, makes them intimate with Him, occupies them with His remembrance and sends them to one of His *awliya'*. He continues to travel with the spirit from stage to stage and from halting-place to halting-place until He says to it, "Here you are with your Lord." That is when the darkness of phenomenal beings is peeled away from the heart and the lights of the unseen are witnessed, the secrets of the Essence appear. The person concerned drowns in the lights, and withdraws from witnessing the effects. This station is called the Source or Eye of Certainty. It is the station of annihilation and its elements are the *dhikr* of the heart and the movement of reflection through the arenas of the unseen worlds while being constantly in the company of the gnostics and serving of those who have arrived.

When a person is firm in witnessing the lights and returns to witnessing the effects, they see them as supported by Allah, having no real existence alongside Allah, this station is called the Truth of Certainty. Its elements are reflection, looking, and necessary company and service. After this there only remains unceasing, everlasting ascent in direct knowledge in both the worlds since the immensity of the Real has no end and so ascent has no end.

Abu-l-Qasim al-Qushayri said, about these three stations – Knowledge of Certainty, Source or Eye of Certainty and Truth of certainty – "Knowledge of Certainty is based on logical deduction. Eye of Certainty is based on direct evidence, and Truth of Certainty is that which is clear in itself. So the Knowledge of Certainty is for the masters of intellects, the Source or Eye of Certainty is for the masters of knowledges, and the Truth of Certainty is for the people of direct perception."

Better than that is what Abu Sa'id al-Farghani said, "Certainty is the stillness and firmness of the heart. When this stillness is ascribed to the self and intellect based on proof and evidence which guides them to the desired matter, it is called the Knowledge of Certainty. When it is ascribed to the spiritual perception by means of removing the veils which comes between it and that desired matter, then you see it and witness it as it is in its lode, it is called the Source or Eye of Certainty. When that stillness is ascribed to the secret, it is called the Truth of Certainty." This is a summary.

An example of that in the visible world is our knowledge of the existence of Makka. As long as man has not reached it, he has Knowledge of Certainty about it. When he looks down on it and sees it, he has the Source or Eye of Certainty. When he enters it and knows its paths, then he has the Truth of Certainty. That is how it is with direct knowledge of the Sublime Essence. As long as the slave believes in the unseen, witnesses phenomenal beings and deduces the Maker of beings from them, this knowledge which he has of Allah is called Knowledge of Certainty. When he devotes himself to Allah and connects himself to a shaykh of instruction, travelling with him until he makes him absent to witnessing phenomenal beings by witnessing the Maker of beings so that the lights of the meanings flow to him and make him absent to witnessing the outward phenomena, it is called the Source or Eye of Certainty. When he is strong in that witnessing and his feet are firmly planted in the witnessing of the Worshipped King, so that he sees that meanings are sustained by outward phenomena, that is called the Truth of Certainty. These three stations are indicated by Ibn 'Ata'allah in the *Hikam* when he says "The light of the inner eye lets you see His nearness to you. The source of the inner eye lets you see your non-existence by your existence. The truth of the inner eye lets you see His existence, not your own non-existence or existence. 'Allah was and there was nothing with Him. He is now as He was.'"

These three stations – Knowledge of Certainty, Source or Eye of Certainty and Truth of Certainty – have their place in all matters about which growth of certainty is desired, such as the fact of guaranteed provision, absence of fear of creation, fixity of the lifespan, and the occurrence of things decreed like the resurrection and what follows it. As for guaranteed provision, Knowledge of Certainty about it is gained by reflecting on the *ayat*s which have come concerning it. There is a lot in the Qur'an, as well as *hadith*s which have come from the Truthful one ﷺ about its being guaranteed.

As for the *ayat*s which have come about it, they are very numerous indeed. The Almighty says: *"There is no creature on the earth which is not dependent upon Allah for its provision. He knows where it lives and where it dies. They are all in a Clear Book."* (11:6) The Almighty says: *"Instruct your family to pray, and be constant in it. We do not ask you for provision. We provide for you. And the best end result is gained by taqwa."* (20:132) The Almighty says: *"How many creatures do not carry their provision with them. Allah provides for them and He will for you. He is the All-Hearing, the All-Knowing."* (29:60) The Almighty says: *"Allah is He who created you, then provides for you, then will cause you to die and then bring you back to life."* (30:40)

These *ayat*s connect creation and trust in Him, so if you do not doubt that Allah is the One who created you and the One who will make you die and then give you life you should not doubt that Allah will provide for you; it is all the same. The Almighty says: *"Is there any creator other than Allah providing for you from heaven and earth? There is no god but Him. So how have you been perverted?"* (35:3) The Almighty says: *"It is Allah who made the earth a stable home for you and the sky a dome, and formed you, giving you the best of forms, and provided you with good and wholesome* things." (40:64) The Almighty says: *"I only created jinn and man to worship Me. I do not require any provision from them and I do not require them to nourish Me. Truly Allah, He is the Provider, the Possessor of Strength, the Sure."* (51:56-58) The Almighty says: *"Whoever has taqwa of Allah – He will give him a way out and provide for him from where he does not expect. Whoever puts his trust in Allah – He will be enough for him."* (65:2)

As for the *hadith*s of the Prophet, he ﷺ said, "If you were to rely on Allah as He should be relied on, He would provide for you as He provides for the birds. They go out in the morning hungry and return in the evening full." The Prophet ﷺ said, "The Spirit of Purity breathed into my heart that a soul will not die until it has received its full provision, so fear Allah and be moderate in asking." The Prophet ﷺ said, "Provision seeks out a person just as his term seeks him out." There are many other *hadith*s which are too many to mention. As for the words of the Prophet ﷺ, "Allah is responsible for the provision of the one who seeks knowledge," what is meant is a special responsibility which is that it comes to him without means or fatigue. Allah is responsible for providing for all of His creatures, but He, glory be to Him, has concealed that with the Cloak of Wisdom, which is the existence of normal means.

The one who is occupied with seeking useful knowledge and is sincere in it will be given his provision without the need of any means, but Allah has concealed this guarantee in the Cloak of Wisdom, which is the existence of means, because the emergence of provision outwardly without causation would entail disclosure of the secrets of lordship and the rending of the screens of Divine Magnificence in this abode which is the abode of obligation, not the abode of direct witnessing. This so that faith in the unseen is maintained. The Cloak of Wisdom must be spread over the disposal of Power and so the secret remains protected and the treasure buried. On the Day of Rising, Power will be manifest and Wisdom concealed and so the secret will appear with clear visible Lights. Then provision will appear from the source of favour, manifest without cloak or covering, because it is the abode of direct witnessing, not the abode of responsibility. Then the fruit of faith will appear openly and profit will be distinguished from loss with respect to what people sowed in this world.

The slaves' knowledge of this guarantee from the *ayat*s and the *hadith*s of the Prophet already mentioned is called Knowledge of Certainty. If someone wants to gain the Source or Eye of Certainty about it, he should devote himself to Allah completely and divest himself of means, both in his heart and body. Allah will bring him his provision without means by His words: *"Whoever has taqwa of Allah – He will give him a way out and provide for him from where he does not expect"* (65:2) and the words of the Prophet, peace be upon him, "If someone devotes himself to Allah, Allah will spare him every burden and provide for him from where he does not reckon. So he should remain still under the force of poverty until he tastes its secrets and obtains necessary knowledge." Allah gives provision through means and without any means. When the knowledge of this is firm and there is no opposition or illusion, that is called Truth of Certainty.

As for absence of the fear of creation, Knowledge of Certainty is gained in it by reflecting about the *ayat*s which indicate the *tawhid* of actions and that there is no actor but Allah, such as His words: *"But they cannot harm anyone by it, except with Allah's permission"* (2:102) and His words: *"If Allah had willed, they would not have fought each other. But Allah does whatever He desires."* (2:253) Another example is His words in which our master Ibrahim says: *"I have no fear of any partner you ascribe to Him unless my Lord should will such a thing to happen."* (7:195) and His words: *"Say: 'Call on your partner-gods and try all your wiles against me and grant me no reprieve'"* (11:55) and His words: *"If your Lord had willed, they would not have done it,"* (6:112) and His words: *"Your Lord creates and chooses whatever He wills. The choice is not theirs."*(28:68) The Almighty says: *"Allah created both you and what you do ."*(37:96)

In the *hadith* of the Prophet ﷺ he said to Ibn 'Abbas: "Know that if creation had gathered together to harm you with something which Allah had not decreed for you, they would not be able to do that. The pens are dry and the pages rolled up..." to the end of famous *hadith*. If he wants to gain the Source or Eye of Certainty, he should go to places of death and places where people fear to settle until he gains it. If he continues to do this, Truth of Certainty will become firm in him and he will realise this in tasting and unveiling. There is no Doer but Allah, no Doer besides Him. Then if he finds someone who can take him to Allah, he will obtain the *tawhid* of the Essence and know that there is nothing in existence except Allah. That is the goal. The Almighty says: *"The ultimate end is with your Lord."* (53:42)

As for fixity of the life-span and the inexorable occurrence of the decree, the *ayat*s which indicate that have already been quoted. If a person reflects on them while freeing his heart, he will gain Knowledge of Certainty. To gain the Source or Eye of Certainty, he should also go to the places of fear and places of death like the land of the plague or be patient in its land until he gains it. The life-span is determined. Someone may gain Source or Eye of Certainty by looking at someone who does that and goes to death traps or lives in places of destruction and yet remains unaffected. If someone remains in such places of fear until certain knowledge is firm in his heart, then he gains Truth of Certainty.

As for the Resurrection and what follows it, this is something well-known. Many *ayat*s in the Qur'an deal with it. Most people have Knowledge of Certainty about them, but they will not have Source or Eye of Certainty or Truth of Certainty, until the Final Hour occurs. However some people will see these things in vision and will gain Source or Eye of Certainty and Truth of Certainty. Indeed, the lights will come one after another to their hearts and the unseen will become visible and their mortal end will become immediate. Everything that is coming is close. Look at the words of Haritha, "It is as if I could see the people of the Garden visiting one another and I could see the people of the Fire seeking help from one another in it." It is as he said. Look at how what is coming was as if it was happening and the unseen was visible. That is why the Prophet ﷺ said, "Hold fast. You have direct knowledge. You are a slave into whose heart the light of Allah has entered," or words to that effect.

The method of gaining certainty is to keep the company of the people of certainty. By Allah none of those who had success had success except by keeping the company of someone who has had success and someone who has achieved a state, which those present with him are not without. In some *hadiths*, "Learn certainty. I teach it." In one transmission: "Learn certainty by sitting with the people of certainty." One gnostic said, "Allah has certain men who, when they look at a person, free him of need." Shaykh ash-Shadhili used to say about his student, Abu-l-'Abbas al-Mursi, "An excellent man is Abu-l-'Abbas! A desert man came to him and urinated on his leg and then he did not leave until he was one of the *awliya'* of Allah." Abu-l-'Abbas al-Mursi himself said, "By Allah, there nothing between me and a man but that I look at him and I free him of need." I say: Every age has men who free people of need by the glance. We have met them – praise belongs to Allah – and kept their company. Allah has made them appear as the lights of a town appear on their lampposts. Or rather as the sun appears on the horizon. However, the sun must have its clouds and a beautiful woman must have her veil.

> How many blamed Layla when they have not seen her face!
>   The deprived say to him, "What was missed is enough
>   for you."

GLOSSARY

adab: correct behaviour, spiritual courtesy.

Anjara: tribe from the mountains near Tangiers.

awliya': plural of *wali*.

ayat: verse of Qur'an, a sign.

Badr: a place near the coast, about 95 miles to the south of Madina where, in 2 AH in the first battle fought by the newly established Muslim community, the 313 outnumbered Muslims led by the Messenger of Allah, overwhelmingly defeated 1000 Makkan idolaters.

baqa': going on by Allah, when the Sufi returns to mankind after annihilation (*fana'*).

barzakh: an interspace between two realities.

bashariyya: human nature, mortality.

Dajjal: the false Messiah whose appearance marks the imminent end of the world. The root in Arabic means 'to deceive, cheat, take in'.

Day of Conquest: the day when Makka was conquered by the Muslims in 8 AH.

Dawud: the Prophet David.

deen: the life-transaction, literally the debt between two parties, in this usage between the Creator and created.

Dhat: the Divine Essence.

dhawq: tasting, experience of direct knowledge.

dhikr: literally remembrance, mention. Commonly used, it means invocation of Allah by repetition of His names or particular formulae.

dhikru'llah: remembrance of Allah.

diwan: a collection of poems.

du'a: supplication.

fana': annihilation in Allah, the cessation of attributes, total withdrawal from the sensory.

faqih: pl. *fuqaha'*, a man learned in knowledge of fiqh who by virtue of his knowledge can give legal judgements.

faqir: pl. *fuqara'*, someone who is needy or poor, used to describe someone following the spiritual path.

fasiq: pl. *fussaq*, impious, someone not meeting the legal requirements of righteousness

fiqh: the science of the application of the *shari'a*. A practitioner or expert in fiqh is called a *faqih*.

fuqaha': plural of *faqih*.

fuqara': plural of *faqir*.

hadith: reported speech of the Prophet, may Allah bless him and grant him peace.

hadith qudsi: those words of Allah on the tongue of His Prophet which are not part of the Revelation of the Qur'an.

hajj: the annual pilgrimage to Makka which is one of the five pillars of Islam.

hal: pl. *ahwal* a transient inward state.

hama: in pre-Islamic Arab superstition, an avenging spirit of a slain person which took the form of a night bird.

hamzah: the character in Arabic which designates a glottal stop.

haqiqa: essential reality.

Haram: Sacred Precinct, a protected area in which certain behavior is forbidden and other behaviour necessary. The area around the Ka'ba in Makkah is a Haram, and the area around the Prophet's Mosque in Madinah is a Haram.

himma: spiritual aspiration,

hiss: sensory.

Al-Hudaybiyya: a well-known place ten miles from Makkah on the way to Jiddah where the Homage of ar-Ridwan took place.

hulul: claim of incarnation.

Ibrahim: the Prophet Abraham.

'id: a festival, either the festival at the end of Ramadan or at the time of the Hajj.

ihsan: the highest level of excellence in worshipping Allah.

ikhlas: sincerity, pure unadulterated genuineness.

'Illiyun: the upper part of the Heavens, where the register of people's good deeds is kept.

iman: belief, faith.

iqama: the call which announces that the obligatory prayer is about to begin.

istiqama: being straight in the *deen*.

'Isa: the Prophet Jesus.

'Isha': the obligatory evening prayer.

Istikhara: a prayer performed by someone who has not decided what to do in a matter hoping to be inspired to do the right thing.

ittihad: claim of unification with the Divine, human individuality passing away in the Reality.

jabarut: the world of Divine Power.

jadhb: Divine attraction which overpowers a person.

jam': gatheredness, combining all into the whole and ignoring structures in existence in an undifferentiated field of awareness by witnessing Allah. Its oppose is *tafriqa*.

Jibril: the angel Gabriel.

jinn: inhabitants of the heavens and the earth made of smokeless fire who are usually invisible.

karamat: marks of honour, miracles.

khalif: khalifa, caliph.

khalwa: spiritual retreat.

khatir: a passing thought which is quickly removed by another.

lahut: Divine Nature.

maghrib: the sunset prayer

Maghrib: the Muslim territories in northwest Africa, especially   Morocco.

mahabba: love.

Makhzan: the Moroccan government.

ma'na: meaning.

maqam: a station of spiritual knowledge, more lasting than a *hal*.

ma'rifa: gnosis, direct knowledge of the Divine Reality.

muraqaba: watchfulness, a permanent state of awareness.

muraqqa'a: a patched cloak worn by Sufis.

murid: a disciple following a shaykh.

mushahada: witnessing, contemplation, vision within in the heart, seeing things in the light of *tawhid*.

nafs: the lower self.

nasut: human nature.

Nuh: the Prophet Noah.

Preserved Tablet: *al-Lawh al-Mahfuz*, also referred to as the *Umm al-Kitab*, the source of the Qur'an, and the place where decrees are recorded.

Qadar: the Decree.

Qadarities: sect who said that people have power (*qadar*) over their actions and hence free will.

qalb: heart

qasida: poetic ode, often sung as a spiritual practice

qibla: the direction faced in the prayer which is towards the Ka'bah in Makka.

qudra: power

Qutb: the pole, the axis of the spiritual hierarchy.

Rafidites: the Rawafid, a group of the Shi'a known for rejecting Abu Bakr and 'Umar as well as 'Uthman. It is a nickname, meaning "deserters".

rahamut: the presence of Mercy.

rak'at: a unit of the prayer consisting of a series of standings, bowing, prostrations and sittings.

rida: serene and joyful contentment with Allah's decree.

ruh: (plural *arwah*) the soul, vital spirit.

ruhaniyya: pure spirituality.

Safar: the second month of the Muslim lunar calendar.

sahw: sobriety, acting in accordance with the *shari'a* rather than inward intoxication (*sukr*).

Salaf: the early generations of the Muslims.

salik: wayfarer, traveller to Allah.

Salsabil: the name of a spring in the Garden.

samt: silence.

Shari'a: The legal modality of a people based on the revelation of their Prophet. The final *shari'a* is that of Islam.

shawq: the yearning of the heart to meet the Beloved.

shirk: the unforgiveable wrong action of worshipping something or someone other than Allah or associating something or someone as a partner with Him.

shurb: "drinking", tasting the sweetness of devotion.

Shu'ayb: the Prophet Jethro.

siddiqun: plural of *siddiq*, a man of truth, the *Siddiq* is the one who believes in Allah and His Messenger by the statement of the one who reports it, not from any proof except the light of belief which he experiences in his heart and which prevents him from hesitating and prevents any doubt entering him about the word of the Messenger.

sidq: truthfulness.

Sifat: the plural of *sifa*, Divine Attributes.

Subh: the dawn prayer.

Suffa: a verandah attached to the Prophet's Mosque where the poor Muslims used to sleep.

sukr: intoxication, rapture.

suluk: wayfaring, journeying on the Way to Allah while maintaining adherence to the *shari'a*.

Sunna: the customary practice of a person or group of people. It has come to refer almost exclusively to the practice of the Messenger of Allah, may Allah bless him and grant him peace.

sura: a chapter of the Qur'an.

Spirit of Purity: *Ruh al-Qudus*, meaning Jibril.

tadbir: management.

tafriqa: separation, separating Allah from creation.

tajalli: self-manifestation, presencing, self-disclosing, the unveiling of a spiritual reality in the realm of vision.

tajalliyat: plural of *tajalli.*

tajrid: divestment, stripping away, detachment from this world and abandoning desires.

takbir: saying *'Allahu Akbar,'* 'Allah is greater'.

tamkin: stability.

talqin: constant change.

Talut: Saul.

Tamim: Banu, one of the largest of the Arab tribes, located in Najd.

tanzih: transcendence, disconnecting Allah from creation. The opposite of *tashbih.*

taqwa: active awe or fear of Allah, which inspires a person to be on guard against wrong action and eager for actions which please Him.

tariqa: the Way, the spiritual Path.

tasawwuf: Sufism

tashbih: comparing or connecting Allah to created things, or making Allah resemble created things. The opposite of *tanzih.*

taslim: submission.

tawaf: the circumambulation of the Ka'bah, done in sets of seven circuits.

tawakkul: reliance, unshakeable trust in Allah.

tawhid: the doctrine of Divine Unity.

tuma'nina: tranquillity.

wajd: rapture, trance, the first degree of ecstasy.

wali: (plural *awliya'*) someone who is a 'friend' of Allah, thus possessing the quality of *wilayah*.

wara': scrupulousness, extending from avoiding the unlawful and doubtful to avoiding anything that will cast a shadow on the heart.

warid: an overflowing experience which overcomes a person's heart.

waridat: plural of *warid*.

wazifa: specific set of prayers which are recited.

wijdan: the second decree of ecstasy.

wilaya: friendship, in particular with Allah, referring to the relationship of the *wali* with his Lord.

wird: (plural *awrad*): a regular spiritual exercise involving recitation of a litany of forms of *dhikr*.

wudu': ritual washing to be pure for the prayer.

wujud: the first level of ecstasy.

Ya'juj and Ma'juj: the people of Gog and Magog who are to burst forth at the end of time to wreak destruction.

Yunus: the Prophet Jonah.

Yusuf: the Prophet Joseph.

Zakariyya: the Prophet Zachariah.

Zulaykha: the name of the wife of the 'Aziz in the story of Yusuf.

zindiq: a term used to describe a heretic whose teaching is a danger to the community or state.

zuhd: making do with little of this world and leaving what you do not need.

SELECTIVE BIOGRAPHIES

'Abdu-r-Rahman al-Majdhub: a Morocco poet and Sufi. He was born in 1506 in Azemmour but moved to Meknes when a child. He died in 976/1568.

'Abdu-s-Salam ibn Mashish: the master of Abu-l-Hasan ash-Shadhili. He was a the Qutb of his age. He was a recluse who lived on the Jabal al'Alam, a mountain in Morocco. All he left was the *Salat al-Mashishiyya*. He died ca. 625/1228.

Abu-l-'Abbas al-Mursi: a Shadhili shaykh in Alexandria, the successor to ash-Shadhili and the shaykh of Ibn 'Ata'allah. He died in 686/1288.

*Abu 'Abdullah at-Tawdi: *see at-Tawdi ibn Sawda.*

Abu Bakr as-Siddiq: 'Abdullah ibn Abi Quhafa 'Uthman, at-Taymi, the Companion of the Prophet ﷺ and the first caliph. He died in 13/634 when he was 63 and was buried beside the Messenger of Allah.

Abu-d-Darda': 'Umaymir ibn Malik, an Ansari Companion who became Muslim after Badr. His virtues are famous and he was known for his horsemanship and piety and wisdom. He was a merchant in Madina before Islam and then devoted himself to worship. He died in 32/652.

Abu-l-Fath al-Busti: a Ghaznavid government secretary and poet who died in Bukhara in 401/1010.

Abu Hamza al-Baghdadi: a famous early Sufi from Khorasan and died in 290/903.

Abu Hurayra: 'Abdu'r-Rahman ibn Sakhr, the famous Companion. He died in Madina in 58/677-8 at the age of 78.

Abu 'Imran al-Barda'i: Musa ibn Abi Hajjaj, a Sufi and prominent Maliki *faqih* of Qayrawan who died in 430/1048.

Abu Nu'aym: Ahmad ibn 'Abdullah ibn Ahmad al-Isbahani, a notable hadith scholar who wrote various works, including *al-Mustadrak* and *Hilya al-Awliya'.* He died in 430/1038 in Isfahan.

Abu Sa'id al-Farghani: an early Sufi.

Abu Sulayman Dawud at-Ta'i: a scholar and Sufi in who died ca. 160/777.

Abu Sulayman ad-Darani: 'Abdu-r-Rahman, d. known for his piety and zuhd. He died in 205/820-21 or 215/830-31.

Abu Talib al-Makki: a Sufi, Maliki *faqih* and scholar. He wrote the *Qut al-Qulub*. He died in Baghdad in 386/998-99.

Abu Thawr: Ibrahim ibn Khalid al-Kalbi who had a school of fiqh in Baghdad and died in 270/883.

Abu Yazid al-Bistami: a celebrated Sufi who was famous for his ecstatic expressions. He died in in 260/874 at the age of 71, either in Damascus or Bistam, Persia.

Ahmad ibn 'Ata'allah: the Sufi Imam and author of the *Hikam* who died in 709/1309.

Ahmad Zarruq: a Sufi, Maliki scholar and *muhaddith* who studied *fiqh* in Fez, Cairo and Madina. Then became a Sufi and withdrew from worldly things and took to wandering. He was a renowned Shaykh of the Shadhiliyya *tariqa* and in died in Libya in 899/1493.

'Ali ibn Abi Talib: the Companion and Prophet's cousin. He was killed in 40/661.

'Ammar ibn Yasir: a famous early Companion who was very close to the Prophet. He was killed in the Battle of Siffin in 37/657 at the age of 93.

'Aqra' ibn Habis: one of the Companions.

Al-'Arabi ad-Darqawi: the Qutb and founder of the Darqawiyya. He died in 1239/1823.

Al-Banani: 'Abdu-r-Rahman ibn Jad Allah al-Maghribi, author of a gloss on the *Mukhtasar* of Khali. He died in 1173/1759.

Bilal: ibn Abi Rabh, the first Abyssinian to come to Islam and meant to be the second adult convert. He became Muslim while he was a slave of Umayya ibn Khalaf and Abu Bakr bought him and set him free. He became the *mu'adhdhan* of the Prophet. He died in Syria in 20/641 at the age of about 60.

Al-Bukhari: Abu 'Abdullah Muhammad ibn Isma'il, compiler of the *Sahih* hadith collection. He was born in 194/810 and died in 256/870.

Al-Buni: Ahmad ibn 'Ali, an Algerian mathematician, philosopher and Sufi who died in 662/1225.

Al-Busiri: the author of the Burda in praise of the Prophet. He was a scholar, calligrapher, teacher and poet and a disciple of ash-Shadhili and al-Mursi and died in 695/1296.

Dihya al-Kalbi: the famous Companion who was one of the most beautiful of people and that is why Jibril took on his form.

Al-Ghazali: Abu Hamid Muhammad ibn Muhammad at-Tusi, the famous Shafi'i Imam and Sufi who died in Tabiran in 505/1111. He was the author of many books, especially *Tahafut al-Falasifa* (The Incoherence of the philosophers) and *Ihya' 'Ulum ad-din*.

Habib al-Ajami: a *muhaddith* and Sufi who transmitted from Hasan al-Basri, Ibn Sirin and others. He converted from a life of ease and self-indulgence to a life of self-denial.

Al-Hadrami: Ahmad ibn 'Uqba, the spiritual master of Zarruq in Cairo. He died ca. 889/1494.

Al-Hakim: Abu 'Abdullah Muhammad ibn 'Abdullah an-Nisaburi, a Shafi'i scholar, hadith scholar and Imam who had many volumes on hadith, of which the most famous is *al-Mustradrak*. He died in Nishapur in 405/1014.

al-Hallaj: Husayn ibn Mansur, Abu'l-Mughith, the famous Sufi. He left a *Diwan* and the *Tawasin*. He was executed in Baghdad in 309/922 because his ecstatic outbursts led people to believe that he was a heretic.

Haritha: ibn Wahb, one of the Companions.

Al-Hasan al-Basri: Abu Sa'id ibn Abu'l-Hasan, one of the most important Followers in asceticism and knowledge. His mother served Umm Salama, the wife of the Prophet. He died in Basra in 110/728 when he was 88.

Al-Hattab: a Maliki who wrote a commentary on the *Mukhtasar* of Khalil. He died in 954/1547.

Ibn 'Abbas: see 'Abdullah, the son of the uncle of the Prophet called the "sage of the Arabs," "the Sea" and the "Doctor (*hibr*) of the Community". He died in 68/687-8 at the age of 71 in at-Ta'if.

Ibn al-'Arabi: Abu Bakr Muhammad ibn 'Ali al-Hatimi at-Ta'i, a *mujtahid*, scholar and Sufi known as Muhyiddin (the Reviver of the *Deen*) and the Shaykh al-Akbar (the Greatest Master). He wrote over 350 works including the *Futuhat al-Makkiyya* and *Fusus al-Hikam*. He died in Damascus in 638/1240.

Ibn 'Atiyya: Abu Muhammad 'Abdu-l-Haqq ibn Ghalib al-Andalusi, an Andalusian who wrote the Qu'ranic commentary, al-*Muharrir al-Wajiz*. He died ca. 542/1147.

Ibn al-Banna' at-Tujibi as-Saqusti: from Fes, author of the poem, *al-Mabahith al-Asliyya.*

Ibn Farhun: Ibrahim ibn 'Ali, author of *ad-Dibaj*, the *Tabaqat* of the Malikis. He was from Madina and appointed *qadi* there. He died in 799/1396.

Ibn Khaldun: 'Abdu-r-Rahman ibn Muhammad, generally known as Ibn Khaldun after a remote ancestor, best known for his famous *Muqaddima*, (Prolegomena), the introduction to the seven volume *al-'Ibar*, the world's first work on social theory. He died in Cairo in 808/1406.

Ibn Sab'in: 'Abdu-l-Haqq, an Andalusian Sufi and philosopher who died in 669/1271.

Ibrahim al-Khawwas: ibn Ahmad, a Sufi author who taught al-Khuldi. He died in 290/903.

'Izz ibn 'Abdu-s-Salam: as-Sulami, "the Sultan of the Scholars", a Shafi'i scholar and companion of Imam Abu-l-Hasan ash-Shadhili. His reputation was the stuff of legends. He wrote a number of books on Shafi'i *fiqh*, *tafsir*, and other legal areas. His masterpiece was *Qawa'id al-Ahkam fi masalih al-anam.* He died in 660/1262.

al-Jilani: Shaykh 'Abdu-l-Qadir, the founder of the Qadiriyya, known as the spiritual pole of his time, al-Ghawth al-A'zam. His most famous books are: *al-Ghunya li talibi tariq al-haqq* (a summary of the Hanbali school); *al-Fath al-rabbani*; *Futuh al-ghayb.* He died in 561/1166.

Al-Junayd: Abu-l-Qasim ibn Muhammad: the great shaykh of his time, known as the Imam of the Sufis. His *fiqh* was taken from Abu Thawr and Sufyan and *tariqa* from as-Sara as-Saqati, his uncle, and al-Muhasibi. He died in 297/910.

Al-Kharraz: Abu Sa'id Ahmad ibn 'Isa, a Sufi in Baghdad who died between 279/890 and 286/899.

Al-Mahdawi: Abu Muhammad 'Abdu-l-'Aziz, a leading Sufi in Tunis and disciple of Abu Madyan. He died in 545/1150.

Malik ibn Anas: Abu 'Abdullah, al-Asbahi, the famous Imam of Madina in *fiqh* and *hadith* and founder of Maliki school who wrote *al-Muwatta'*. He died in Madina in 179/795.

Ma'ruf ibn Fayruz al-Karkhi: Abu Mahfuz:, a famous Sufi of the Baghdad school. He had a great influence on as-Sari as-Saqati and taught hadith to Ibn Hanbal. He died in 200 or 204 (815/6 or 819/20).

Moulay al-'Arabi ad-Darqawi: *see al-'Arabi.*

Muhammad ibn Ahmad al-Buzidi al-Hasani: the Darqawi shaykh of Ibn 'Ajiba.

Muhammad ibn Sirin: a Follower who is reliable in *fiqh* and is related from by the Six Imams. He was known for his scrupulousness and dream interpretation. He died in 110/729 at the age of 80.

Al-Muhasabi: Abu-l-Harith al-Harith ibn Asad, an excellent scholar, held in high esteem among the people of his time in both outward and inward knowledge, and wrote many books. He died in 243/857.

Muslim: Abu-l-Husayn Muslim ibn al-Hajjaj, a Shafi'i scholar and hadith master, the compiler of the famous hadith collection, *as-Sahih*. He died in 261/875.

An-Nawawi: Abu Zakariyya Yahya ibn Sharaf, , the Imam of the later Shafi'ites who wrote many books, including *Minhaj at-Talibin*, *Kitab al-Adhkar*, and *Riyad as-Salihin*. He died at the age of 44 in 676/1277.

Al-Qastallani: Abu-l-'Abbas Ahmad ibn Muhammad, an Egyptian Shafi'i, author of *Irshad as-Sari*, a commentary on Bukhari. He died in 923.1517.

Al-Qushayri: Abu-l-Qasim 'Abdu-l-Karim ibn Hawazin, the shaykh of Khurasan in his time in asceticism and knowledge of the *deen*. He wrote various books, the most famous of which is the *Risala al-Qushayriya* about *tasawwuf* and the biographies of the Sufis, and the *Lata'if al-Isharat* on *tafsir*.

Ar-Rifa'i: Abu-l-'Abbas Ahmad ibn 'Alid, the founder of the Rifa'i *tariqa*. He died in 578/1182.

Sahl ibn 'Abdullah: ibn Yunus at-Tustari: famous man of right action, unique in knowledge and scrupulousness, Sufi shaykh and ascetic. He also wrote a short *tafsir*. He had famous miracles (*karamat*) and kept the company of Dhu-n-Nun al-Misri in Makka. He died in 282/896.

Salman al-Farisi: Abu 'Abdullah, the client of the Prophet ﷺ and renowned Companion. He died ca. 32/652. The Messenger of Allah said of him, "The Garden yearns for him."

As-Sanusi: Muhammad 'Ali, Abu 'Abdullah as-Sanusi, founder of the Sanusi *tariqa*, a Maliki scholar and Sufi. He produced more than 40 books and travelled a lot. His main centre was near al-Bayda in Libya. He died in 1859.

Sari as-Saqati: Abu-l-Hasan ibn Mughallis, said to be a pupil of Ma'ruf al-Karkhi, in the Baghdad circle of Sufis. He was the maternal uncle and teacher of al-Junayd and one of the first to present Sufism in an organised form. He died in 253/867 at the age of 98.

Ash-Shadhili: Abu-l-Hasan 'Ali ibn 'Abdullah, the famous Sufi and murid of 'Abdu-s-Salam ibn Mashish. He wrote *Hizb al-Bahr, Hizb al-Barr, Hizb an-Nasr* and other litanies. He died on the Red Sea coast in 656/1258 on the way to Makka.

Ash-Shafi'i: Abu 'Abdullah Muhammad ibn Idris, the founder of the Shafi'i school of fiqh. He wrote *al-Umm* and *ar-Risala* and was the first to formulate the principles of abrogating and abrogated verses. He died in 204/820.

Ash-Shibli: Abu Bakr Dulaf ibn Jahdar, a Maliki *faqih* who joined the circle of al-Junayd and became noted for his eccentric behaviour which led to his commital to an asylum. He died in 334/846 at the age of 87. He left his *Sayings* (*isharat*).

Ash-Shustari: Abu-l-Hasan ibn 'Abdullah, an Andalusian Sufi, *faqih* and poet. He died in Egypt in 667/1269.

Sufyan ibn 'Uyayna: a scholar from of the Followers of the Followers. He met eighty-six of them. He lived in Makka. He died in 198/813.

Suhayb ibn Sinan: a Companion of the Prophet ﷺ. At the age of 5 he was captured by Byzantines and sold as a slave and spent 20 years there. He escaped and went to Makka and became an ally of a Qurayshi and wealthy merchant. He became Muslim with 'Ammar ibn Yasir and ended by giving Quraysh all his wealth so that he could emigrate to Madina.

As-Suyuti: Jalalu-d-din 'Abdu-r-Rahman ibn Abi Bakr, a Shafi'i *mujtahid* Imam, Sufi, hadith scholar and historian. He wrote books on almost every subject. He wrote a large number of books on different subjects. He died in 911/1505.

At-Tawdi ibn Sawda: a Moroccan scholar scholar and Sufi. He died in 1210/1795.

At-Tirmidhi: Abu 'Isa ibn Muhamma, one of the great scholars. He was proficient in *fiqh* and had many books on the science of *hadith*. He died in Tirmidh in 279/892.

At-Tustari: *see Sahl ibn 'Abdullah.*

'Umar ibn al-Khattab: the Companion and second caliph. He was murdered in 23/643 when he was 63.

'Umar ibn 'Abdu-l-'Aziz: the Ummayd caliph. He died in 101/720 when he was 40. His virtues are famous.

Umm Salama: Hind bint Abi Umayya al-Makhzumiyya, the wife of the Prophet ﷺ. She was the last of the Prophet's wives to die during the reign of Yazid in 62/681.

'Uthman ibn 'Affan: the Companion and third caliph and one of the ten promised the Garden. He was murdered in 35/655.

Uways al-Qarni: He lived in the time of the Prophet but did not see him since he was looking after his mother. He died at Siffin in 37/657.

Yaqut al-'Arshi: a slave from Abyssinia who became the student of Abu-l-'Abbas al-Mursi. He was the shaykh of Ibn 'Ata'allah after the death of Abu-l-'Abbas al-Mursi. He died in Alexandria in 707/1307.

Al-Yusi: Abu 'Ali Hassan ibn Mas'ud, a Moroccan Sufi scholar of the Qarawiyyin who died in 1102/1691.

Az-Zayyat: 'Abdu-r-Rahman ibn al-Husayn al-Madani, the shaykh of Ibn Mashish.

www.ingramcontent.com/pod-product-compliance
Lightning Source LLC
Chambersburg PA
CBHW021218090426
42740CB00006B/272